The United States of Adventure

by Anna McNuff

Contents

Prologue

Part I

Part II

Epilogue

The United States of Adventure

Maps and illustrations lovingly designed by Kim and Sally at
Off Grid. www.somewhereoffgrid.com

For Jamie and Jonty, the best brothers a girl could hope for

The United States of Adventure

by Anna McNuff

The United States of Adventure

Start

Great Plains

Anna

Rocky Mountains

Los Angeles

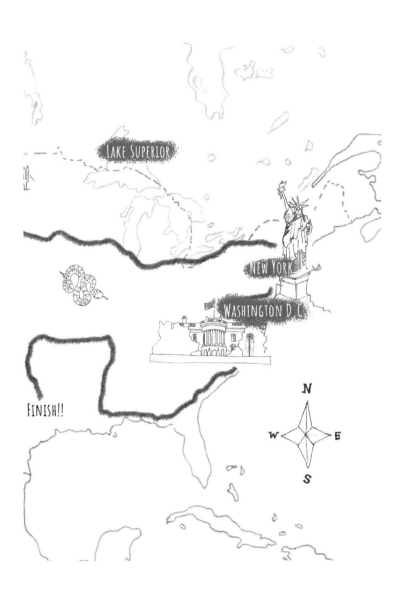

Prologue

For all its oddities, the desert is a serene and beautiful place. As my journey across it gets underway, I settle into a rhythm: basin, fault, range. Up, down, along. I stop in the small towns (if you can call them that) which appear on the horizon every 60 to 80 miles. Each morning I wake at 4.30 a.m. and hit the road as soon as possible in a bid to beat the heat. I revel in the precious hours just before sunrise, when the Great Basin is at its quietest, its unforgiving weather systems still sleeping, and I could well be the only person on the planet.

Each day, I heave and haul myself up two or three small mountain climbs. My knees ache, my legs are tired. My body is weightless but my bike is heavy, its bags laden with the memories of the person I was before starting this journey, and the one I will be when it is all over.

I crest the first pass just in time to see the dawn light up a vast basin below. I stop briefly to stare out across the flat plain, which stretches for 30 miles to the foot of the next mountain. I look to the ghostly outlines of the peaks beyond, and wonder how long it will be before I get to meet them too. During the day, I see lizards, chipmunks and small blue-grey birds that dance playfully alongside me, twittering away. Every now and then a snake crosses the road in front of me, slithering and wriggling like a possessed shoelace. As each day draws to a close and the sun slinks below the horizon, the last of its rays collide with the dust from the surrounding scrub and create a majestic haze, making the cinder landscape glow.

Out here, I am miles from anywhere, miles from anybody, but I don't feel lonely. I am riding side by side with the ghosts of the Wild West. I have the company of the spirits of miners, bandits and the pony riders of the past. I am pedalling through their history, and into my own.

PART I

1

The Sausage that Broke the Camel's Back

It was approaching 3 p.m. on a very ordinary Wednesday. I was sitting in an office on the outskirts of London, staring at the screen on my computer. I had been trying, and failing, for the past 30 minutes to get the boxes in a PowerPoint presentation to line up with one another, but they refused to follow my commands. They were, it seemed, in cahoots with the little numbered circles who, despite my repeated efforts, refused to grant my wish to have identical formatting. I can only assume that the numbered circles appreciated the importance of maintaining a sense of individuality, of not getting lost in the crowd – which was more than I could say for myself at that point.

In a bid to jazz up the view that greeted me for eight hours of every day, I had adjusted the settings of my computer so that each programme was surrounded by a bright border of magenta. Usually this small amendment to my daily vista brought about enough amusement to make it to 5.30 p.m., but not that day. That day, the magenta offered no salvation.

I narrowed my eyes and sat forwards once again, fuelled by a renewed determination. For a moment the presentation boxes slotted into place and I rejoiced. Sweet alignment, hallelujah! Alas, the joy was short-lived – moments later they reverted to their original, misaligned position and all hope was gone. I slouched back in my chair and took a deep breath, fighting every urge to throw the computer and its disobedient accomplices out of the office window.

Just then, a train of thought rumbled into motion and a soft voice asked me a question. It was almost a whisper. 'What are you doing here?' it said.

'You are building a career, Anna,' came the reply from another voice, which sounded like that of my secondary school chemistry teacher.

'But are you building a life?' said the soft voice again. And for that I had no answer.

At 27 years old, there were a number of choices that had led me to that office block. After leaving secondary school, I had decided to study psychology at the University of London. There, I mostly immersed myself in the world of university and international rowing. After graduating, I decided that the life of an aspiring Olympian felt restricted when there was a big world out there to explore. So I hung up my oars and took a leap into the unknown.

The unknown led me to believe that I might like to try a career in advertising. The first issue with this plan was that I had nothing on my CV that was remotely related to work – all my spare time had been dedicated to sport and, funnily enough, it didn't seem to matter to my prospective employer what my O2 max was or how fast I could cover 2 km in a rowing boat. Still, if you don't throw your hat into the ring, you don't get picked, so I applied to dozens of graduate advertising schemes, with varying degrees of success. In one of my interviews at a high-flying digital advertising agency in south London, I was presented with a banana and asked to 'sell' it to the interviewer in a 'fascinating and thought-provoking way'.

'You've got thirty seconds to make me believe that I need this banana in my life – go!'

I failed in selling that banana. In fact, I failed at getting accepted on to any of the graduate schemes, but I was offered a role as a receptionist in a PR company based in Soho, west London. Working in PR in Soho! I had made it! I was to be paid a meagre salary and live it up in the heart of it all! Most importantly, I manned a desk that was situated behind a huge curved wall of pink wood, a bubble, if you will. As queen of the bubble, my duties included greeting clients as they came into the office, arranging meetings, running upstairs to turn computers on and then off again, and keeping an eye on the guest toilet – which was next to my desk and often (illegally) frequented by those in the company who needed a little quiet time for a number two. I also had to make sure there were enough biscuits for each meeting. I always bought the fancy ones with chocolate chips in because I liked to eat them too when no one was looking.

It soon became apparent that PR was a world I didn't

understand. Cold-calling spreadsheets of journalists was my idea of hell. And, besides, people were mean. Or rather, they seemed mean. It was likely that the journalists I was calling were rather busy and having a bumbling PR rookie interrupt their day wasn't entirely welcome. Still, there were some good eggs at the company and some whom I really liked. Things went well and after six months I was promoted from receptionist to account assistant, so I moved from my pink bubble to a desk upstairs. However, I no longer had a say over the biscuits chosen for client meetings and I had to attend things called development reviews. These reviews involved questions such as,

'Where would you like to be in four years' time, Anna?' Well, I guessed that I should want to be where the account manager was sitting. Account managers were god-like mythical creatures, after all. They had life figured out. They were doing things like getting married, buying their own homes and going for lunches with journalists.

'I would like to be an account manager,' I said, firmly. Which, in a way, was true. I would progress; I would be paid more money. I would be happy.

The account manager nodded in agreement and looked back at her list of questions.

'And, what would you say are your key weaknesses?'

***

Despite my assertion that I wanted to move on up in the world of PR, a few months later it began to dawn on me that life in Soho wasn't all it was cracked up to be and perhaps I wasn't cut out for a life of PR. The tipping point came when I was assigned to 'sell in' sausages. I was a vegetarian at the time. I had been since I was six years old, when I declared to my mum that 'I like aminawls and I dunno wanna eat 'em'. I knew as much about sausages as a bull does about ballet. If I managed to run the gauntlet of not stuttering through my first few sentences on the phone to the journalist, and they had actually been interested enough to hear more about said sausages, they would inevitably ask me: 'And what do the sausages taste like?'

There would be a long pause, while I contacted the part of my brain which fabricates information, and then I'd reply, 'Oh, well, one is packed with nutmeg and a little spice – it's sooooo delicious. And the other flavour, the venison with smoky chilli, well, that's just divine. You really *have* to try them to see what I mean. May I send a packet to your office?'

This had to be rock bottom. I was lying about the taste of sausages. It wasn't the straw that broke the camel's back – it was the smoked venison and chilli infusion sausage that broke it.

I jumped ship from PR and spread my wings to more general 'marketing'. Again, I applied for graduate schemes and, out of 1,800 applicants and following several rounds of *X-Factor*-style auditions, I was one of six selected for a role at a large

UK household brand. I still have no idea why the recruiter chose me, but choose me they did.

I was 23 years old. I had a swipe card, a new laptop and it was time to start climbing the corporate ladder.

***

At my desk on that ordinary Wednesday, I picked a piece of fluff out from between the keys on my keyboard and inspected it. I discovered that it wasn't fluff at all, but a piece of the baguette I had eaten for lunch on the Monday that week. In a vain attempt to avoid working on my presentation, I looked up and around. I was based in an open-plan office and there were dozens of people milling about. I could hear desk phones ringing and the low hum of multiple voices; someone was wrestling with the printer in the corner of the room, trying to free a jammed piece of A4 paper. I knew most of these people and, more than that, I knew that most of them loved their jobs – a fact that made it all the more apparent that I didn't, not anymore anyway. I was not the same bright-eyed graduate who had walked through the oversized glass swing doors four years earlier. Life had changed a whole lot since then. Not just my mindset, but my personal circumstances had too, which opened up a world of possibility.

Eighteen months earlier I had been in a long-term relationship. I thought it was a done deal. I was blindly in love and living with the person whom I would spend the rest of my life with. Only, I made an error all too common to those in love: I forgot to put myself first. So when things between us began to falter, I shoved my needs further and further into the background, believing that I could fix it if I could just make him happy. Unfortunately, he no longer wanted me to try to make him happy. In fact, he could likely see that I was making myself miserable trying. It takes two to tango, and he wanted out.

In a last-ditch attempt to save our relationship after five years together, I wrote him a letter. A handwritten, old-fashioned, ink-on-paper letter. It spanned four A4 sides (front and back) and said everything I felt I needed to say. It spoke of all that we had been through together in years of a stop-start relationship, one which rumbled on like a car engine almost out of fuel – spluttering, jolting, lurching – but still just about moving forwards. The letter spoke of my hopes, of my belief that we might have been able, and we still were able, to make it.

The words in that letter extended from my heart like branches of a tree, desperately clinging on through the winter in the hope that it might see another spring. I did not give up easily on anything in life, least of all the thing most important in it – love. I would not give up on love, even though it had chosen to give up on me. I wrote the letter so that I could look back and have no regrets. So that I could know that I had done everything possible to make it work, and that if it wasn't meant to be, I could let it go. Of course that letter was laced with hope; it reeked of it. When I went to the apartment we shared together to collect the last of my things, I left it propped on the mantelpiece, nestled against the smooth belly of a wooden carved rhinoceros which he had bought me on a trip to Africa.

A year and a half after the inevitable breakup, I was an independent single woman who had rediscovered the joy of putting herself first, and I craved adventure. The break-up had shattered me into a thousand tiny pieces, but being in bits had opened me up to letting a little light back in. And now my life was beaming. I was beaming. I had no one else to think about except me, so I started to think about all of the things that made me happy, the moments when I felt complete, like the real me, the me I was supposed to be. I soon realised that I felt like the best version of myself only in the moments I was cramming into life around my day job. I would fill my weekends with sporting competitions, I'd enter races abroad. I would take 'holidays' which involved swimming down the coast of Croatia, or Greece, or cycling up mountains in the French Alps. These were the things that made my soul sing.

I wanted to travel, to see the world. To hike, run, swim, cycle for thousands of miles into an endless horizon. Only… I couldn't do that. Why couldn't I do that? Could I? And then I realised, I could. The only person making me be here was me. I was here by choice. What a revelation! I could at any moment, entirely of my own free will, get up, walk out of the door and never come back. I could even steal the entire box of teabags in the communal kitchen while I was at it.

That night I left the office (without having stolen any tea-bags) and tumbled through the door to my house. I called up the stairs to check that my housemate Ed wasn't home. Ed was one of my friends from university and we had bought a crumbling Victorian terrace house together last year in a bid to be 'grown-up'. It was purely a ploy to buck London's extortionate rental prices and get 'on the ladder'. There was no reply to my call from Ed – I was alone.

I laid a world map out on the living-room floor and began to move around it, like a tiger stalking its prey. My mind was set on a cycling adventure somewhere, but where? My stomach bubbled and fizzed with excitement. Within this map was (quite literally) a world of possibility, a world of unknowns. I would be doing this. It *was* going to happen. I hovered momentarily over countries, running through each of them that piqued my interest. Africa? Dancing, big animals, dusty roads and deserts. India? Eclectic, vibrant and lots of people. South America? Mountains, beauty, jungles and a little scary. And then my eyes stopped on the USA.

I looked from corner to corner, from the Atlantic Ocean to the Pacific, from national park to national park, from mountain range to mountain range. And then I browsed the big cities. *But isn't the USA just like the UK?!* I wondered. *Is it?! I mean, do I know that?* Beyond the bright lights of New York City and tourism adverts of Arnold Schwarzenegger knee-deep in the Californian Ocean, how much do I really know about America? What about all that space in between? The Midwest, the

Deep South – what goes on there? I had absolutely no idea. That settled it. The USA it would be. And logically it followed that I should travel through all 50 states. There was no sense in doing things by halves, after all. In for a penny, in for a pound. The challenge was set – I would cycle through all 50 states of the USA.

***

I decided it would take me a year to save up for my cycling adventure. Over the months that followed, I set about putting a plan into action. I paid close attention to the voices that screamed at me, barking all of the reasons not to go. I never ignored them, and I felt that I should hear them out. I needed those voices on my side by the time I left the UK or they would only drag me down. Besides, those voices had some very valid points.

I decided that the reasons not to go were less scary when they were down on paper, in black and white, so I made a list of all the things that could prevent the trip becoming a reality. The list was long. I had a good job for a start. However, I decided that a job is only good if I deem it to be fulfilling, so perhaps I had a bad job, after all. I would hand in my notice. I didn't know anything about long-distance cycling or how to fix bikes. I reasoned that I could learn that. I had no money. I concluded that I would either earn more or spend less. Or do both. I was terrible at saving, so I would likely need to find a way to do both. I had to tell my parents, and what if they didn't approve? I hoped they would, eventually, and if they didn't then I had to be the master of my own happiness. Lastly, and this was the ugliest one – I had a mortgage. Yikes. I decided that I could rent out my room to cover my portion of the mortgage payment.

Suddenly, as if by magic, all those reasons not to go didn't really seem like reasons at all. In fact, when put next to the terrifying notion that I might carry on with an unfulfilled life, they weren't terrifying one bit. The reasons were pussycats. They were no match for the sensation that came from having made the decision to leave. I felt in control. I had purpose. I had a mission. From that point on, the adventure clung to me. It was by my side through every struggle. It was my guiding light in the darkness of the resistance I faced. Nothing mattered more than it. I was going on an adventure and no one was going to stop me.

I took a second job in a local bike shop and for nine months I worked seven days a week. From Monday to Friday I was a marketing manager, and on Saturday and Sunday I was a sales assistant in my local bike shop. My marketing job was easier. Being on your feet in a shop from 9 a.m.–6 p.m. with only a short break for lunch was exhausting. The second job meant I didn't go out and I didn't spend money. I learnt how to fix bikes and received a discount on cycling equipment. Win. Win. Win. On the downside, I gained a bit of weight in those nine months. I was sleep deprived, not doing any exercise and living on a diet of baked beans, cheese, toast and croissants. But the pounds that piled onto my body mirrored those that were stacking up in my bank accounts and so that made it okay.

A few months down the line, I bit the bullet and handed in my notice at work, giving my boss six months' warning. Colleagues told me I was crazy to do that. 'They'll fire you!' they said. But I decided that it was important to be honest and to give my boss a decent amount of time to replace me in the team. Just because I didn't think that my job was what I was supposed to be doing with my life didn't mean I didn't like the people I worked with – they were the only reason I'd not left sooner.

It was around that time that I decided to tackle what was quite literally the mothership of all barriers – telling my parents. I was racked with guilt of the worst kind – middle-class guilt. How could I turn around to my parents and say: 'Mum, Dad, thanks for everything you've done for me in life, for the roof above my head, for the university education 'n' all – but really I'd just quite like to go and ride my bike and sleep in a tent'?! But that's exactly what I did. Mum, prone to worrying as mothers are, gave a surprisingly positive initial response. 'You're going to cycle the fifty states? That's fantastic, Anna!'

'Is it?! Yes, it is. Thanks, Mum.'

'Because I am going to come and drive fifty states behind you. In a van.'

There was a long pause while I checked her face for signs of a joke. This was no joke.

'Mum! You cannot drive behind me for all fifty states. That is so uncool.' She looked hurt. Eventually Mum came to terms with the idea, and we settled on my parents coming to see me in the final state of the journey – Hawaii. Yes, I dangled the Hawaii carrot. All mothers are calmed by the dangling of a hula-dancing, volcano-erupting, Mai-Tai-drinking, Pacific-paradise Hawaii carrot. In truth, I felt a certain amount of guilt about the worry I would no doubt bring to her in the months to come. It ate me up inside to think that after all she had done for me I was about to put her through months of sleepless nights. But I resolved that I couldn't take her worry from her – all I could do was my best to minimise it.

In between work in the bike shop and the day job at the office, I sat up late into the night on my laptop, building a website for the ourney, planning the route and researching what kind of kit I might need for all the seasons I would be passing through. Deciding on a route was the most challenging part of all the planning. But in a sick way, I loved it.

I decided to draw stars on a map of every location in the USA I wanted to visit, then I placed some tracing paper over the top and traced a line through each of the stars. I say traced – I traced and retraced and traced again. Have you ever tried to draw a semi-continuous line through the 50 states of the USA?! They should add it to the Mensa test. Thankfully, there was an organisation called Adventure Cycling Association that had some cycle-friendly routes already mapped out, so I stuck to these where I could. It was like a never-ending game of Tetris. Just when I thought the blocks were stacked up so high that I might explode, one would slot into place, followed by another, and another, and I saw a way through to the next level. I am a planner at heart, after all, and being a planner means I get to be excited about the prospect of a journey ahead of time, and then again while I am on it. Planners get to double down on excitement.

When I sat back from my trace-a-thon, I was greeted by a very long, wiggly line – a line that was 16,000 miles long. It took in every nook and cranny of the states and saw me heading down to Florida's Key West for a little cocktail time. I realised that 16,000 miles was too far to cover within the six months my visa would allow, so I went through the soul-destroying process of hashing out sections of the route, of cutting corners and missing out certain national parks. Oh, how my soul wept.

By the time I was satisfied, I had a route that was 11,000 miles long. To sum it up, I would begin with a little pedal in Alaska. I would then fly to Seattle on the west coast of the mainland US and complete a very long wiggle all around the country to Dallas, Texas. And from Texas I would fly to Hawaii. It was a route that terrified and excited me in equal measure. I would aim to average 75 miles per day, with extra time allotted for days exploring some of the big cities and resting. I also added a few contingency days to the schedule – because it was likely that there would be many disasters en route. As an added bonus, and seeing as how I would be working every hour God sent in the lead up to landing in the states, I decided that I would spend a month 'warming up' in Canada. It would be a month to ease myself into life on the bike, and it would perhaps serve to settle my ever-growing nerves too.

Somewhere in the midst of all the planning, I had also decided that going off on this big adventure to fulfil my own life was all very well and good, but that it had to serve a purpose beyond that. I thought about the new direction in which I'd chosen to take my life, and how grateful I was to have even considered a big adventure as a possibility. So I decided that I would visit schools along the journey – one in every single state if I could – to talk to the kids about how beautiful their country is, to encourage them to cling on to everything in life that makes them happy and to dream up big ideas of their own.

The final piece of the puzzle was to select my companion for the journey, a trusty steed that would carry me through my darkest days. I did some research, read many cycling blogs that made my brain hurt and came across a few brands – Surly, Santos, Koga, Genesis – which most seemed to trust for round-the-world journeys. I have always liked Dutch people and they sure do know how to ride bikes, so I went with the Dutch-made Santos. An aluminium, long-framed bicycle beauty. When I went into the shop on the south coast of the UK to discuss my final requirements for the bike, I was asked to pick a frame colour. I scanned those on offer on the wall – blues, reds, bright greens, yellows, whites…

'Which colour do most people go for?' I asked the shop owner.

'Dark green or black,' he replied.

Urgh. How dull.

'Why do they choose such dark colours?!' I asked, half in disbelief, half wondering if the 'happy colours' were more expensive.

'Oh, well, they like to blend in, to not be seen when they're camping, et cetera,' said the man.

Sod that, I thought. I have not come here to blend in. I am not going to the USA to blend in. I will blend in no longer.

'I'll take the pink one,' I said firmly. 'And I shall name her Boudica.'

In one sense, the aim for the 50-state journey was simple: I would do what I believed would make me happy and I would do it every single day to see how that felt for a while. I would put myself, ultimately and selfishly, first. Yet, in another sense, this journey was just the tip of an iceberg. My plans and intentions were the only parts visible to others. Lurking beneath the surface, hidden from daylight, was a frozen mass of complex emotions. An unfulfilled dream to be an Olympic athlete. A failed relationship. An overwhelming belief that I had more to contribute to the world. And so out of multiple inadequacies, the journey rose like a triumph.

I wondered what I hoped it would bring me. Perhaps I would find that elusive thing called inspiration? Perhaps I would find what I was supposed to be doing with my life? Perhaps I would find love? Although I wasn't sure I was ready for that. Perhaps I would find lust? I would settle for lust, at least. Perhaps I would find a place where my restless mind could be at peace? I hoped that I would find all of these things. Whatever my hopes, whatever the reasons, one thing was true: I had to go.

***

I should have known better than to have my leaving party two nights before I was due to fly. In 28 years of life, I thought that I'd have grown wiser, that I'd have moved beyond letting the excitement and free flow of champagne and company of long-time friends get the better of me. But at 4 a.m. I was lying in a bush at the end of my parents' road in south-west London. I had spent the whole taxi ride from Fulham expressing my deep disgust that a work colleague, whose face I had attempted to attack with my own, had politely declined my advances. Fancy that. After exiting the taxi and deciding that a wee couldn't wait the extra 40 steps to the house, I had attempted to relieve myself in a lucky nearby bush. Alas, the bush was behind a calf-height wall, so I'd fallen backwards over the wall, into the bush. Legs akimbo, pants down, chuckling to myself.

Upon righting myself, I decided that this was probably a good time to go for a 'TC', a tactical chunder, as my peers termed it. Not being much of a drinker, I wasn't really versed in such late-night endeavours, but I'd heard it was the thing to do when one realises one's alcohol consumption has gone a little beyond redemption, and, in my case, I was far beyond that.

The following morning, I opened my eyes to a world of pain. I lifted my leaden head off the pillow and tried to calm the sloshing of cerebral fluid inside my brain, which was matched by a sloshing sensation in my stomach. I felt a wave of nausea build and lunged for the en-suite toilet, depositing whatever remained in my stomach into the ceramic bowl, with a topping of bile for good measure.

That day I was supposed to be packing and sorting out all the last-minute important stuff for seven months away from home. Instead, I spent the entire day in bed. Well, half in bed and half clutching the toilet. That in itself was terrible behaviour, but it was made even worse by the fact that my friend Lydia, who would be joining me for the first part of the 50-state journey, had now arrived at my parents' house. I had invited her over to 'get the last-minute things sorted'. But Lydia was now hanging out with my family downstairs while I secreted champagne from every pore in my hot and stuffy teenage bedroom.

Mum seemed more upset than usual at my alcohol antics. She, quite rightly, didn't approve of hangovers as a general rule, but today there was an extra look of disdain in her eyes. At 6 p.m. I managed to crawl out of bed and present myself for what Mum had told me was going to be a 'special dinner'. As I swayed and swallowed down a final attempt from my body to eject any form of evil, Mum led me to the dining room.

'Ready?' she asked.

Ready for what? I thought. But I nodded all the same as she shoved open the dining-room door to reveal my entire family, plus Lydia, sitting around the table. The room was dripping with Christmas decorations. Great swathes of tinsel were suspended from the ceiling, stars were pinned where the picture frames usually hung and I spotted our Christmas tree in the corner of the room, laden with sparkles and fairy lights. The table was covered in everything you would expect of a perfect Christmas dinner – stuffing balls, crispy roast potatoes, parsnips, cranberry sauce, turkey. And in front of each person's place was a cracker. I looked at Mum, and then at the rest of my family, who were already fully in the mood and wearing paper Christmas hats.

'Well, I realised that you were going to be away for Christmas this year,' Mum said, 'so I thought that we'd have our own Christmas while you were still here.'

It was 30 June 2013, the start of summer and as perfect a time as any for my last pre-adventure supper in the UK.

CANADA

CHURCH HOUSE

WHISTLER

CAMPBELL RIVER

COURTENAY

VANCOUVER

PORT ALBERNI

DUNCAN

VICTORIA

2

The Land of Moose and Maple Leaves

Distance Cycled: 0 miles
States Completed: 0

Head down, abs pulled in tight, elbows locked in position – I was doing all I could to engage my glute muscles to help me push my oversized cardboard bike box through the arrivals lounge of Vancouver airport. It was a great post-flight workout. Lydia parted the crowds in front of me like a modern Moses and I followed her snaking path, making a loud 'ssssh-hhhhhhhhhhh' noise as the cardboard scraped along the grey tiled floor of the airport.

There was an excitement bubbling in my belly. This was it; we had arrived! Let the warm-up portion of the journey commence. After a 10-hour flight we were both hideously jet lagged, me especially it seemed. I'd gotten overexcited with the array of films on offer on the flight and, aside from dozing off briefly, I hadn't slept a wink. I'd now been awake for a full 24 hours and my left eye was starting to twitch.

After what felt like an eternity of shoving, we reached the automatic glass doors that marked the airport's exit. Lyds stood up from her hunched position and turned to me, grinning. I grinned back.

27

I first met Lydia Birch when I was 16 years old. We were running alongside each other one morning during a 5k at Club La Santa, a holiday resort on the island of Lanzarote for sports-mad people who can't keep still. We saw each other once a year at Club La Santa over the years that followed, but our friendship wasn't solidified until we were 20 – when we ended up at the same boat club back in the UK at the University of London and lived in student housing next door to one another.

I had always been a little perplexed by Lydia's mix of unshakable cheeriness and steely determination. If you didn't know her well enough you might assume she was a little ditzy, but she is far from it. I will be forever envious of her luscious thick dark hair and dark pool-like eyes, topped off with a soft Liverpudlian accent. There was a rumour that went around the university boat club once that one of Lydia's eyes was made of glass, on account of a parasite she'd picked up from a cat when she was young. It was a fantastic rumour, one that I believed for many years, but I later found out that this was only partially true. Yes, she was blind in one eye, but both of her eyes (much to my disappointment) were real.

I couldn't quite recall how it came to be that Lydia would join me for the first eight weeks of my North America journey, but I think it had begun with me divulging my plans and Lydia casually offering to join me for a portion of the ride. She was a teacher and had a long summer holiday to fill with adventure.

'How about we assemble Boudica and Zena outside?' Lyds suggested, referring to our bikes in their boxes and motioning to the wide pavement just the other side of the airport sliding doors. I was pleased that Lydia had chosen a suitably warrior-esque name for her own steed and, although somewhat less pink than Boudica, I hoped that our bikes would become good friends too in the months to come. Exiting the airport was like walking into a greenhouse. Thick clammy air wrapped itself around my body like a blanket. In the Canadian heat, I felt fat and unfit. My lack of training, recent sleep deprivation and a disproportionate amount of time dedicated to eating croissants had left me less than svelte for the start of the journey. I had piled on 8 kg over the past year, and my legs and ass now felt uncomfortable crammed into cycling kit – legs and ass that had lain dormant in the lead up to the ride as I worked every hour God sent to make it to the start line.

I'd rather have gouged my eyes out than assembled my bike at that very moment. The lack of sleep on the plane was starting to catch up with me, and at the point when I dropped one of the tiny bolts which secured the bike's water bottle cage to the frame for the fifth time, I feared that I might lose my rag. We took it in turns – one of us ducking off to slip into cycling clothing, while the other continued to assemble the bikes. At last we stood back from the bikes and inspected our handiwork. To my amazement, everything was in place – nothing had snapped, bent or broken on the flight over and Boudica looked resplendent in the Canadian morning sun. We set about tearing the cardboard bike boxes up into smaller strips and crammed them into three nearby bins. Cardboard deconstruction complete, we were at last ready for the off.

***

'Ummm, Anna?'

'Yeah, Lyds?'

'Which side of the road do they drive on in Canada?'

I paused. I'll confess I hadn't really thought about it, but the answer had to be the obvious one.

'Errrr… the same side as America, I'm guessing?'

'Are you sure? Because I thought it was the left,' said Lyds, looking confused.

I wavered. Well, now I wasn't sure. I mean, Canada is part of the Commonwealth, and we drive on the left so perhaps the tradition of driving on the left was part and parcel of taking on the Queen as a head of state too. A sort of 'buy one, get one free' on British rules. I looked up to the airport slip road for confirmation, only to find that it was a one-way street. I tried to reason out loud.

'It has to be the right, I mean – how would that work at the border? They can't just switch sides of the road as cars cross from Canada to America…?' I conjured an image in my mind of the bedlam that it would cause. 'It's got to be on the right.'

'Well… I don't know…' Lydia continued. 'I'm going to go and ask the bus driver.'

'Lyds! You can't ask the bloody bus driver what side of the road we should be on! We'll look like complete idiots!' I protested, overwhelmed with the embarrassment of both of us not having thought about this before.

'But I want to know,' Lyds continued matter-of-factly.

'Oh, dear God, go on then,' I sighed. 'Go and ask in your best Queen's English which side of the road we should ride out of here on.'

She skipped off to a parked-up shuttle bus and, after a short exchange and a bit of gesturing, she returned to the bikes.

'Well?'

'It's the right,' she shrugged. 'Makes sense, I suppose.'

And we were off.

The plan in Canada was to have no plan. This extra month tacked on at the start of the USA trip was for us to get used to the bikes, to one another's company and to the daily mileage I'd need to crank out for the six months that followed in the 50 US states.

Naturally, we got lost within the first hour. My body groaned and creaked in the heat as we climbed over hills to catch the ferry from Horseshoe Bay. From there we would head to Vancouver Island, which (according to my thorough googling) was a beautiful place to ride a bicycle, and there was less traffic than in mainland British Columbia. My pasty English skin glowed, almost translucent, in the bright Canadian sunshine, and my legs told me to sod off on several occasions. But onwards we trundled. Physically, I felt uncomfortable; mentally, I was anxious. I was concerned that I had bitten off more than I could chew and cursed myself for not having done more training. But overriding all of that discomfort was a sense of freedom. Complete, refreshing, lighter-than-air freedom.

After getting off the ferry at Nanaimo on Vancouver Island, our first evening of riding and camping didn't exactly go to plan. I realised that I'd left my favourite sunglasses in the toilets on the ferry for starters, and so after a short ride being blinded by the evening sun, we arrived at a campground. Only the ground was so hard that we'd have needed a jackhammer to get the tent pegs in. I then set fire to our brand-new cooking stove, melting the metal edges of it… largely because I hadn't taken the time to work out how to use it before leaving.

I lost my rag a fair few times, all the while knowing that these were not things I should be losing it about. And to make it worse, Lydia was cool as a cucumber. I had always thought that it would be the physical side of this journey that would challenge me, but on that first evening I realised it was going to be much more than that. There was so much beyond my control – an exploding camping stove and lost sunglasses were just the start.

Still, at least navigating over Vancouver Island was a cinch. The island is 290 miles long, but in the northern, less populated half, there are approximately three roads. Okay, I exaggerate – there are at least six. They splay out like fingers from the East Coast, meaning that we needed to follow the main highway up the East Coast and then duck off to the west, before returning to the east to carry on north, to explore anywhere on the West Coast. Confused? Me too.

We made a vague plan to head north and explore as many places on the East Coast as we could. We picked a few place names we liked the sound of – Port Alberni, Comox, Courtenay, Gold River, Hot Springs Cove – as well as those that sounded exotic, such as Tofino and Ucluelet, which we couldn't pronounce and so referred to it as 'Cluedo', 'Ukulele' or 'Yooky'. Still, we both knew what we were talking about, so that was A-okay.

The limited network of roads led us through a largely unspoilt part of the world. Being in the midst of such vast expanses of wilderness, surrounded by towering pine trees, and passing snow-capped mountains and lakes, it was impossible not to feel humbled. Over those first few days it was like Mother Nature herself was standing right in front of me, beating her grand chest and saying, 'Aren't I just fabulous? I've been here for thousands of years – what took you so long?'

We ducked and weaved our way around the island, riding among towering evergreens, in bright sunshine and past soaring bald eagles. I'd never seen an eagle before, not in the wild anyway, and I don't think that London Zoo counts. So when I spotted the first one, gliding above me against a backdrop of blue sky, I almost drove my bike off the road. I followed its flight path with my eyes, watching as it flexed and fluttered its vast outstretched wings. It made flying look effortless, which wasn't surprising given the size of its wingspan. 'Baldy', as Lydia and I named our very first eagle friend, was close enough that I could see the ruffle of white feathers around his neck, slightly raised from his body at the point where the white head feathers transitioned into brown, and then back again to white on its tail. Its beak was less yellow than I had imagined it might be from all the cartoons I'd watched over the years, but its talons were just as terrifying. They looked like they could pick me up and carry me away, let alone any smaller prey.

As the days wore on, I got used to seeing eagles, and they became our companions on Vancouver Island. There we were, two girls, just hangin' with the eagles. They soared, we rode, and we all enjoyed the same sense of freedom. In between eagle spotting, we pedalled past lake after lake after lake. Most of the campgrounds were situated on the lakeshore so we got into the habit of beginning each morning with a dip in the watering hole, and using them to do our laundry too. We received some odd looks from day-trippers as we slipped into bikinis and set about scrubbing our wardrobe items one by one. Sometimes the lakes were more like large ponds, but more often than not they were at least 10 miles in length and a mile wide.

In those early morning dips, surrounded by cool, fresh water, my body still felt uncomfortable and unfit, but it was beginning to relax. My mind was too. The lake water of Vancouver Island was washing away the grime and stress from a life in the City of London. With each day on the bike, my muscles relaxed and my eyes seemed to open a little wider. I heard more of the birdsong; I noticed the rush of the wind through the leaves of the trees, the sun felt warmer on my skin. I had always thought that freedom was one thing, a single sensation, but in reality it was a series of little things. Tiny changes in the atmosphere that combined to deliver an overwhelming sense of contentment.

***

Over the course of two weeks, we averaged cycling 80 miles a day on Vancouver Island. It was more than we'd expected to do, but when there was nothing to do but cycle all day, and there was so much to see, it was hard to do less. I had bought an old-fashioned-style British-made leather saddle which, according to the manufacturers, would take 1,500 miles to mould to the shape of my own derrière. So it wasn't surprising that it had yet to get to the comfortable stage and had left me with a few saddle sores. Those sores were accompanied by a strange rash we both seemed to have picked up from one of the lakes. We looked a mess, red patches all over us, scratches and dirt, little areas of sunburn where we had missed applying sun cream, but despite all of this I had grown extremely fond of Vancouver Island, so when the time came to return to the mainland, I was sad.

After catching the ferry from Courtenay to Powell River, we worked our way down Vancouver's Sunshine Coast. A fair attempt at a name – there was indeed sunshine and coastline, although 'Sunshine (roller)coast(er)' would be more apt.

After two days of ascending and descending on the Sunshine Coaster, we rolled into the town of Gibsons. While hanging out in a fast-food chain, using the free Wi-Fi and chomping on an obligatory doughnut, we began discussing our camping options for that night. We were gawking at the cost of the campsite on a road just out of town, which was billed at $35 for a camp spot – pretty much our whole budget for the day. I was up for wild camping, going rogue, but Lydia still didn't really like the idea and I knew not to push it. Just then, a man came over to our table, clearly drawn to it by our scintillating camping chit-chat.

'Say – you girls would be welcome to come and camp in my back garden?' he said, tentatively interrupting our conversation in an accent that was unmistakably English. I looked at the man; he looked nice. Nice face, nice brown hair, not a hint of the serial killer about him. And then I looked at Lyds who shrugged.

'Really?!' I asked.

'Yes, of course, although – let me just check with my

wife first!'

'Cool!' said Lyds.

And so, following a phone call to his wife to check that she didn't mind him bringing home two strange British girls, we were properly introduced to Paul and were left with instructions on how to cycle to his house, 2 miles up the road. That night we 'mild camped' in Paul and Claudette's 'back garden', which was set in five acres of open forest (I'm still claiming it was partially 'wild'.) The fact that Paul spent the first 10 minutes telling us just how many bears he'd seen in his garden, and I spent the night with Lydia clutching my leg, swearing she'd heard a bear, just added to the wildness of it all. Paul also told us with glee: 'If you walked out of the backyard right now, into the forest, you'd only cross one more road before you made it to the edge of the Arctic Circle. It's pure wilderness out there.'

See, like I said: wild camping.

In the morning we were woken by the sound of a male voice that didn't sound like Paul. The man was in the garden and on the phone to his dad, it seemed – delivering an update on life and letting his dad know just how much he loved him. It was all quite sweet, and Lydia and I listened longer than we should have from beyond the flimsy ripstop walls of our tent, before we emerged and found 'Ben'. We knew it was 'Ben' because Ben had been mentioned many times in dispatches the previous night by Paul and Claudette. Ben lived in the spare room in the house and was, for want of a better term, a hippy. Ain't no two ways about it, Ben was an absolutely lovely, hug-delivering, earth-worshipping hippy.

Ben the hippy took us for a short barefoot walk down to the nearby stream in the forest, before returning to a circle of stones on the ground in the back garden, not far from where our tent was pitched.

'Stand here,' Ben instructed Lyds and me, and we dutifully obliged, placing our bare feet within the circle of arranged rocks. 'Can't you just feel it?' he said. 'Feel the earth, the stones? It's like they're talking to me.' All I could feel was that my feet were starting to get a little cold with the lack of sock and shoe action, but I was trying to hear what they were saying.

During the 20 minutes we spent packing up our tent, Ben returned three times. The first time he shared some of his homemade kombucha (an all-natural drink made from fungus – sounds disgusting, tastes delicious) with us, before scurrying off again. The next time he returned with a loaf of bread and a block of cheese.

'I know you girls said you like cheese,' he said, grinning as he handed it over. From our earlier conversation as we'd walked into the forest, I knew that Ben earned very little wages working in a logging farm up the road. He was saving to go to Ireland, to learn more about the Gaelic and Druid places of worship, and here he was giving us food. Even as we wheeled our bikes out of the garden he ran after us, delivering a final gift of organic cherries for the road. Each item had come with a big hug and the cherries were no exception. In all this hugging, I'd started to notice that Ben was actually rather good looking, so in the end I didn't mind an extra hug one bit. It'd be rude not to hug back, after all.

***

Leaving Paul and Claudette at Sunshine Coast, we began a pedal-pilgrimage to the world-renowned ski resort of Whistler. Given that there's only one main road in and out of Whistler, navigation was a cinch. Rebuilt for the Winter Olympics in 2010, Highway 99, or the Sea to Sky Highway, is 63 miles from the ferry port to the town centre, which stands 670 m above sea level. It was halfway through the 63-mile journey that I considered putting in a complaint at the Ministry of Road Naming. The highway, which does start at the sea and move in a general sky-like direction, in fact takes the sea-sky-sea-sky-sea-sky route to get there.

It'd now been just nine days since we'd stepped off the plane at Vancouver. We'd covered 612 miles so far and I was really starting to feel it in my legs. And when you're really starting to feel it in your legs, there's nothing more frustrating than to discover that there is a descent after each uphill effort. Thirty miles in, and having been plunged back to sea level for the fifth time, we finally began to climb consistently. At this point, as if by magic, a little tailwind arrived. I stand strong in my belief that this was the sheepish Highway 99's doing

– trying to make up for its miles and miles of deceit. 'Sorry about that,' it whispered, pushing us gently towards the sky and Whistler, at last.

Whistler is a town brimming with life. Traditionally a ski town, the place had transformed into a mountain-bike mecca, as it was now nearing the height of summer. We couldn't help but be swept along with the hordes of men, women and teeny kidlings, wheeling bikes around with a constant look of glee on their faces.

There was, however, one other thing that we noticed very quickly about Whistler: the cost. Having set ourselves a daily budget of 50 USD, including food and accommodation, Whistler was hammering our wallets. We opted to stay at a campground just outside town and hop on a shuttle bus into the centre to save the pennies. On day two, we decided to take a day off the bikes. The prospect of the first day off our bikes in 10 days was a real treat.

We took the cable car up to the top of one of the nearby mountains and set out on the narrow and winding High Note Trail. The scenery was mind-blowing. At lunchtime we stood at a clearing in Garibaldi Provincial Park and looked out onto the valley below. In front of us was Cheakamus Lake, the most vibrant turquoise blue in colour. It looked as if someone had poured acrylic paint into a mould and left it to set solid, such was the concentration of colour. The clouds were casting shadows across the surface of the lake, which were ever so slightly distorted by the waves on its surface, whipped up by the wind. On the far side of the lake were three snow-capped peaks, framed by surrounding evergreens which occupied every other available scrap of land.

All this Garibaldi exploring had made me think of Garibaldi biscuits, and thinking of biscuits had made me hungry. So we plonked ourselves down on one large rock each and began to unpack the supplies we'd brought up for lunch. I set about steadily cramming salami into the cavern I'd created in a bread roll, and realised it'd been a long time since I'd eaten salami, if ever. Having been a vegetarian for 22 years to this point, it was like discovering food all over again and, if I was honest, it all looked a bit rank. Still, I'd decided just before the trip started that being a vegetarian on the road was going to be more trouble than it was worth. And seeing as my aversion to eating meat was wearing thin and precariously balanced on the principle of 'I just really like animals' and 'I wanted to be a vet when I was younger', I decided that perhaps this trip was as good a time as any to let meat back into my life.

'We better not stay here too long!' said Lyds.

'Why not?' I asked, stuffing the now fused mass of dough and salami into my awaiting pie-hole. It still looked rank, but I was ravenous. Lydia was doing the same and it took her a good few chews before she could begin to speak.

'Thw eeers!' she said, her mouth still full and not able to fully form any sound that even remotely resembled the

English language.

'The what?' I said. Lyds chewed a few more bites and swallowed hard before gasping for breath.

'The bears!' she clarified.

'The bears?! What do you mean the bears?'

'I mean, if we're out here, eating salami, the bears will smell it and come and find us. And then they'll eat us. We'll be their salami. Human salami!'

'Lyds. I think the bears have got more things to be worrying about than our salami sandwiches. And besides… we'd see them coming up here, wouldn't we?' I glanced around nervously.

The truth was she had a point. We knew there were black bears around here, but equally the chance of running into one was nothing to be overly worried about. I was fast learning that Lyds was terrified of the prospect of running into a bear unannounced and, although I had some mild concerns, I thought it best to play down my bear anxiety, if only to reassure her a little. It's one of the things that I loved about our friendship – in many ways Lyds mothered me, and in other ways I mothered her.

Bear-free picnic complete, we continued on our hike. There was some light snow on the trail, a leftover from the spring snowfall, and I had been finding it tricky to negotiate in the thick-soled trainers I'd packed, which had little to no grip on them. We arrived at a narrow section that required a semi-scramble over a boulder and placing my foot between two boulders on the other side. I put my left foot down in the snow, on what was a small incline, and it slipped immediately.

'Wooahhh!' I yelped, as the rest of my body slid forward and then… thud. My left knee collided with the boulder.

'You alright, McNuff?!' Lyds shouted back from where she was on the trail ahead.

'Yeaaaap!' I called back, inspecting my knee, which was now bleeding. 'Just slipped, nothing major… it really hurt though!'

'Is there any blood?' Lyds shouted back. How sweet that my friend is so concerned for my safety, I thought.

'Errrr – a little. It'll be alright.'

'Bears. They'll smell the blood, you know?' Lyds said matter-of-factly, before turning and continuing on down the trail, as I hobbled after her.

***

The following morning, we waved a fond farewell to Whistler and headed back down the 99 towards Vancouver. Forty miles into the return ride and something in my left knee just didn't feel… right. The fall on the High Note Trail the previous day had left a deep cut and my knee felt bruised. When I set off on the bike that morning, I assumed the dull ache on the outside of the knee was just the bruising. Only now I began to wonder. Bruising shouldn't hurt the more you cycle, in fact, if anything, the adrenaline rush from exercise should make the pain from the bruising subside. It was then that it started to dawn on me, like a dark cloud creeping slowly across the front of my mind – my knee was more than just bruised.

I didn't want to tell Lydia, and I was hoping against hope that the pain would miraculously disappear. *If I ignore it, the pain doesn't exist,* I told myself, pushing on in silence for the following 10 miles. I thought that if we could just make it to Vancouver, then I could give it a little rest and it would all come right again. But the pain continued to get worse. Every time I turned the pedal it felt like there were two bits of sandpaper moving against one other beneath my knee cap. Eventually I cracked and decided to investigate the issue. Moving in a nonchalant fashion (so as not to raise any suspicion from Lydia), I lowered my hand to have a feel around the knee cap. My fingertips were greeted with a sensation that made my heart sink. It felt as though someone had slipped gravel beneath the surface of my skin: cruuuunch. I moved my fingers away and tried again, testing out a slightly different area: cruuuunch. It was tendonitis. Tendonitis is a common injury among rowers, who often suffer from it in their forearms, and so I knew the dreaded symptoms well. I'd never had it in my knee before, but it was the same sensation nonetheless. The game was up. I turned my head back over my shoulder: 'Lyds, I need to stop.'

I sighed, now searching for the right words. 'I've totally buggered my knee.'

***

For the following week, we holed up in Vancouver – both of us sleeping on a pull-out bed in the hotel room of a mutual friend from the UK, who happened to be in the city for a science conference that week. I wrestled with the angst of willing my knee to get better, or fall off – one of the two. My mind was swimming, and although I tried my best to distract myself, I couldn't help but feel useless. And foolish. Having averaged those 80 miles a day on Vancouver Island, I was cursing myself for doing so many miles so quickly. I knew the injury was a result of the collision with the rock, but the underlying issue was that I had gone too hard, too soon. What a prat.

If there was one thing I knew, it's that there was no way I wasn't carrying on. I would find a way, there had to be a way, but right now I couldn't see beyond this week. My mind was foggy. I had published one blog so far about riding in Canada, but I wasn't feeling brave enough to admit to everyone that I'd damaged myself so early on, so I decided not to share much on social media or online at all that week. As far as everyone back home knew, all was still well.

We all know that it's best to rest with an injury, but to try to make me do absolutely nothing is near impossible. So I filled the week with Google searches about tendonitis and various applications of ointments to the knee. I tried everything: ice, heat, gels, stretching. I even went to yoga classes. I had never done yoga before; it wasn't my kind of exercise. But over that week in Vancouver, I went to a yoga class every day, convincing myself I was 'rebalancing' my body. The reality was that the yoga gave me some kind of structure to my days; it made me feel like I was progressing with the injury somehow and it took my mind off my knee. I told myself to stay positive. 'It'll be right in a week,' I repeated each night before bed. Every morning I woke up and poked my knee, just to see how it was doing. Every morning, it hurt.

I felt for Lydia during that week because I was away with the pain-fairies. She joined me each morning at yoga and spent the rest of the day reading and catching up on prep for the new school term. All the while, I continued to obsess about my knee. All my fears about the trip came piling down on top of me. I had told everyone I was off to cycle the 50 states, and here I was, having not even hit state one, with a potential showstopper of an injury. I decided that I best go and see someone. Because that's what you do when you hurt things – you seek out some advice. The plan was to arm myself with some exercises or something, anything that would make the knee manageable so that I could carry on. I googled 'physio Vancouver' and booked in to see one of the people who popped up in the search results.

Sitting in the physio's office in downtown Vancouver, I

looked at the walls, which were adorned with pictures and sports memorabilia from signed professional athletes. I was impressed. If this physio had treated all these stars then she would surely understand that I wasn't giving up. I explained my plans for the next six months very thoroughly. As we went through the treatment, she poked, prodded and took out a magic machine, which put some electricity in my knee – it was all very encouraging. At the end of the session, after some more questions, the physio asked me to sit down in the chair next to her desk. I readied myself for the remedy that would set me right and put me on a positive trajectory for the next six months.

'So, it's clear you've got tendonitis,' she said firmly. I nodded as she continued with her diagnosis. 'But you also have hyper-mobile joints.'

'Hyper-mobile?'

'Your joints move a lot outside the normal range of movement. It's quite common.'

'Okay, right…' I was beginning to wonder how this knowledge would help me battle my knee pain. Perhaps I needed to know about the limits of my body before I could start cycling again? I absorbed the information and readied myself for the solution to the past week of mind games and misery.

'As you have hyper-mobile joints, I would suggest that you don't do any exercise which continues for an excessive length of time.' My mouth dropped and I stared at her as she gave the knife one extra twist in the wound. 'You'll just damage your body if you do a lot of exercise. It's not designed to cope.'

As I left the treatment room, I wasn't angry so much as disappointed. What a waste of time, of money, and a waste of faith in a professional. Rule number one of endurance exercise: no one knows your body better than you. I reminded myself of this, threw her advice pamphlet in the bin outside the practice, and walked back to the hotel. Whatever anyone else said, it didn't matter now. I was out of time. Lyds and I packed up the bikes and jumped in a taxi back to Vancouver airport. I was heading to Alaska without the faintest idea of how I was going to carry on.

HEALY

CANTWELL

Mt. McKinley

DENALI NATIONAL
PARK & PRESERVE

DENALI STATE PARK

TALKEETNA

SKWENTNA

WASILLA

Start

ANCHORAGE

ALASKA

3

Meals on Wheels

Distance Cycled: 832 miles

States Completed: 0

I had always been mildly concerned about being granted a full 180-day B2 visa for the United States. My experience at the US embassy in London had been tense and unpleasant to say the least, and I was expecting a similar level of interrogation at the border. Having come this far and scrambled my way over a jumble of messy fears, excuses and logistical shenanigans to actually get to the start line, the visa stamp in my passport was to be the final hurdle. Unlike many of the aforesaid challenges, it was one aspect over which I had little to no control. My fate was in the hands of the border official, and as I had been informed multiple times on the phone by the US embassy when back in London, 'Only the border official can decide how long to grant your visa for.'

As such, I had set aside a whole flight from Vancouver to Anchorage, Alaska, to worry myself senseless about whether I would be granted the full 180 days I needed to complete the ride. (Well, I had neatly scheduled some worry in between the in-flight meals and movie-watching. I wouldn't want my worry to interrupt the enjoyment of many Disney films, but, rest assured, somewhere between a limp beef curry and my second free diet coke, I would let my imagination run amok and do some catastrophising.)

When I moved towards the gate in Vancouver airport and came upon a huge sign that read 'US border control', I as good as peed my pants. Not now?! Now?! I was still in Canada and definitely not prepared. What if they interrogated me as hard as they had in London?! What if I fluffed my words again when I tried to explain that I intended to cycle from Alaska to Hawaii, only to be told, 'It is physically impossible to cycle across the Pacific Ocean to Hawaii, ma'am.'? What if, what if, what if… oh jeepers. I was at the front of the queue. My heart began to beat fast, the hairs on my arms stood on end and my temples began to tingle as I approached a stout-looking man encased in his glass cocoon of decision-making. I decided to name him, in my mind at least, because then perhaps we could be friends. Otherwise, he was a nameless man, with my fate in his hands. I decided he looked like a Joe. Joes were kind, Joes were rational, Joes would grant me my full 180-day US visa.

I took a deep breath and swallowed the lump in my throat as the person in front of me moved away from the booth. I waited, patiently. Joe looked up from his desk and motioned for me to move forwards. I pulled out my passport and slid it through the little slot in the glass and smiled. Well, I was *trying* to smile, although I think the result must have looked like the smile given by someone who has had an awful lot of Botox. Or one who was plotting a murder. My lips moved, but my face remained frozen.

'Mornin', ma'am,' said Joe, taking the passport from my hand and turning to the page which contained my beloved B2 tourist visa.

'G-good morning,' I stammered.

'Heading to Anchorage, are you?' he enquired. *Here we go*, I thought.

'Yes,' I said, sternly, making sure I sounded as if I knew exactly what I was doing.

'And what are you planning on doing in Alaska, ma'am?' he asked. I was ready, I had the full spiel on the back burner. I launched into motion.

'I'm cycling. I mean, we're cycling. Well, my friend Lydia – that's Lydia over there – we're going cycling in Denali National Park and th–'

'That's fine. Thank you, ma'am,' said Joe, stamping my passport and handing it back to me through the little slot in the glass.

'But I– Oh, right! Yes, yes! Great. Thank you, Joe.'

'I'm sorry, ma'am?'

'Oh, I mean, thank you… J… eepers! I'm just so excited to get there,' I said, doing my best to disguise the fact that I had called this man by his imaginary name. He stared at me. I stared back, and then he motioned for me to move.

'You can go on now, ma'am,' Joe said.

'Oh yes, good! Bye then.'

That was it. I hastily flicked to the page that Joe had stamped in my passport, and there it was, in blue ink, clear as day: '14 January 2014'. He had in fact stamped my passport for three days longer than I'd expected. Today's date was 22 July 2013, and I now had until January 14th to make my way through all 50 states and to Hawaii.

***

Flying into Alaska, I was overcome with emotion. It was hard not to be. The view from the plane window, through a blanket of cloud and onto the snow-covered mountain ranges below, teeming with ice fields and glaciers, was breathtaking. I had always thought of Alaska as one of the last true wildernesses left in the world, but I hadn't expected to experience it until I was actually on the ground. But from way up here, from my throne in the sky, I could already see that it was a very special place indeed. Alaska was beautiful, in the purest sense of the word.

Our accommodation for that night had come courtesy of a website called WarmShowers.org. I'll admit that the name sounds a little dodgy. It is not actually a soft-porn site used by people who would like to meet up to pee on one another; it is, in fact, a site where cycle tourists around the world can connect and offer to host one another. I'd become aware of the website earlier that year and tentatively set up a profile. I couldn't quite believe how many people were registered on the site, and especially within the USA. At the time of writing, there are almost 83,000 members worldwide. That's 83,000 people who are willing to offer a bed (or patch of grass for your tent), a (warm) shower and sometimes dinner for the night, completely free of charge. If that doesn't restore your faith in humankind, I don't know what will.

WarmShowers member Linda and her housemate Angie had been insistent on meeting us at the airport in Anchorage. Despite my protests and us offering to ride to their house in the hills, just behind the city, they had told us that riding through downtown Anchorage was not a fun experience, especially after a long flight. I was confused and mildly uncomfortable at the idea of Linda and Angie collecting us from the airport. Back home, to get a friend or relative to take time out of their day to give you a ride to an airport was asking an awful lot, and here were two women I'd never met, not only giving us bed and board for a few days, but also coming to collect us from the airport as if we were long-lost daughters.

Linda and Angie pulled up outside the airport in a large grey station wagon. Linda got out of the car first and was wearing a Hawaiian shirt, loose khaki shorts and had her silver-white hair cut close to her head, disrupted only by a pair of sunglasses nestled on top. Angie was similarly dressed, although she had opted for a loose yellow T-shirt under a

Hawaiian shirt and was wearing long beige trousers as opposed to shorts. Angie's hair was darker and more grey than white, but cut almost as short. These two were practical to a tee.

In a rather formal fashion, we all shook hands and I awkwardly bumbled my way through some profuse thanking for the ride, and in advance of them having us to stay. They both busied themselves, hauling our bikes onto the back of the wagon, and brushed every thank you off with a 'well, of course' and carried on their mission to treat Lydia and me like princesses. They were warm, open and friendly, but equally matter-of-fact. There was a job to do, and these two weren't stopping until it was done. When the second bike was safely stowed on the rear car rack, Linda clapped her hands together: 'Let's get you two home and fed,' she said.

Linda and Angie's home in the hills above Anchorage was an extension of their personalities. Pulling into the driveway, there were brightly coloured wind turbines planted out the front. One was a rainbow-coloured bicycle whose wheels spun as the wind passed through them, making the makeshift rider sway in the breeze. Another was a large ladybird, surrounded by circles of red that spun each time a gust of wind caught them.

We followed Linda and Angie through the door, up a set of stairs and into a first-floor living room. Almost every surface was coated in adventure items. Clothing, backpacks, sleeping bags, dehydrated food… I even spotted a camping stove perched on the edge of the couch. The walls were adorned with paintings and pictures of far-flung places around the world, and the shelves were brimming with trinkets and carvings from countries to match.

After being shown to our room on the ground floor of the house, we made our way back up to the living room and got chatting about Linda and Angie's lives and how they'd come to hosting two strange cyclist-touring Brits.

'I didn't take up cycling until I was sixty-four years old, you know…' said Linda, and I could tell there was hint of pride in her voice.

'What?! Hang on, how old are you now? I asked, incredulous.

'Sixty-nine years young,' she smiled, now busying herself in the kitchen, chopping up pieces of avocado for dinner. Linda hadn't sat down since we crossed the threshold. After showing us to our room on the ground floor of the house, she'd promptly set about tidying a few things, before making a start on dinner.

'We only got halibut,' she said, stopping mid-avocado-chop and looking up.

'Halibut?' I asked.

'For dinner, I mean. That's all we got. That okay?'

'Ooo, lovely!' said Lyds, piping up from the sofa next to me.

'I love halibut!' I announced, just delighted that someone was making me dinner.

'Caught fresh, mind,' said Linda. 'From Prince Rupert Island.'

'Lovely,' Lyds and I said in unison.

'Lewis caught it,' Linda added. 'You'll meet him soon; he's our lodger – stays in the room downstairs next to yours. Real outdoorsy fella. Does all the bits around the house that we don't like to.' She smiled.

'He's always fixing something,' Angie added.

Over a dinner of freshly caught halibut, asparagus, potatoes and avocado, Linda told us more about her life. A grandmother of six, she is relentless in her mission to tick off a bucket list of things she wants to do while she can, in her words, 'still walk 'n' talk'. And she does each one with the equally adventurous Angie by her side. Each year, Angie and Linda pick one big trip to do together. A few years previously, they'd cycled Route 66, covering 2,100 miles in just 24 days. 'We averaged eighty-seven miles a day. Not bad for a grandma, hey?' Linda winked.

That wasn't bad for anyone, let alone a grandma, but by now I wasn't surprised. Since their journey along Route 66, I learned that the adventurous duo had gone on to walk large parts of the Great Wall of China, visit the Galápagos Islands, not to mention other smaller hiking, cycling and canoeing trips. The way Linda talked about the adventures in her 'golden years', as she called them, made me think that these journeys had changed her in some way. This adventurous streak, her lifestyle, her love of cycling – it seemed to define her. She was very proud to be a cyclist and it led me to wondering who Linda would have been had I met her before she turned 64 and took up cycling. Would she carry the same exuberance as she did now? And as for me worrying about being a bother, it seemed that hosting rogue cyclists was just all part 'n' parcel of their lifestyle. They estimated that they'd had over 300 visitors cross their threshold in the past few years. How they had the energy to host that many people, I couldn't quite fathom.

We were midway through enjoying a proper Alaskan fish supper, when I heard the front door open downstairs.

'Ah, that must be Lewis. He's been out hiking up glaciers with friends,' Linda said.

In my mind, Lewis was a man in his 50s, with greying hair, dusty clothes and a fading smile. We carried on eating and chatting, until a figure appeared at the top of the stairs. I almost choked on my avocado. Lewis, as it turns out, was a dish. Early 30s with tousled brown hair, a strong jawline and a set of piercing blue eyes, all balanced neatly with a broad chest on a set of wide shoulders – he was fresh out of a Hollywood movie.

Introductions were made, and we all chatted for a while. I have no recollection of anything Lewis said, but I did note that he was rather quiet and extremely polite. And I'll confess, I don't think I hid my affections well at all. I felt myself grow rather red. Not only that, but, suddenly out of nowhere, I had a far stronger British accent than I had five minutes previously, began giggling at intervals and sat rather more upright than was natural. It was then I realised that I was staring, and no one was talking. I quickly looked away and down at my plate.

Later on in the evening, as we busied ourselves downstairs – unpacking, and getting showered and ready for bed – Lewis offered to take us through his photos of the trip to the glacier he'd just returned from. This did nothing to dispel my affections. He was gorgeous and outdoorsy, and he took photos. I was a little bit in love. As Lyds and I sat either side of Lewis on the blue couch in his room, adjacent to ours, I wondered how many times this had happened. How many WarmShowers ladies had he shared his photos with in the past, after returning to find them staring at him over an empty plate, with a dinner full of halibut he'd caught for them on his latest glacial jaunt? I knew we weren't the first, and we wouldn't be the last. I had to face facts – I was just a notch on Lewis's couch-post.

It was nearing midnight when we finished the Lewis, I mean… glacier slide show, but the sun was showing no signs of going down. We said goodnight to Lewis and returned to our own room, just across the hall. It was mid-summer in Alaska and we could expect 23 hours of daylight at this time of year. I wasn't sure I'd be getting much sleep tonight anyway. I was far too excited. After all, we were in ALASKA!!! The taped sheets across the window weren't keeping much of the daylight out, but the bed was covered in flannelette sheets, and it was soft, so very soft – I was asleep in an instant.

When we came up the stairs the following morning, Linda was busying herself in the kitchen, fixing us breakfast. There was a mug of freshly brewed coffee for each of us already laid out on the table. I knew Linda was headed out that day, down to New Mexico to visit her children and also look at the potential of setting up a cyclists' B&B down there.

'Eggs and avocado – that okay?' she asked, turning around with a plate in each hand.

'More than alright! Thank you!' I chirped back. As Linda moved towards us, I noticed that on her T-shirt was a picture of a cyclist being chased by a bear, and below it read 'Meals on wheels'. I nearly spat out my coffee.

'Nice shirt,' I said and Linda smiled. I could tell she'd been waiting for us to notice it. Her mischievous grin gave the game away.

'Ah, yeah. That's one thing I forgot to mention about the bears. When you see one out there, if it chases you, stop cycling. If you're cycling, they'll treat you like prey. They love to chase things, bears. And they can run real fast. Stop and put your bike between it and you, and make yourself as big as you possibly can.'

Lydia turned a shade of white and looked at her eggs. She

had a fear of bears at the best of times, but this was next level.

In a bid to distract Lydia from her thoughts of death by grizzly, Linda began to share some of Alaska's geographic and historic background with us. Bought by the USA for 7.2 million dollars from Russia back in 1867, Alaska is the most northern and western state in America. In fact, Alaska reaches so far west that it almost touches the eastern date line. If, like me, it blows your mind how that can be true, it's because of Alaska's 'Aleutian arm'. The Aleutian Islands are a chain of small land masses that stretch out from western Alaska, like a half moon, into the North Pacific Ocean. With or without that Aleutian chain, Alaska is enormous. To put it into context, it's eight times the size of Great Britain. In Anchorage, you'll see T-shirts for sale that state: 'Alaska – Pissing off Texas since 1867'. This is because Texas was the biggest US state until Alaska joined the party.

Linda went into more detail about the native Alaskans. We learned that there are 229 native villages still in existence in Alaska, and 20 individual languages spoken across the native population. Those numbers amazed me. In a world which seems to be moving at a rapid pace towards much of the population speaking just a few languages, it seemed ever more important to keep the native ones alive, if only, in this case, as a window into the history of Alaska.

Linda checked her watch and stood up. 'Well, I've got to run,' she said with a smile, then her expression changed to excitement. 'Oh! One more thing before I go!'

She moved past the piles of camping gear and over to a small cabinet in the corner of the room. She seemed to pick something up and then turned sharply on her heels. She moved towards us with her hands behind her back.

'Shut your eyes, girls,' she said. And we obliged. 'These are for you.'

I un-scrunched one eye and then the other to see that in Linda's outstretched hands were two small brown stuffed bears.

'These can be your mascots,' she said. 'They'll keep you safe against the real ones.'

I'd never seen Lydia so delighted to see a bear! She was grinning from ear to ear as we accepted a handful of brown faux-fur each and thanked Linda for the gifts. I then took my bear downstairs, tied a pink ribbon around his forehead and christened him Rambo.

In the lead up to the trip, Lydia and I had debated whether to make a visit to Denali National Park. Alaska was so huge, and rumoured to be so beautiful, that I felt it wasn't enough to simply 'tick it off' the list with only a visit to Anchorage. So we planned to spend a few days cycling in Denali National Park, which is 240 miles north of Anchorage.

Later that morning, Lewis drove us to the Anchorage railway station. I flirted as best as I could before we loaded our bikes onto the Denali Star train for the eight-hour journey north. Did I feel guilty about putting our bikes on a train? A little. But I'd made the call a long time ago that this trip was about adventure, exploration and satisfying curiosity. It wasn't about cycling every single mile, although that remained the general aim. There were no rules and, as we were short on time, we decided to board the Star train, eat salted cod and chat to all the tourists on there.

I settled into being gently rocked back and forth by the surge and glide of the train tracks. Staring out of the window, I watched as the buildings and blocks of Anchorage softened into hills and trees. Within 30 minutes of leaving the city, we were transported to another world. This was the Alaska I had read about – wild, rugged, untamed, untouched. The train chugged on, softly gripped by a track that meandered like a river, past small, disused railway stations – no more than free-standing white wooden shacks with short platforms. And with each bend the scenery became even wilder and even more beautiful. Lydia was soon asleep in the large leather seat next to me, being gently rocked like a baby in a crib, breathing in the fresh Alaskan air through a slightly open window. I moved from my seat and stood in the hallway of our carriage, sticking my head out of the window, just as the train curved around a long bend. A chain of carriages stretched out in front of me, twitching from side to side, jolting, hissing, clunking, dancing to their own rhythm. The wind smelled of pine fir and fire smoke. Fresh mountain air whipped my cheeks and made my eyes water. I blinked the water away and looked beyond the train, to a backdrop of snow-capped mountains and endless green. Trees, upon trees, upon trees. I inhaled a long, slow breath and let out a sigh. I was in a postcard of my own design.

After five minutes of dangling my face out of the train window, the jewel in Alaska's crown came into view on the horizon and my wild little heart skipped a syncopated beat. It was Mount McKinley or, to use its native Alaskan name, Denali. And it was glorious. Denali means 'the high one', which is appropriate as it is the highest peak in North America, standing at 6,190 metres above sea level.

I spent the rest of the journey alongside Lydia, drifting in and out of sleep on a warm leather recliner chair. We didn't say much during the eight hours on board. We simply sat and absorbed it all, finding a deep sense of comfort in the arms of the Alaskan wilderness.

At 4 p.m., the wheels of the Star train ground to a halt and we pulled into the railway station on the edge of the national park. Our plan was to camp for the next few nights and immerse ourselves in all Denali had to offer. Wild camping was an option in the park, but given that this was our first visit to grizzly territory, we decided to ease ourselves in gradually by camping in one of the six official campgrounds in the park – although we had opted for the ones with the most basic facilities, i.e. a bear lock-up to put your food in and a toilet block.

I was in high spirits as we straddled Boudica and Zena, to

begin the 23-mile ride to Sanctuary River Campground.

After almost an hour of cycling, it was 5 p.m., but the sun was still shining brightly – it would be 10 hours before it slid below the horizon, and even that wouldn't last long. It felt wonderful to be moving again. I soon found myself at peace with the simple motion of turning pedals. I was lost in the joy of it all, and still adjusting to the fact that I was here, in Alaska, really here! How many times had I sat on my big red sofa in London and watched the Discovery Channel, or National Geographic, or my favourite *Ice Road Truckers* show, and thought about Alaska? How many times had I marvelled at the vast expanse of it on a world map, yet here we were, just us and our bikes, in the middle of it all.

In many ways, Alaska was a world away, and yet all it had taken was one decision to get here. Of course, that big decision was made up of a thousand smaller decisions, just like a galaxy full of stars, but ultimately there was one driving force, an overwhelming urge to see this wilderness with my own two eyes, and that had landed me here.

I was rudely awakened from my dreamlike reflective state by a sharp pain in my left knee. Dammit! In all the excitement and fun with Angie, Linda and dishy Lewis, in my nervousness about the visa, in my self-congratulation at actually having made the trip a reality, I had completely forgotten about my knee. The knee injury had lain dormant, like a silent assassin, watching, waiting for a moment to strike and be heard. And now the injury was speaking to me in a sinister, barely audible snake-like hiss. 'Thought you'd escape me, did you? Forget about me?' Lydia was on the road up ahead of me, so I sighed alone and said nothing.

After 15 miles, the road turned into gravel track, and I decided to come clean with Lydia and let her know that my knee was still causing me some grief. Lydia was as sympathetic as ever about the news, and so we stopped every 30 minutes for me to go through a new routine. I would stretch my quad muscles, then apply more ibuprofen gel around my kneecap. By the second stop, I had discovered that if I jammed my thumb really hard into the muscle to the left of my knee, it went some way to alleviating the pain. I'm sure it's not a technique you'd see in any medical journal, but it worked, so I did it at every chance. I tried everything to ignore the pain, but, in the back of my mind, the fears about not being able to complete the trip were tugging in unison with the ligaments around my knee. It was very clear now that my knee hadn't healed since leaving Vancouver. In fact, it was now actually worse.

The last 3 miles to Sanctuary River Campground were agony. Each pedal stroke felt like someone was jabbing a large screwdriver into the side of my knee and turning it. Arriving at the campground, we spotted three boys in a tent pitch nearby. Lydia and I had a serious conversation about the chances of being eaten by a bear and decided to camp close to the boys, because surely a bear would try to eat three nice juicy boys, before going for two girls? It was a flawless plan. After pitching up, we got chatting to the lads and learned that they were using their summer holiday to ride from Alaska all the way back home to Mexico. They were 18 years old and I was in awe of their bravery. There is no way I would have had the gumption to take on a trip like that just out of school. It wouldn't have even crossed my mind that it was possible, and so I wondered who had helped give them the belief that it was? Midway through getting to know the boys, Lyds spotted a stuffed bear, hanging off the back of one of their bikes.

'Hey, look, they've got a bear too! They look just like ours.'

One of the boys smiled. 'Did you stay with Linda too?' he asked. It turned out that the boys had left the company of Linda and Angie in Anchorage a week earlier. They were now headed in the opposite direction to us, out of the park, to make the long trek through Canada's wild Yukon territory.

We chatted on and off with the lads for the rest of that evening and, after parting ways, I followed them on social media for the remainder of their trip. I watched, open mouthed, as they reported encountering 27 grizzly bears on the Yukon portion of their journey. Yikes! I chose not to tell Lydia.

Back on the road the following day, I forced my mind from the pain in my knee and opened my eyes to the landscape surrounding us. The road through the park was quiet. It was closed to cars and if you weren't on a bike, the only other way to travel along it was on one of their official park buses. These looked like old school buses, painted in a mixture of cream and green horizontal layers. Many tourists stayed on the bus all day, peering through the wilderness from the comfort of the glass, just as we had done on the Star train. Others got off and went for a hike, returning to the road to be picked up later in the day. Every 30 minutes or so, one of these buses would roll on by. Lyds and I would hear it coming and manoeuvre ourselves to the edge of the road, preparing to be coated in a fine layer of dust like sweaty little human truffles. In between the truffle dusting, there was only us. No sound beyond the crunch of wheels on gravel. It was a perfect happy medium for both of us – there was the great outdoors, the open road and the safety of knowing someone would come by eventually should anything happen to us out here.

Denali is a true wilderness, the likes of which I'd never experienced before. If you don't happen to be from the big, wild landscapes of North America, the only way to describe it would be to imagine that someone had given the UK's Yorkshire Dales permission to take steroids. Voluptuous green mounds rose from the ground, covered in blocks of trees, as if someone had delicately draped a blanket of evergreens over the landscape and gently tucked the material into the many folds of the earth. The evergreens gave way to sharp peaks and ridge lines, which rose higher still, standing tall and proud against a backdrop of grey-blue sky. Glacial rivers snaked and weaved their way in between the mounds, like arteries feeding the heart of the wilderness. And over the top of it all, sprinkled like hundreds and thousands, were red squirrels, foxes, marmots, Swiss firs, bright purple flowers and lakes. From every angle, the vista in Denali was picture-perfect.

Not only were there impressive views on either side of the road, but the road itself was a marvel too. There was an element of mystery to it, as we could only ever see far enough along it to wonder what occurred around the next bend. But, oh, how I loved to wonder. So, for the next two days, we followed that road blindly. We put our journey in its hands, as it wound over mountain passes, round sharp, steep-banked bends and under low-hanging thunderous clouds into the distance. On and on the road went, escorting us silently across vast river plains and swamp land, carved out by glaciers thousands of years before. It never rained in those days in Denali, but it always seemed to threaten to, as if Mother Nature were reminding us that we were in her kingdom now, and that she was in charge.

'This is the kind of road that makes you feel like you're on a real adventure!' Lydia turned to me and shouted over her shoulder one afternoon. Her voice was barely audible above the ever-growing wind, and I couldn't agree more.

At mile 45 on the road, we both popped our grizzly cherries. I spotted it first and my stomach just about turned 1,000 somersaults in under a second.

'Lyyyyyyds!' I shouted up the road. 'Lyd-i-a!'

'Yeah?!' she hollered back.

'Bear! I think it's a bear!!'

'Oh, very funny, Anna. Very funny.'

'No, really!' I shouted louder, putting in a few hard strokes to catch up to her. 'There!' I said again, pointing to a slope to our right.

'Oh. My.' Lydia said, and we both pulled on our brakes to bring the bikes to a halt. Just there, less than 100 metres from where we were stood, was a big ole grizzly bear. And he looked enormous. He was engaged in sniffing the ground and didn't seem much interested in what we were up to, but we dropped our chatter to a whisper, just in case.

'It doesn't look real,' I said.

'Looks real enough to me,' Lyds replied, a mixture of concern and excitement on her face.

'What do you think he's doing?'

'I dunno… Sniffing things? Maybe he's looking for berries.'

'Do you think he can smell us?' I asked, thinking it had been a few days since I'd had a shower.

'He can probably smell *you*.' Lyds grinned. 'Look! Sshhhhh!'

The bear looked up and turned his head towards us.

'Maybe we should get going,' I said, deciding that although it was all very wonderful to see a bear this close up,

I didn't fancy getting any closer. Lydia nodded in agreement and we pedalled off, watching the bear as it watched us back.

Later that day, we heard a bus coming down the road behind us, so as usual we braced for a truffle dusting, but the bus pulled up alongside us and stopped. The driver leaned out the window.

'Hey girls!'

'Hello!' we beamed back, smiling at him and the busload of tourists in tow.

'We've just heard on the radio here that there's a grizzly on the road up ahead, just round this bend. You might wanna sling your bikes on the bus from here and hop on, so I can take you past him.'

At first, I intended to protest. How cool would it be to see a bear *that* close?! It would be a sighting even closer than the one we'd had that morning. But the driver's words seemed to sound more like a statement than a question, so sense prevailed. We duly obliged, took our panniers off the bikes and lifted them onto the rack at the front of the bus. Boarding the bus, we nodded and smiled at the other tourists, who looked a little bemused to have the wildlife joining them. The bus drove two minutes further on, taking us around the next bend, and, sure enough, there was the grizzly. It was a little way up from the road, on a hill to the right-hand side, but it was close enough to warrant getting on the bus. The other passengers lunged to the right side of the bus in a frenzy, so much so that

I feared the speedy transfer of weight might cause it to tip over entirely. A large Texan man and his wife pressed themselves against Lydia and we became pinned against the glass. Had I been able to move under the weight of the excited tourist's bosoms, I might have reached for my camera, but, as it was, my arms were pinned to my sides, so I took pictures with my eyes instead, storing them in the greatest hard drive of all – my mind.

Three minutes later, we were back on the road, having been dropped off by the bus a good half a mile past the bear. We waved at the passengers as the bus pulled away. After being coated in a familiar layer of grey road dust, we set off again, pedalling towards the final campground in the park – Wonder Lake.

Wonder Lake is situated right at the very end of the park's 92-mile road, and in the shadow of the mighty Denali itself. It was rumoured that on a clear day you could see Denali reflected perfectly in the glassy waters of the lake. I looked up at the grey cloud-filled sky and suspected we wouldn't get such a view today.

Beyond the potential for a spectacular view of the mountain, there was another aspect of Wonder Lake's reputation that caught our attention even more – the number of mosquitos. Apparently, there were swarms of them. 'Worse than the midges in Scotland,' one fellow traveller in the visitor centre had told us. Having experienced midge misery in the

Highlands, and as one of life's 'tasty ones' (the official name for those who get bitten by anything and everything), it was a description that filled me with terror.

Instead of becoming an evening meal for the mozzies, we elected to stop and cook up our dinner by the side of the road, just a few miles shy of the campground. It was a great idea. A great idea that was until we realised we were out in the open, cooking up food with grizzly bears wandering around. As a result, we broke a new noodle inhalation world record, slurping and swallowing as fast as we could in complete silence.

'Done?' I said to Lyds.

'Done,' she said, draining the last bit of noodle soup from the bowl. 'Let's get out of here.' Fuelled by adrenaline, we leapt back on our bikes and made the final few miles to Wonder Lake in no time at all.

The 20 pitch sites at the lake were all set apart from one another, scattered in the undergrowth so that only the tips of brightly coloured tents peeked above the shrubline. After putting up the tents, I began efforts to 'mozzie-proof' myself. I pulled on all of my clothing, a buff, a hat, everything – to the point where all that was exposed was my eyes. I sat on the picnic table and did my best to 'enjoy' the view of the surrounding mountains, but the mosquitos drove me nuts. They buzzed and hummed and landed on me frequently. At 5 p.m., Lyds and I had both had enough, so we crawled into bed. Because it was a warm night, I slept on top of my sleeping bag.

Whether those Alaskan mozzies had bitten me through my thermal leggings or had pulled my pants down in the night to expose my naked rump, I will never know. But when I woke up in the morning, my bum was on fire! I tried to look at it and, in my attempt, I even flashed Lydia a section.

'Woah! Mate, that is not good!' she said. 'Here, give me your phone.'

Lydia proceeded to take a picture of my behind and show it to me. The mosquitos had gorged themselves on my buttocks. I counted 37 bites on my bum and on the back of my legs, and each one had swelled up beautifully like mini Mount McKinleys. I contemplated deleting the photo from my phone, but decided to keep it for posterity.

Having 'experienced' Wonder Lake, and without enough time to take a hike, we set out on the return journey to the park entrance. The bear sightings had evidently opened the wildlife floodgates for us and we went on to spot three moose, a few caribou, several wild hares and an Arctic squirrel. The bears were cool, but it was the moose that captured my imagination the most. I couldn't get over how long their legs were and how big their heads were and their antlers! How in the world was it even possible to hold up that much weight?!

Despite the distraction that the scenery and wildlife brought about, I had to be honest that my knee was still driving me nuts. I had gone through several phases of injury emotions: self-pity, anger, resentment, denial and hopelessness. I was worried I was being terrible company for Lydia, but when I apologised for being such a grump, she said she didn't think I was being grumpy at all.

I tried to take it steady, which didn't help. So I then tried sprinting as fast as I could to see if I could break through the pain and come out the other side feeling fine – like a Concorde bursting through the sound barrier. Funnily enough, that didn't work either and just exacerbated the searing pain. We began to brainstorm ways to rest and ride at the same time, and investigated whether perhaps strapping one leg to my crossbar and riding one-legged for a month or so was a possibility. I tested this out by unclipping one foot and resting it on the pannier over the front wheel. It worked perfectly well, and served to stop any pain, until I slipped on the gravel and almost fell off. This sent me into fits of giggles and distracted me from the pain for at least a moment.

On returning to Anchorage, I decided to get a second opinion on my knee. I searched for a chiropractor online again and found Alex, who worked in a downtown clinic. From her profile, it seemed she was a real outdoorsy sort herself. She'd moved from Chicago to Anchorage to be closer to the mountains and wilderness, and was a keen snowboarder. That made her cool by association. Anyone who is associated with boards is cool by default. Alex was my girl, I just knew it. As I walked into the treatment room, Alex offered me a seat and asked me the usual questions about where I was from and what I was doing in Anchorage. I told her that I was from England, and nervously followed up with the fact that I had the intention to cycle the 50 states. Alex opened her mouth to speak and I prepared myself for the usual spiel about 'resting' my knee with the affirmation that I wouldn't be going anywhere for a while yet.

'So you need to keep going, right?' she said, and I couldn't believe my ears.

'Yes, Alex! I have to keep going!' I exclaimed. 'I can't stop, I mean, I won't stop.'

I wanted to smooch this woman's face!

'So you just need something to make it manageable then?' Alex said.

'Yes, please. And maybe just your opinion on whether I'm making it worse by carrying on. I don't mind pain, pain is fine, but I guess I don't want to do any irreparable damage to the knee.'

'Okay, got it!' said Alex cheerily, and with that she began rummaging around in her drawers, before picking up a roll of blue tape and returning to my side.

'I'm going to say two things to you, Anna.'

I waited and nodded.

'Magic tape!' She held up the blue reel of physio tape.

'Magic tape!' I repeated.

'And ice! You've gotta ice whenever you can!'

Alex did a little bit of treatment on my knee before showing me how to strap it up to take the pressure off of the tendonitis. She rigged up a network of tape that lifted the knee cap slightly away from the socket, and sat back to look at her handy work.

'So, you can do this yourself every few days on the road,' Alex said. 'And other than that, just ice it as often as possible.'

'Got it,' I said.

'One thing though, if it does start to get a whole lot worse, or if you start to feel a clicking instead of a crunching feeling, then you've got to stop. Promise me?'

'I promise!' I said to Alex, unable to stop myself from engulfing her in a hug.

'And you should take just a couple of days of rest before you start cycling again. Promise me on that one too?'

'I promise!'

I skipped out of the surgery. Armed with magic tape and renewed hope, I felt that the 50-state crusade was back on track. After a brief stopover back at Angie and Linda's pad in Anchorage, Lewis dropped us back at the airport with our bikes so we could fly to Seattle to begin the journey through the remaining 49 states. Only on take-off did I realise that I had left my phone in Lewis's car. And that if he opened up the photo album, the first images he would see would be the ones Lydia had taken of my swollen, red, ravaged buttocks.

WEST COAST

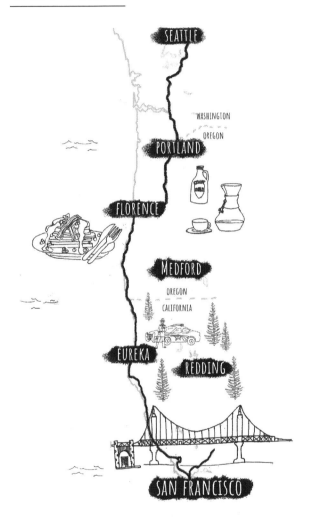

SEATTLE

WASHINGTON
OREGON

PORTLAND

FLORENCE

MEDFORD

OREGON
CALIFORNIA

EUREKA

REDDING

SAN FRANCISCO

4

Breakfast with the Boys

Distance Cycled: 1,024 miles
States Completed: 1

On the plane from Anchorage to Seattle, I made a decision about the weeks that lay ahead down the West Coast. Lydia and I were due to meet up and cycle with Laura, an old friend of ours. Laura lived in Washington DC but was on holiday in Oregon and eager to ride a portion of the famous Highway 101 into San Francisco. It was 1,000 miles from Seattle to San Francisco and I wanted to give my knee the best chance possible from here on in, but I was also conscious that this might impact Lydia's trip or cause us to miss our planned rendezvous with Laura. She only had another month of the adventure left before going home and I didn't want to be responsible for keeping her from doing as much cycling as she could. So we agreed to part ways for the next ten days. I would spend an extra few days in Seattle, staying with some friends of friends, while Lydia continued on down the coast to meet Laura on her own. Somehow, some way, I'd catch them up in a week's time.

I was glad to be given the chance to explore Seattle – mainly so I could visit the movie set of *10 Things I Hate About*

You, one of my favourite films of all time. The lead actress, Julia Stiles, is my hero. Largely because she has curly hair and makes those curls look awesome. Her curls came into my adolescent life at just the right moment when I was deciding whether to fight them or embrace them. Julia taught me to embrace them. As if that isn't enough, in the film, Julia is the ultimate modern soccer-playing, poetry-writing, guitar-slinging femme fatale. She was my role model in my teenage years, and not much had changed since.

Movie-set visits aside, after three days of rest in Seattle, I was chomping at the bit. My knee still hurt like heck, even with the tape on it and icing it five times each day, so I threw the rest and recovery rule book out of the window. I simply couldn't let it hold up the trip any longer. I would rather cope with the pain of moving than the agony of sitting still. I was busting out.

It was getting late in the afternoon as I entered the town of Spanaway, 50 miles south of Seattle. The ride wasn't an entirely pleasant one; it was the first time I'd realised that getting out of cities on a bike is an ugly ordeal. I made my way through the city outskirts, navigated some rather nasty roadworks and finally settled into a rhythm. It felt incredible to be back on the move again, like a weight had lifted even within the first 10 miles. I felt positive about the road ahead. Whatever happened, I was moving towards the goal I'd set myself.

Every mile that ticked by built up my confidence and

mood a little more. I had decided to switch to riding in train-ers, rather than my usual cycling shoes that clipped me into the pedals. It meant I wasn't being as 'efficient' as I could be, but it did allow my knee to sit in whatever position it felt comfortable in as I pedalled, and that seemed to be helping. Better still, I discovered that 7-Eleven gas stations were great places to ice my knee. I would stop every two hours and use the small sack that usually held my Puffa jacket as a makeshift ice bag. Once the sack was filled with ice from the drinks dispenser, I would then sit on the kerb outside, icing and eating any snacks I'd bought inside. This icing ritual broke the day into neat little chunks of time, and each time I set off, my knee was just about ready for the ride once again.

In my eagerness to leave Seattle, I hadn't done enough research on where I might camp that night. I'd googled 'camp-ground Spanaway' and a few things had popped up. I found one which looked to be about the right distance for the day and headed there. Only when I arrived at the address I'd found online, I was led down a creepy, narrow gravel track. All I could see were ramshackle trailers on both sides. There were a few dogs barking, each of them straining on their leashes, lunging forwards to the gap in the fence as I passed. I felt un-easy, unsafe and like this really wasn't a place I wanted to go and ask someone for a cup of sugar, let alone whether I could camp there for the night. So I pedalled back up the track and onwards, contemplating my options. It had been a long day and the energy that had buoyed me through the first half had started to fade. I was now tired, mentally and physically, and I wanted nothing more than to just pitch up my tent and crawl in for the night.

Looking around me, beyond the road, all I could see was grass, lush fields and what looked like small farms. It seemed ridiculous that there was so much space to camp, but I wasn't allowed on any of it. Maybe I could camp in one of those fields – would anyone mind? I'd read and heard about cycling tourists knocking on doors and asking strangers if they could camp in their garden, but that was mostly in the European countryside. Come on, Anna – be brave, I told myself. What's the worst that could happen?

I really hated asking for help. In fact, I really hated to be a 'bother' to anyone. The thought that someone might go out of their way to offer me aid left me feeling wholly uncomfortable and guilty. I'd never been so acutely aware of it until this trip, especially having ridden with Lydia, who had absolutely no qualms in strolling up to a stranger and asking for help. I, on the other hand, preferred to just sort it out myself. I think I get that one from my mum.

On this occasion, I grew a pair of bravery lady-balls. I turned off the main highway and down a small road, leading to a series of farms with wooden houses clad in white boards. One of them looked like a good place to approach and ask for a spot to camp. The grounds were neatly kept, there was a play-ground in the white picketed field next door, and I spotted some kids' toys on the back lawn. *They must be nice*, I thought. Anyone capable of rearing youngsters has to be nice. Them's the rules. So I parked my bike a respectful distance from the front door, just so as to give the impression I wasn't assuming they'd help, and shuffled my way up to the front porch. I stood there for a moment, feeling rather nervous. I took off my hat (that's only polite after all), and smoothed my hair a little. I reached forward with my right hand and rapped lightly on the white wooden door. Then I leapt back. What had I done? Help!

I heard some commotion inside and a man opened the door. I immediately pulled my 'apology' face, which I'd honed finely over the years. It involved a squinting of the eyes, a semi-frown (one of those frowns that's doing its best to escape up your forehead) and a biting of the lower lip. I began the blurt immediately.

'I'm *so* sorry to bother you. But um… I'm on a bicycle tour and the campground I was heading for tonight doesn't seem to exist. I wondered if it might be possible to pitch my tent in your garden for the night.'

The man took an inward breath as if he were about to speak.

'I'd be gone by sunrise tomorrow,' I blurted, and then at last paused.

During my very British apologetic rant, the man's face had changed expression several times. I waited, until he said, 'I tell you what. Why don't you pitch up over there, in that field.

There's a tap with running water you can use.'

Phew. Sweet relief. What a nice man. I looked past him to a young boy and a mother in the living room and waved. Then I thanked them all profusely and rolled my bike over to the field next door.

I'd just finished pitching the tent, when a woman came out of the house and made her way over to me. She introduced herself as Kim and asked me whether I needed to come inside and use the bathroom. I accepted the offer and followed her indoors. There I met the couple's young son, Jackson, who was playing with a train set and all smiles. I explained what I was doing – cycling every state and all that – although I had begun to notice that it was a difficult thing for people to grasp when I was only on state number two. The response was normally subdued. Many people had said 'oh, that's lovely' when you know full well they're thinking 'oh, bless the love, she'll not make it, but that's a great aim'. Kim's reaction was the strongest I'd had in a while. She was full of enthusiasm for the task at hand, as was Jackson when Kim put it into context for him.

'You know when we go to visit grandma, and we drive allllllllll the way to California? Well, Anna here is doing that on her bicycle.'

Jackson fell silent and looked up at me.

'Woooooooooowwwww,' he cooed. 'You're going to see my grandma!'

Returning to my pop-up palace in the field, I checked what was on the menu for that night. Noodles and nuts. Excellent. I went to light the stove, before realising that Lydia had the only lighter between us. So there I sat, crouched behind the tent, so that no one in the house would see what I was doing, crunching on dry noodles. After three mouthfuls I decided it was pretty disgusting and offered little to no nutritional value, and so I settled for a pot of Greek yoghurt and a few nuts instead. I'll add at this point that, had I read the instructions for my newly purchased Jet Boil stove (having melted our first one), I might have clocked on that there was a self-ignite button on the side. Then again, I'd never have experienced the culinary delights of raw noodles if I had known that. That night, I fell asleep feeling safe and content, albeit a little hungry. I'd only cycled 56 miles, but that was 56 more than yesterday, and 56 miles closer to the next state.

In the morning, Kim came over to my tent as I was packing up. She'd googled my trip overnight and had established that I was in fact telling the truth. We chatted about their shared family love of climbing, and about trips Kim had made to Mount Rainier, which I could see beyond the trees behind the field. Just before I left, I went inside to use the bathroom and hand them a little thank-you note, because as my great aunt says, 'A thank you is an invitation for another gift.'

Later that day, I received a Facebook message from Kim:

'Thank you for the note and the card with your route map… Jackson

is amazed at all the places you will be going and says he would like you to stay inside next time you visit. Do look us up if you ever come back. All the best to you!'

Kim's note made me feel just a little bit warm and fuzzy inside. With Lydia gone on her mission down the coast to meet Laura, I was still getting used to travelling alone. And having plucked up the courage to ask a stranger for help, I felt encouraged that the stranger really did seem to care about me and the journey. And better still, a four-year-old boy was impressed by my exploits. It was official – I was down with the kids.

After leaving Spanaway, I wound my way through the endless pine trees of Washington State, down small grey dusty farm roads, past lone houses with tattered US flags hanging on flag poles. I was chased by a few dogs, which made me poop myself in fear. I guessed that there was no need to tie them up around here, as everyone used cars due to the distances between the houses being so vast. The whole area had a distinctive smell and it took me a while to put my finger on it, but something about it flooded my mind with memories of primary school. Then I realised that it smelled of pencil shavings, an oddity which made sense when I passed a number of timber yards, watching as a steady stream of trucks pulled in and out of the forecourts, unloading their stacks of felled timber trunks, before going out with empty lorries to collect a fresh batch. Away from the main highway, with all this space and so little traffic, I was beginning to get a sense of just how vast the USA was.

I made my way further south and crossed into state number three, Oregon, before heading to the city of Portland to stay with friends of a friend. Since leaving Seattle, I had hatched a new plan to take a shorter, inland route, which would slingshot me onto the south coast and allow me to catch up with Lydia and Laura.

Getting into the city of Portland was quite a mission. In fact, I took it as a test of my wit and patience to navigate the webs of roads that surround the city. There are no fewer than 12 bridges into the centre and, attempting to follow the cycle routes, which twist and turn back on themselves, weaving in amongst them with no apparent clear direction, was testing to say the least. I got lost several times and had to stop and ask for directions when I ended up back at the same spot by a highway underpass after 30 minutes of cycling. Still, I made it.

My hosts Joe and Drea were headed out for the night, but there was a Portland Timbers soccer game going on at the local stadium, and Joe had offered me his season ticket so that I could go along and experience a slice of the real Portland. He and the eldest of their two young girls, Lucy, promised to teach me some of the chants (including the rude ones) and two hours later I was sat on a bench in Providence Park, yelling, 'When. We. Root. We Root. For. The. Tim-bers!'

That night, I strolled back to Joe and Drea's in the warm Oregon summer air and decided that I rather liked Portland. Despite having navigational issues into the city, it was one that sat well with me. During a rest day that followed, I visited a cycling exhibition at the Portland Art Museum and learned that Portland has a strong cycling culture. Portlanders also love craft beer and artisan coffee. It was a city full of culture; bustling but not too busy, friendly, but calm and with a healthy dose of laid-back suburban living.

I was having a gay old time in Oregon, but it was time to head back to the West Coast, to find Highway 101 and intercept Lydia and Laura. I sent Lyds a message and told her that I'd meet her and Laura at a campground in Crescent City in three days' time. A reply came straight back. She was delighted that we'd be meeting up again and said that she missed having me ride with her. I'd missed her too in the time we'd been apart. Her message ended with:

'I've met up with Laura. She's got everything shipshape and on schedule already.'

Lydia's message made me smile. Laura was a wiry, strong, intelligent and assertive woman with bright blonde hair who had rowed for Great Britain as a lightweight during and after her time at university, and had gone on to channel her endurance talents into bike racing after moving to the US. She mixed a no-nonsense approach to life with an air of sweetness which made her loveable and, without a doubt, Laura was always dedicated to her training – never late and always organised.

After passing through Eugene, I turned west and headed

for Highway 101. It was to be a 60-mile ride along a busy narrow highway from Eugene to the 101, but gradually the traffic began to thin out. Upon making the town of Mapleton, I was still 15 miles shy of hitting the 101, but it was approaching dusk so I decided to look for a place to pitch up for the night. Wild camping seemed out of the question as most areas to the side of the road were dense forest and fenced off with scary 'NO TRESPASSING!' signs. Just then, I spotted a caravan park. I was just about to go in and be charged a disgusting sum of money for a camping pitch when, to the right-hand side of the park entrance, I spotted a large mound of gravel and, just behind that, out of the ray of light cast by the nearest streetlight, a patch of flat(ish) ground. It was almost big enough to fit my tent in. If I stayed crouched, and moved around only on my hands and knees, I would be out of view of the road. I waited an hour for darkness to fully descend before putting my tent up. I had to tie the front ends of the tent to Boudica, who was lying on her side in the brambles, but once I was in, it was comfortable enough. Comfortable or not, I barely slept a wink that night. To my right was a large patch of forest, where I could hear the noise of animals moving around. I was also half-petrified that someone from the caravan park would come wandering around the gravel mound and find me camped there. And, of course, when you are in a sleepy state, all the possible catastrophic scenarios are magnified tenfold. In my head, I was about to get raided by the police and attacked by a giant racoon, who would then ride off on my bike, all at once. I decided that this wasn't wild camping; it was more just 'free'. But I was okay with that.

I woke from the little sleep I had managed to get at 6 a.m. to find that it was still dark out. Staying crouched and out of sight, I packed up my tent and was on the road by 6.30 a.m., in search of breakfast. At 7.30 a.m., I hit the outskirts of the town of Florence and knew that just beyond it was the 101 and the West Coast. I spotted what looked like a nice cafe, or one that was open at least, and parked the bike up out the front. I decided that I had time for some pancakes, especially as it's a well-known fact that pancakes make you go faster.

Walking into the modest cafe, I headed for a table in the middle of the room. I clocked two men sitting at a table to my right, and I could feel them looking at me. The younger of them, with long dark hair, called over to me as I pulled out a chair to sit down.

'Early start for you, hey?' he said.

'You bet, nothing like it – gotta get crackin'!' I smiled.

'Where did you start this morning?' his friend asked.

'Mapleton.' (I felt the detail of 'behind the mound of rubble in the caravan park' was a little surplus to requirements.)

'No wah-hey,' the first man said, sitting back in his chair and looking me up and down.

'Yes way.' I smiled and set my helmet down on the table, as he continued.

'Say, why don't you come over here and join us for breakfast?'

The two men were both grinning like Cheshire cats. They seemed kind, so I accepted. I ordered a stack of three thick blueberry pancakes and a coffee, and got chatting to Rick and Bill, who were to be my breakfast-time entertainment.

Bill, aka 'The Captain', as he asked me to call him, was in his mid 60s. He was in the midst of refurbishing a boat – which he'd transported to Florence from his home in Maine. When I looked down at Bill's hand, I noticed that one of his thumbs was missing, and there was just a tiny stump where it once had been. When I asked Bill about his thumb, he said he'd lost it in an accident once upon a time.

'Say, Anna,' he said, holding up his stump in front of his face, proudly. 'Do you wanna hear The Captain's rule of thumb?' he chuckled.

I smiled. 'Go on then, Bill. What is it?'

'Be patient or become a patient.'

Bill's chuckle erupted into belly-busting laughter as he leaned back on his chair, showing me a mouthful of pearly white teeth.

My other breakfast companion, Rick, struck me as the mischievous kind. He was in his early 40s, tanned, and had dark brown eyes and long brown hair, tied in a neat, low ponytail. He had a cheeky smile that reached from one ear to the other and an infectious laugh that sounded like Graham Norton and Goofy had produced a lovechild. But the best part was his voice – it reminded me of the turtle in *Finding Nemo*. I liked Rick instantly.

Rick, it emerged, was quite well-established on the nightclub scene. Although semi-retired, he specialised in designing and fitting lighting systems for the clubs, which was one of those jobs that I'd never really thought about until now. Rick was rather coy, but I had the feeling that he was well-connected.

'Yeah, this guy's loaded,' Bill joked, pointing at Rick. 'Hangs with all the celebs,' he continued, and I couldn't tell if he was being serious or not.

Rick looked too young to be semi-retired, so I was intrigued by what he'd done to warrant such an early release from a full working life.

'Rick, tell me about the lighting. What do you do exactly? Do you have to sit at a computer a lot, or are you out and about using your hands?'

'Me? Oh, I mostly just plug things in, turn 'em on and boom! Disneyland!' he laughed.

I had a feeling I wouldn't get a serious reply on the ins and outs of life as a nightclub lighting designer. I had no idea why I had expected one. It no longer seemed to matter so much what had brought Rick to this moment, sat at this table with me. All that mattered is that we were here, and he was a dude.

Rick went on to talk about his various conspiracy theories, including how people stored money in banks. He didn't trust banks, not at all.

'Silver's where you want to be putting your money,' he told me with a stern face. And again, I couldn't tell if he was joking or not. These two had thrown my sarcasm radar all off kilter. 'In things like this,' Rick said, pulling a large silver coin out of his wallet.

'Woah! That thing is huge!' I said, watching the morning sun reflect off its shiny surface.

'Here, you keep it,' he said, thrusting it into the palm of my hand. It felt ice cold and was heavier than I'd expected it to be.

'When it all goes belly up, you've at least got something.' He laughed again.

I tried to refuse but Rick was insistent and wasn't taking no for an answer.

'We've got this covered too,' he carried on, gesturing to the empty plates on the table.

'Oh, what? No, I… I mean, I should be getting *you guys* breakfast!' I replied.

'Don't be so silly, it's our treat. It's been a pleasure having you as company this morning, Anna from England,' said Rick.

I grinned, a little embarrassed but humbled all the same. I'd enjoyed the company of these two men just as much as they'd enjoyed mine.

'Well, I better get back on the road,' I said, shoving back my chair and starting to stand up. 'I've got some miles to mak—'

'KOMBUCHA!' Rick interrupted. 'Now, have you ever had Kombucha?'

'Kom what?'

'Hang on…' Rick shoved back his chair and darted off to the cooler at the back of the cafe. I chatted to Bill for a minute or so until Rick returned. He thrust two bottles into my hand. It was the same stuff that hippy Ben had given us at Sunshine Coast, but I'd not seen it in glass bottles, like average soda, until now. 'Here you go. It's good for ya. Kombucha. You'll love it!' He laughed that laugh again, and I giggled too.

We said our goodbyes, exchanged contact details and I promised to go and party with Rick in one of his Miami clubs someday. They both came outside the cafe to wave me off. Bill waved his thumb stump and smiled.

'Remember the rule of thumb!' Bill called after me, and I was on my way. I shook my head in disbelief. What on earth had just happened?! I had a belly full of blueberry pancakes, a hoard of silver and a new 'be patient' life motto to live by. It was only 9 a.m. but my day had already veered wonderfully off course.

Five miles down the road from the cafe, I began to notice that there were grains of sand, creeping out from the forest and spilling onto the tarmac. I knew that the Oregon Dunes National Recreation Area was somewhere around here, so I figured that I was on the edge of it. An internal conflict raged. I desperately wanted to stop, to pull into one of the many parking bays and take a proper look. But after a long breakfast with Rick and The Captain, I really needed to keep moving in order to make my rendezvous with Lydia and Laura in Crescent City tomorrow. *But what if I never came back?!* I thought. And what about the kids I'd be speaking to in the schools?! I would need to tell them about the national parks I'd seen en route, and to describe what I'd seen. I couldn't tell them I'd been in too much of a hurry to stop and marvel at one of the world's greatest natural wonders – that would never do! Sod it. *I could at least spare five minutes*, I told myself. I spotted a dune through the trees off to my right and set Boudica down at the side of the road. I kicked off my socks and shoes and slogged my way up a pile of sand 30 feet high.

Halfway up the dune I remembered that I had a sore knee, or rather the knee reminded me, so my attempted dune sprint turned into a hop, then a one-legged drag, and finally a crawl, but I still went up. Reaching the top, I peered over the crest of the dune and got slowly to my feet. I couldn't believe my eyes. Stretched out in front of me was what looked like a full-blown desert. I looked back down at my bike and the grey road, surrounded by green trees, and then out again across the sand. The contrast in landscape was beyond belief. How in the world had Mother Nature cooked up such beauty?!

Piles of pastel yellow sand extended from my feet into the distance, rising and falling like waves on an ocean. Two crows swooped above the dunes, gliding for a few seconds and dropping in height before flapping their wings again and returning to the grey and overcast sky. I shut my eyes for a moment and felt the onshore breeze gently sprinkle grains of sand across my nose and cheeks. Although I couldn't yet see it, I could smell the salty air from the Pacific Ocean, and so I took a deep breath, filling my lungs with it. Wiggling my toes, I burrowed them deeper in the sand, feeling them cool as they moved away from the heat of the surface and met with wetter, darker sand below. Opening my eyes again, I looked out at the furthest dune. I could well slip into a trance here. I wanted to slip into a trance here. Standing up to my ankles in sand, this landscape had become a part of my journey, and I had become a part of it. Someone, something, pressed the pause button on my mind. My thoughts were like commuters rushing to and fro in a crowded and busy railway station, and then, all of a sudden, they stopped. There was no rushing here; speed seemed a foolish thing to pursue. There was only me, the sand, the salty air and the birds.

Had I not been so acutely aware that I'd left Boudica on the road, alone and unwatched, I might have answered the deep urge I had to wander across the dunes. But after five more minutes of gawping and blissful quiet, I dragged myself away.

I knew full well that I'd likely never come back, and there was a sadness in that realisation. So, I shrunk the scene into a bite-sized video that I could play over and over in my mind at will when I needed to find a peaceful place. I half stumbled, half slid back down the dune to Boudica, and set off again.

I'd been looking forward to meeting the Pacific Ocean for over a week now – it was what had kept me going as I rested in Seattle and battled with knee pain. In my head, it was to be a spectacular affair. Uninterrupted ocean views, endless sun-shine, Highway 101 sweeping dramatically close to cliff tops as I weaved among the clouds. Unfortunately, when the 101 cata-pulted me beyond the Oregon Dunes to the edges of the West Coast, it was foggy, spitting (not even real rain) and I couldn't see a speck of the ocean. I felt disappointed at first, but then I realised that there will always be times like these, where the things you hope to see don't reveal themselves, but are instead replaced by hidden treasures you could never have imagined – like endless sand dunes and strangers with half a thumb who will buy you a blueberry pancake breakfast.

The following day I let out a little cheer as the 101 led me over the California border line and into state number four of the journey. I stopped to take the obligatory sign-selfie, an art I was perfecting by balancing my camera on Boudica's leather saddle. Each one of these pictures was a part of a puzzle. They would form a square in a large frame I would one day hang in the living room of my home, which would show me next to each and every state sign in the US. It might seem crazy to be thinking so far ahead, but placing myself in a time when I would have completed this journey was something that gave me the daily strength to believe it would come true.

I was now just 15 miles shy of Crescent City, where I would finally rendezvous with Lydia and Laura. It was starting to get dark and I was determined to make it before nightfall, so Boudica and I were hammering down the road with gritted determination. Fifteen miles and I would be back on track, back with Lydia. I was going to make it! All of a sudden, I felt a huge jolt, followed by the sound of my back tyre exploding. There was a loud hissing noise, as the air in the tyres made a swift bid for freedom into the outside world.

'Oh crap!' I shouted, pulling the bike to a halt and getting off to investigate the damage. To my dismay, I finally found out what the noise in my rear tyre had been over the past few days. There had been a weak spot in the rubber wall and the inner tube had forced its way into that spot and burst through it, leaving a large split in the tyre. Sigh.

As if by magic (I'm honestly not sure where he came from), a Highway Patrol Officer appeared. Was this section of the 101 like The Room of Requirement? Could I just shut my eyes and summon whatever I needed to get me out of a fix?! I could tell the man was a Highway Patrol Officer because of his light brown uniform (I had seen that in the movies) and the fact that it said 'Highway Patrol' on the side of his white car. Detective McNuff strikes again.

'You okay there, ma'am?' the officer said, leaning out of the window.

I babbled something about my back tyre and that I'd be fine. The officer got out of his car and came over to me and the bike. He was dark-skinned, broad-shouldered and looked to be of Hispanic descent. His face remained stern as he approached.

'That looks like it's a problem for you, ma'am,' he said. 'Are you sure I can't offer you a ride?'

I was about to protest again, and tell him I'd be okay – the last thing I wanted to do was take four-wheeled assistance. But then I stopped, and thought it through. I was an unwanted item on the highway, and it was his job to keep the highway free from 'obstructions'. Plus, I was losing light, I hated riding in the dark and, besides, I had no way of fixing the tyre. I had some things with me to plug small holes, but not a full-on tear like this one. The reality was if I didn't accept his offer I would be walking my bike the final 15 miles. So, after some deliberation, I graciously accepted the officer's offer to throw my bike in the boot of his patrol car and drive me to Crescent City.

I have no doubt that the Highway Patrol Officer, who I learned was called Matiás Torres, regretted his decision to allow me into his vehicle within about five seconds. Officer Torres relayed something rather official into the radio back to base which sound like, 'Um, this is 90214, niner, we have a 1148, chaperone to the shoreline RV park for drop off, and return to post, over.' *Well. How exciting*, I thought. Looking around the car, I started to notice all the pretty lights on the dashboard and wanted to know *everything* about them.

'What does this do?' I asked, pointing to a black lever.

'Turns the siren on, ma'am.'

Then there was silence.
'Ooooo. And this?!' I said, pointing to red dial.

'Tunes the radio,' said Matiás again.

More silence.
'What's a 1148? Am *I* a 1148?' I asked.

'Yes, you are, ma'am,' said Matiás again, keeping his face straight and staring ahead at the road.
There was a really long silence now.
'Soooo… Are you into sports?' I asked, trying to make polite conversation.

'No, not really, ma'am,' said Matiás, cutting my line of questioning dead.
'Oh. Well. You must go to the gym or something,' I said. 'I mean, you look like you pump iron…'

Wow. Those words actually just left my mouth, and at last Matiás cracked a smile. He muttered something about spending all day picking his kids up, possibly to ward off any inclination I might be making advances with my 'pumping iron' chat. Officer Torres finally dropped me off 15 miles down the road with a smile and a nervous wave. I lifted Boudica out of the boot of the car, and set her down on the pavement, ready to wheel her across the road to the Shoreline RV Park. I thanked him again and off I went.

'Anna!' came a call across a darkened patch of grass.

'Lyds? Lyds, is that you?'

It was well into nightfall now and I couldn't see a thing. Three figures appeared out of the gloom, one of whom was especially excited and lolloping toward me like a puppy dog. 'You're here!' Lydia exclaimed as I greeted her with a huge hug – it was so nice to see her. 'Oh my gosh,' she said. 'I was so glad to make it down the coast and get to Laura. I only spent one day riding on my own, and I nearly went MENTAL!' she blurted as we walked back to where they had pitched their tents. Once Lyds and I had stopped wittering, I hugged Laura, whom I hadn't seen in six years.

I was absolutely exhausted, but somehow I needed to find a new tyre. We were due to leave at 8 a.m. the next morning – long before any shop would be open. We discovered our only option could be a nearby Walmart. I'd read a book where a guy had survived a long tour on a Walmart tyre, so I figured it was worth a try. After a fraught conversation with a rather clueless Walmart employee, Lyds offered to ride the few miles down there and pick up the tyre so I could get some sleep. She seemed excited at the prospect of a night cycle and insisted she wanted to 'try out her lights' anyway. So off she went into the darkness.

I must have gone out like a light because the next thing I remember was waking up the following morning. It was freezing. I poked my head out the tent to see the campground shrouded in a low-hanging fog. We had 450 miles to make to San Francisco and 6 days to do it.

Over the next week, we three adventure amigos followed Highway 101, as it skirted close to the shores of the Pacific Ocean. The Californian coast was different from how I had imagined it would be. We saw nothing of the white sandy beaches, endless sunshine and abundance of beautiful bodies that Arnie likes to tell us about on California tourism commercials, so I concluded that all of that business must happen south of San Francisco. Instead, I learned that northern California is rugged, foggy, damp and windy. For the most part, the sands on the beach are a dark shade of brown and the currents of the ocean are too dangerous to take more than a quick dip. At one point, when the route left the coast and entered farmland, I turned to Lydia and Laura and said, 'I love this – it reminds me of home!' I'm not sure if it was the whiff of cow turd in the air, the terrible road surface, the drizzle or the rolling fields, but something out here, in California, screamed of England.

The fog continued as we wound our way further south. We rode together for miles along the Avenue of the Giants, in the Redwood National Park, clad in high-vis jackets so that passing vehicles could see us on the road, surrounded by some of the biggest tree-beasts I've ever seen. Each one seemed to be watching over us like old grandfather time himself. I thought about the things they must have seen in the 800 years they'd been standing. If only trees could talk...

In between the national parks, we passed through quaint little coastal towns, such as Eureka, Mendocino, Fort Bragg and Jenner, all of which provided ample opportunities to stock up on eggs, potatoes, pancakes and ham.

There was a mystery to the constant fog and it added an element of mindfulness to the riding. I couldn't see much beyond the end of my bike, so I concentrated hard on not crashing into the back of Lydia's or Laura's. The days were torturous for my body, but I very much enjoyed being in a three. Somehow in the week we'd been apart, Lydia had picked up a tonne of speed. In between resting my knee and taking it steady, I hadn't picked up any speed at all. Couple this with the fact that Laura was an actual bike racer and I was destroying myself to keep up with the others.

Still, we settled into a rhythm together. We averaged 75 miles a day and finished by mid-afternoon, each taking it in turns to be absolutely shattered and decide that one member of the group was going too fast. The steep inclines on the 101 made the going a little tougher than I'd expected, but when the fog parted like an oversized theatre curtain and gave us a glimpse of the Pacific from time to time, I was rendered speechless. We rode above the clouds, next to swooping birds of prey, dipping into small sandy coves and whooshing up the other side.

Every night as I tried to sleep, my legs throbbed. We took advantage of cheap camping on the West Coast by paying hiker/biker fees at rough campgrounds – most of which offered a prime camping spot for less than $10 between us. One particular site, Westport, cost just three bucks and let us camp right on a cliff edge. That night, watching the sun go down over the Pacific Ocean, we chowed down on a curry-esque concoction, followed by our traditional hot chocolate and marshmallows. I was like a pig in poop. Life truly couldn't get much better.

SAN FRANCISCO

CALIFORNIA
NEVADA

RENO

CARSON CITY

YUBA CITY

NEVADA
CALIFORNIA

SACRAMENTO

SANTA ROSA

SAN FRANCISCO

PALO ALTO

5

Smashin' It to Sacramento

Distance Cycled: 1,850 miles
States Completed: 4

Seeing the Golden Gate Bridge for the first time is a moment I will treasure for the rest of my days. I had thought it would be no big deal. I'd seen 'Old Golden' so many times in the movies, after all. Yet, as we emerged from the bustling suburb of Sausalito and the bridge came into view for the first time, I was dumbfounded. It was beautiful! As much as a huge red steel structure can be, that is.

On the day we arrived at the bridge, it was shrouded in characteristically low-hanging San Francisco cloud. The tips of its art deco steel spires were lost somewhere in a ceiling of grey. I thought back to one of the first books that had stirred up a sense of wanderlust in me as a kid – a book where characters from my favourite childhood cereal (Weetabix) would dress up and visit the Great Wonders of the World. Being here and looking out at the bridge made every available hair on the back of my neck stand to attention. It felt like this was the first major landmark in the journey. However, it was more about just seeing the bridge – it was about doing something that I had always wanted to, going to a place that I had always wanted to visit, so very badly. It was that I had put myself on this bike and ridden the 1,850 miles to this point, to enjoy this very moment. Through the haze of excitement and the jumble of thoughts and feelings, I recognised the emotion – it felt a lot like pride.

Lyds and I waved Laura goodbye as she made her way back to Washington DC, and we spent a couple of days exploring San Francisco. I went down to Pier 41 to meet up with some friends, Jenny and Dan, who were from the UK but happened to be in San Fran at the same time as me. We went for a slap-up meal at The Bubba Gump Shrimp Co., and while inhaling my 'Jenny burger', I was reminded of another adventurer I'd heard about a month previously via social media. He was called Jamie McDonald and had just set out on a record-breaking 5,000-mile run across Canada. I was pretty new to social media. I only had a handful of followers, most of whom were friends or colleagues, but I had decided that it was a good way to help share the journey. Social media also offered the opportunity to peer into a whole other world of people doing crazy, adventurous things – people like Jamie McDonald. I'd recently donated to his fundraising efforts, and had decided that he was the UK's answer to Forrest Gump, so I tweeted: 'Ashamed I just ate a Jenny burger at Bubba Gump Shrimp Co. at Pier 41. Not ashamed that I thought of @MrJamieMc-Donald. #RunJamieRun #PeasNCarrots'.

Unfortunately, my initial excitement at reaching the bright lights of San Francisco began to wear thin, and soon I found the city to be overwhelming. Having spent seven weeks exploring wide open spaces and living in our tent for most of it, a big city like San Francisco was an assault on the senses. The smells, the noise, the anonymity of it all. Wandering down the street passing hundreds of people who didn't venture so much as a smile. Lyds was feeling the same as I was. She longed for the open road and big skies again, so we elected to leave the city a few days early and skipped town via ferry to Vallejo.

It was late in the evening when we got off the boat at Vallejo, and the change of scenery was stark. From the ferry terminal, we followed baby-smooth tarmac roads away from the Pacific Ocean, heading eastwards across inland California. We wound over soft rolling hills, where both sides of the road were lined with the distinctive rows of vineyards – thick, luscious purple grapes, waiting patiently on green-leafed vines for their turn to be warmed by the mid-summer sun. From time to time, the vineyards gave way to fields of golden grass – slim, feathered towers swaying gently in the early evening breeze. We whizzed past long driveways, leading away from the road and to large detached homes, and I wondered what it would be like to live out here among the vines and the golden fields, nestled in the shadow of the small mountains just beyond. Every now and then, we'd catch sight of a pack of cyclists, zig-zagging their way through the vineyards, out for an evening social ride. We'd get a passing hello as our mini peloton merged with theirs, but they were going at a considerably faster pace, and we were quickly alone again. I let out a long sigh. This is the

California I had hoped to experience. One that was peaceful, calm, and with ever such a slight breeze to move away the stifling August heat.

The following morning, the temperature has already crept over 30°C, and it was humid to boot. It was like riding through treacle. Every intake of breath singed my windpipe and filled me with so much hot air that I feared someone might attach a basket to me and I'd float on up into the atmosphere, never to return. We had 90 miles to cover before reaching the town of Folsom that day, where the brother of a friend from home had offered us a bed for the night. The conversation over breakfast that morning about the day's plan had gone as follows:

'How far to Folsom?' said Lydia.

'Ninety miles,' said I.

'Is it flat?' said she.

'As a pancake,' I replied.

'Smash it?' said she.

'Smash it,' said I.

That settled it: we would be 'smashing it'. That is, riding as hard and as fast as we could to make it to Folsom as soon as possible. Passing through the town of Davis, we happened upon a bike path. We checked the map and the path seemed to lead in the direction that we needed to head that day. Best of all, it was no ordinary bike path. This was the finest bike path in all of earth-land. Upon stopping to chat to a local, we discovered that the path was 50 miles long. It had its own speed limit signs (15 mph), road markings and even some mini roundabouts (or traffic circles as Americans call them). I couldn't believe my greedy little eyes! The notion that Lydia and I could ride freely side by side, winding through light woodland, chatting away with no fear of being mowed down by traffic was a delight.

Shortly after Davis, the temperature rose to 38°C and I felt like my blood might be ready to boil. I unzipped my short-sleeved cycling jersey the whole way (I'd seen the pro cyclists in the Tour de France do this to help cope with the heat, so it had to be a good idea) and emptied the remaining contents of my water bottle over my head. The water released the salt from the encrusted padded rims of my helmet and it trickled down my face and into my mouth. It made me gag a little, but the cooling sensation of the icy water running down my sticky neck was glorious. We followed the bike path over a river and dropped down the other side on the opposite bank. Just as we did, a man in his mid 60s on a bike appeared on the path ahead of us.

Lyds and I trucked past, looking sideways as we went and both shouting, 'Morning!'

The man looked startled.

'Oh. Um. Good morning!' he replied, and a few minutes later he appeared beside us, panting. 'Girls, I say girls! Where are you headed?!'

'Lyds!' I called. 'Slow up a little, will you?'

Seventeen miles into our 90-mile day we picked up Mike, a retired surgeon, who decided that he'd like to ride with us, just for 20 miles or so. Mike was out on his usual loop that he did three times a week, and so welcomed the company of two British girls. As we rode for the next hour, Mike talked to us about his career, his girlfriend, and the local history. He reminded us that we were going to cycle right by Folsom Prison later that day, the place which lent its name to Johnny Cash's 1956 single 'Folsom Prison Blues', and where he performed the hit to inmates in a concert in 1968. Given that both Lyds and I are big Johnny Cash fans, we rewarded Mike for his tour-guide efforts by singing Johnny Cash songs at him for much of the afternoon.

Seventy miles further on, and now only 3 miles shy of Folsom, Mike was still with us. He had insisted at every short stop that he'd like to keep going. Only now Mike had fallen silent.

'Say, you alright there, Mike?' I asked, calling back to him, as Lyds turned to me – a concerned look on her face.

'I think I might just need to stop for a bit. To, you know, rest, in the shade,' Mike rasped back.

I didn't blame him. It was the hottest day we'd had on the bike so far, and Mike had only come out with enough water for his originally planned 20-mile ride.

Until now, Mike had been refusing the extra snacks and water Lyds and I were offering him, insisting that he'd be okay. He didn't even eat lunch when we pulled into a big university campus to fill up on food from their college canteen. But now when we offered snack bars to Mike, he inhaled them. We gave him all the water we had left and watched as he poured half of it over his head before gulping down the rest. We waited while Mike took a second phone call from his girlfriend, his short grey hair now plastered to his face and cool droplets dripping from his nose. Lyds and I tried to look 'busy' as an awkward debate ensued on the phone. Apparently picking up two girls in their 20s on a trail and riding with them for 70 miles, when you're supposed to be having lunch with your girlfriend is not cool, not cool at all. I didn't blame the girlfriend – I'd have been pretty hacked off too, but I had a sense that Mike had a streak of mischief in him, and he had found the call of adventure that day a little too much to resist.

Lyds and I had long since decided that we would go for a refreshing dip in Folsom Lake before presenting ourselves at our hosts' house for tea, so that was the end point for the day's ride. Mike got off the phone and insisted that we push on without him, and assured us that he would follow on and meet us there. I could sense there was an element of him protecting his pride. Perhaps he needed to recompose himself. Whatever his reasons, he wanted to be left alone and so we granted him that and pushed on reluctantly, wondering whether we'd gone ahead and fried poor Mike with our 'smashing it', and whether we'd see him at the lake at all.

It was another hour before Mike showed up at the lake, where he found us laughing and splashing in the water, as if at a seaside holiday resort, although we were swimming in our sweat-encrusted cycling shorts and sports bras, and not bikinis. Folsom Lake was a strange and eerie place. There was a vast expanse of blue-grey water set in a barren, orange, dusty surround and flanked by steep reservoir-style walls on one side and a softer, sandy beach at the other end. I was perplexed by the lack of anyone in sight – there was a small cafe at one end, but that only had one person in it too. Mike said that he'd managed to sweet talk his girlfriend into coming to collect him, and that she was on her way. We both got out of the water and gave him a hug, thanking him for the company that day.

'Are you going to be in a bit of trouble when you get in?' I asked, referring to the fact that he'd missed lunch with his girlfriend. Mike paused and took a long sigh.

'You know, girls. Sometimes life sends a freight train your way, and you've got no choice but to hop on board.'

***

My watch bleeped 6 a.m. as we rolled out of our hosts' driveway in Folsom. We'd arrived at their home last night and were greeted with open arms, despite full kid-juggling family chaos being in full swing. The temperature was set to hit 38°C again that day and I knew that an early start was going to be key to making it through the summer heat in any kind of fit state. Especially as we were headed for the biggest climb of the trip so far – Carson Pass.

Carson Pass had been hanging out quietly on the map in my front pannier for the past 7 weeks. We both knew it was there – the first pass of the Sierra Nevada mountain range was lying in wait for us. I'd glanced at the profile once whilst we were in Canada and seen an ascent from sea level to 2,600 metres high. I'd then decided that I wouldn't worry about it until absolutely necessary. And so here we were. Given that my knee was still sore, and on account of the heat, we decided to split the climb over two days, and camp at 1,500 metres on the first night.

The first day on the pass was long and arduous. Going in an upwards direction for over 60 miles was just not something I'd experienced before. I'd done alpine climbs on a lightweight carbon racing bike in the past, but at most those had taken two hours to reach the summit. This one would take us the best part of two days. I was finding the heat unbearable, and Lydia seemed to have found a new burst of speed. The hotter and more uncomfortable I got, the more my knee seemed to hurt, so I flitted between passive attempts to distract myself from the pain and swearing in sheer frustration. Every now and then, I'd go a little berserk. I would get up out of the saddle and pound on the pedals like a savage animal, gnarling and spitting, foaming at the mouth, raging my way up the climb. After a minute of madness, I'd run out of puff, the pain in my knee would return and my rage would retreat – battered into submission by the searing pain.

We were entering the final 15 miles of the day, but I was

a mess. Not even an Eton Mess, but a hot mess to be precise. We decided to split the final section into three 5-mile stints and focus on just those 5 miles at a time before taking a rest in the shade. I'd just about expelled all possible salts from my body onto my shirt and even Lydia was now starting to tire.

We knocked off one 5-mile stint, and I was beginning to wonder how on earth I was going to make it through the next two when we came across a sign locating a general store. By all accounts, we were in the middle of nowhere, so we as good as fell off our bikes and whooped and cheered at the prospect of purchasing some chilled goods to propel us through the final few hours of cycling for the day.

After ringing a bell to summon the shopkeeper from what I presumed was her house next door, Lyds and I took our time surveying the small selection of available items in the store. I chose well. A packet of cheesy puffs, an apple, a banana, a litre of chocolate milk and an ice cream with a respectable hundreds-and-thousands-to-ice-cream ratio. Anything we didn't have to carry up the final section of the climb was surely a bonus, so we opted to ingest everything we bought rather than carry it. It's a well-known fact that everything is lighter once in your belly. That's just sensible survival tactics, if you ask me.

The stop was just what we needed to refresh both our battered bodies and weary minds.

'Ice cream POWERRRR!' Lyds yelled as she jumped back on Zena and pedalled to the main road, with me following closely behind. Those final 10 miles whizzed by in a flash, thanks to the snacks and the middle of nowhere store; we even managed to find the breath to resume the singing of Johnny Cash tunes.

When we rolled into our campground for the night at Cooks Station, it was deserted. There was a large wooden building which looked like a restaurant, surrounded by decking, and an old picnic bench. We peered through the windows of the restaurant, but it was all locked up, and no one was inside. In the back garden were a few small sheds, and the broken and rusted remnants of old trucks and motors. Five hundred metres further into the woods, I could see what looked like a logging station with piles of timber all neatly stacked.

We made our way around the back and set up our tents, before returning to cook up the usual nightly feast of noodles and tuna on the decking. It was only during the dinnertime water-boiling process that we realised we'd left our camping cutlery in the dishwasher at our hosts' house in Folsom. Instead, we used our tent pegs as chopsticks, which really isn't that bad once you scrape the mud off of them. I emptied the remainder of the noodle broth into my mouth, put down my 'chopsticks' and looked at Lydia. She was sitting opposite me on the picnic bench, slumped with her head and arms on the table. She looked up.

'I'm *really* tired,' she groaned.

'Me too.'

'Bedtime?'

'Bedtime,' I affirmed.

It was 6.30 p.m.

***

'Anna!' Lyds woke me with a hoarse whisper. 'Anna!'

'Mmmmm?' I peeled my face off of the camping pillow, wiped the dribble from my cheek and squinted at my watch. It was 2 a.m.

'Can you hear that? That noise?'

I stopped my breathing and listened. I could hear the ruffle of bags, the scuff of paws and some form of squealing. It seemed to be coming from the decking where we'd eaten dinner.

'Oh crap,' I sighed. 'Lyds, did we leave the food out by any chance?'

'I can't remember if we… oh, yes. We did.'

'That'll be racoons having a feast on it then. I'm going for a pee. I'll see what they're up to.'

I unzipped the tent and stepped outside. Sure enough, there they were. Three racoons having a whale of a time, rummaging through our food bag. We would be going to a town the next day, so it wouldn't be too long before we could get more supplies, and I had a couple of emergency cereal bars stashed in my panniers in the tent, so it wasn't the end of the world. I was too tired to bother shooing them away, so, instead, I just stared at them as I peed. It was sort of like an extreme wildlife programme – live and uncut. As they gorged on our food, I imagined them sat around a table in little paper hats with miniature racoon knives and forks, passing food amongst themselves. Fair play to them. We'd left our food out, they'd found it. It was the natural order of things. I finished my pee, pulled up my pyjama shorts and was just about to step back towards the tent when a thought crossed my mind. I looked up. There, stretched out above me, like a blanket encrusted with diamonds, was the most incredible night sky.

I sat back down (taking care not to sit in the spot I had just peed in) and lay on my back atop twigs and rocks. The air was warm, Lydia had by now fallen back to sleep and (apart from the mid-swing racoon feast) there wasn't a sound. I focused and refocused my gaze, each time spotting new clusters and galaxies that weren't there 10 seconds earlier. I breathed out. A long slow breath. I'd been obsessed with stars and planets since I was a kid. I used to sit on the windowsill of my bedroom and use binoculars to look at the craters on the moon. I had always found solace in how insignificant the planets and the stars made me feel, and tonight was no exception. If we are that tiny, if we are that insignificant, then what can the purpose of life be, except to be grateful for it and enjoy as many precious moments of it as possible? I must have fallen asleep mid gaze, because I woke 30 minutes later, my teeth chattering from the cold. The racoons had clearly finished their petit fours and dessert wine, and then returned to their beds, and it was time I did the same. I sat up, brushed the twigs from my hair and crawled back to the tent.

The following morning, we consulted the map over a breakfast that had been gathered from the scraps left by the racoons. We still had a few sachets of porridge and that'd do for now. We agreed that, after covering the final 36 miles up Carson Pass, we would take a more 'scenic' route, via Lake Tahoe. I say 'we agreed'; the reality is that I pressed the idea on Lydia. The thought of passing so close to Lake Tahoe, and not actually taking a ride along the shore seemed a real shame. It would mean climbing another Sierra Nevada mountain pass, but I thought that was a small price to pay for, what I hoped would be, magical scenery. Eventually, Lydia agreed and the new route was set.

Lydia had enjoyed the descent off of Carson Pass, but she was now having a sense-of-humour failure as we climbed Luther Pass. The gradient of the climb was similar to Carson Pass, at a steady 6% incline, but going uphill for three days in a row was a tall order, especially in the heat. We weren't precious about always riding together, so I trundled on ahead, leaving Lyds to deal with her personal storm. It was rare for her to be in anything other than a great mood, so I knew that she must be having a really bad day. I was beginning to think that Lydia was an invincible cycling goddess, so I was actually relieved that she had a breaking point. After 5 miles or so, I looked back and saw that she was no longer alone. She had another cyclist by her side, a man on a racing bike who was making his way up the pass too. I looked towards the road ahead, continued riding and, five minutes later, the man appeared alongside me.

'Awesome day for a ride, isn't it?' I said, looking on in envy at his light, red and white carbon bike and noting his lack of panniers.

'You bet. Your friend back there doesn't seem to think so though?' he replied in an accent that told me he was Australian.

'Ha! She's enjoying it really. She just doesn't know it yet.'

We carried on chatting for a few minutes and I learned that Brett was a semi-pro triathlete. He was sponsored by a major bike brand and travelled around the world to compete in major triathlon competitions. The sponsorship wasn't enough to mean he could give up work entirely, but he worked in IT and so could do that from anywhere. He flew from his home in Australia to Lake Tahoe every summer to train. Now that's a cool life, I thought, wondering whether I had given up the path of being an elite sportswoman too soon. Then again, rowing wasn't a sport I could have done semi-professionally, but perhaps there was still time to pick up another sport that would allow me to do that?

Brett was lovely. Friendly, open and with a clear sense of

drive. I admired that he was fitting work in around his passion and finding a way to create a life he loved. He seemed to have the best of all things – freedom, financial security and lots of time spent out among the mountains. Although I did wonder whether it might get a bit lonesome, spending four months on your own in a foreign place each year. Lyds must have felt like she was getting a little lonesome too, because after 10 minutes of continuing to truck up Luther Pass and chat with Brett, she appeared alongside us. And now she was looking much more like her chipper self.

After a few more miles of chatting as a three, I began to wonder whether we were messing up Brett's training ride – I mean, he was having to average a whopping 4 mph to stay with us up this hill, a pace I am sure was half his usual lick.

There was a moment of silence before Brett said, 'Umm. Girls. I know this is a bit strange…'

And then there was a pause.

'We like strange, Brett… go on?' I said.

'But I'm renting this house just on Lake Tahoe. It's only me in there and there's a spare room. You're welcome to save yourselves some money and stay there tonight?'

Lyds and I looked at each other and grinned.

'That's not weird at all!' I exclaimed.

'We'd love to!' finished Lyds.

I thought of what on earth my mother would say, but I'm a firm believer in trusting your traveller's gut (I will add that 'traveller's gut' is very different from 'Delhi belly'). I could tell that Brett was a nice man and was extending an offer out of kindness. I might have thought a little longer if I were travelling alone, but trusting the good vibes in my gut and being a two, we accepted his kind offer immediately. Brett was a little taken aback by our instant acceptance.

'Oh! Great!' he said. 'The only thing is…' he trailed off. I waited for the catch. Did he live with his mum? Was he into swinging? Was he a nudist at home? At last Brett put us out of our misery. 'My house is at the top of a twenty-per-cent hill. I mean, you can get off your bikes and walk them up?'

Phew.

'Nah,' Lyds and I chorused. 'Twenty per cent?! Sounds like fun!'

'Ha! Well, I'll give you my number. I live in a place called Heavenly. What time do you think you'll make it there?'

'Heavenly?! Is that for real?!' Brett nodded and I smiled at Lyds before saying, 'Well, however long it'll take you to get home, it'll take us twice as long.'

'Okay, I'll be home in an hour from here. So see you two in two!'

And with that, Brett was gone.

We crested the top of the pass shortly after Brett left us

and enjoyed a long descent into south Lake Tahoe. Well, Lyds enjoyed it – I mostly clung to my brakes and prayed for it to be over. When we made town, we were both absolutely starving. It was now 3 p.m. and we hadn't eaten since our 'racoon leftovers' that morning. Not wanting to turn up on Brett's doorstep and immediately demand access to his fridge, we decided to pull into a supermarket on the outskirts of town and take the edge off the hunger, just a little. We took it in turns to watch the bikes, while the other one went inside the supermarket to pick out a selection of goodies.

I took my turn first and stocked up on chocolate milk (which was downed immediately), some dates (in preparation for the up-and-over assault on Mount Rose the following day) and a 250g block of cheese. I always craved cheese, but I was especially craving it today. I sweated out absolute buckets and there was something about the salt content in cheese that put my body back in balance. I only intended to take a few bites of the cheese block, but 20 minutes later, I looked down at my hand to discover it was empty. I'd just consumed an entire 250g block of cheddar: even I was impressed.

The 20% climb to Brett's house was brutal, but it was nice to add in one final challenge to make us work for our bed 'n' board. When we arrived, Brett offered us a welcome snack (which we welcomed despite our supermarket trip) and we started chatting.

'Aren't you girls afraid?' he asked.

'Afraid of what?' Lyds replied, a small morsel of baguette dropping from her mouth and onto her lap. She quickly retrieved it and returned it to her mouth.

'I don't know? Of people? Of the roads?'

'No,' said Lydia. 'The only thing that scares me are the bears.'

'Oh, the bears! Lyds hates bears!' I chimed in.

'Really?! You know we get a lot of bears around Tahoe,' said Brett.

Lydia's face went as white as the inside of her baguette.

That night Brett took us out for pizza and beer in the small town of Heavenly. On the stroll, I asked him how far we were from the Nevada border. I was eager to know how long it would be before we would cross into state number five of the journey. Brett laughed.

'You're kidding, right?' he said. I looked at him blankly. 'It's just round the corner. C'mon, I'll take you there!'

I looked at Lyds, eyes wide, and squealed.

The road at the border was a bizarre sight. The Nevada side of the street was lined with casinos and on the side where we were stood, in California, there were none.

'Welcome to Nevada!' Brett said, gesturing across to the other side of the road. 'Where gambling is legal and they don't waste a second in letting you know it!'

I pranced around between the borders for a few minutes, running back and forth across the road shouting 'California!… Nevada!… California!'

After two minutes, the novelty of border dancing wore thin, so I returned to Brett and Lydia's side. 'Which state shall we eat in tonight?!' I asked, grinning. We settled on staying in California, because they did good pizza in California.

The following morning, we waved goodbye to Brett, crossed the Nevada state line again and rode along the western shore of Lake Tahoe. Once out of town, the scenery changed dramatically, from high-rise casinos, restaurants, bars and shops and back into tall trees, winding roads and snow-capped mountains in the distance. I guessed that this was the appeal of spending time in the towns around Lake Tahoe – they had everything you needed but were just a stone's throw from the beauty of the Sierra Nevada mountains.

I was struck by the vastness of the lake. It was such a deep shade of blue, which turned almost green at some points and purple in others. The morning sun danced on the lake's surface, making it sparkle, and the land at the shore was lined with rows of evergreens. We took the chance to stop at some of the lookouts along the way and to marvel. I was so glad we'd made the detour, and I knew that Lydia was too. We were looking out on the lake in the height of summer, but I wondered what it might look like in winter, where the rich patch of blue would be surrounded by a carpet of white snow.

It wasn't only the scenery that caught our imagination; the houses of Tahoe did too. On the northern shore of the lake, we got off our bikes several times to press our faces up against the 6-metre-high black metal railings that surrounded each mansion. One house had three giant fountains in the front garden – fountains that wouldn't look out of place in a public park. It was decadent to say the least. Beyond the fountains and down the side of the house, I could see a dock leading straight down to the water's edge, where there was a parked jet ski and a speedboat. Floor to ceiling windows revealed a sleek wooden interior, a large staircase and a chandelier in the lobby. I wondered about the people who lived in these homes. Were they happy? Did these homes make them happy? Or were they just as confused as the rest of us, but living in a larger house, so that their confusion at their purpose in life had more space to roam?

After a tour of the mansions, we pulled in at a small cafe at Incline Village, just shy of the start of the climb up to Mount Rose. We sat and digested everything we'd seen so far, and I mean everything – from the time spent in the wilds of Canada to watching grizzly bears forage in Denali. Riding late into the evening in 23 hours of Alaskan daylight, singing Shania Twain and Johnny Cash tunes at the top of our lungs, enduring mosquito bites, stifling heat, and endless pots of porridge and instant noodles cooked up on campfire stoves together. The journey down California's Route 101, amber sunsets over the Pacific Ocean and riding above the candy-floss clouds with the birds of prey. It felt like leaving this side of Sierra Nevada would be closing a chapter, so I wanted to savour it a little longer, because after the 10-mile winding slog up and over Mount Rose, we would arrive at Reno. And it was in Reno that Lydia would be going home. Term time at her school was due to start next week, and she was needed back there. She *wanted* to go back there, although she did consider staying for a fleeting moment.

Two days later, I waved Lydia off from the doorstep of my temporary home in Reno, as she piled Zena, packed neatly inside a bike box, into a taxi and headed to catch her flight home. We said goodbye with a simple hug because I felt that anything more complex, too many words, too many thoughts, would have weakened the bond that now existed between us. I had a feeling that Lyds and I would be telling stories to our kids in the years to come. It had meant so much having her alongside me for a portion of the journey. I knew a laid-back, cheery temperament like hers was hard to find in a travel companion, and so I was grateful I had found it in mine. Although I would welcome the extra space in our small, two-man tent, it felt weird to be carrying on without her. I would have to find new routines, a new rhythm of my own, and, aside from that, I'd have to cook my own porridge in the morning. As I watched Lydia roll away down the driveway, the feelings of sadness and excitement collided like two giant waves in my mind. She had been a safety blanket for me. She had eased me into the transition from home to here in spectacular fashion, but it was time to face the remaining 45 states alone.

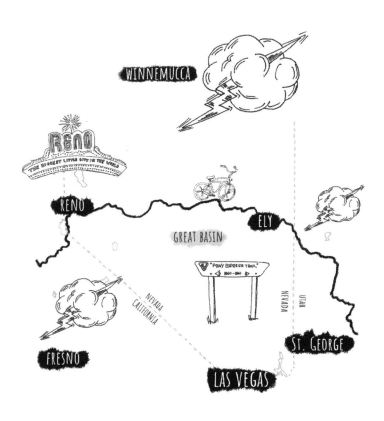

WINNEMUCCA

RENO

GREAT BASIN

ELY

NEVADA
CALIFORNIA

NEVADA

UTAH

FRESNO

ST. GEORGE

LAS VEGAS

GREAT BASIN

6

America's Loneliest Road

Distance Cycled: 2,000 miles
States Completed: 5

Faffing is a quintessentially British word. I had learnt over the course of my two months spent so far in North America that it was a word which did not easily translate to American English. Locals would simply repeat it back to me: 'Faaaffing? What is this faffing?'

Despite its lack of existence in the American-English dictionary, I was somehow managing to faff in my bedroom in Reno. Thanks to a local fig bar company, whom I had connected with before I left the UK, I had spent my few days in Reno being treated like a princess. I'd been treated to massages at the local posh hotel, introduced to the local cycling community, Reno Cycling Club, and had sorted out a place to stay with one of their members, Grant. I'd also got up at the crack of dawn one morning to pay a visit to Billinghurst Middle School, who made me an honorary co-anchor of their weekly student news broadcast.

When the time finally came to ride out of Reno, I was nervous. After two months on the road, I had found some comfort in being in one place for a while, where my pannier bags were untouched and clothes freshly laundered. I had enjoyed the days spent immersed in the more stable lives of others, carried along by their energy as I restored my own. But I now thought about the road ahead and wondered how I would cope as a solo traveller with only my energy to propel me forwards.

I had been fully expecting to leave town quietly, to slip out alone in the light of the early dawn, but I got the feeling that Jon Pettengil, who was the head of the Reno Cycling gang, was having none of it. In the few days spent in town, I'd grown really fond of JP. He is a doer, one of life's 'yes' men. I'd found him to be generous with his thoughts and kind with his actions, always quick to praise others and extremely modest. To say he inflated everyone around him was an understatement. Our friendship had started well ahead of my arrival in Reno, when we'd exchanged a few emails in which JP had well and truly taken the micky out of me. If there's one thing a Brit loves more than a cuppa and a slice of cake, it's sarcasm. And JP had bags of it to dish out.

'What time you thinkin' of setting off?' he asked me over dinner, a few nights before my departure.

'It'll be an early one, JP,' I said, between mouthfuls of buttered chicken and coleslaw. 'Likely 6 a.m.,' I said. 'I've got a long way to ride.'

JP didn't even seem to draw breath before saying, 'We'll be there. In fact, we'll all be there,' he continued, referring to the rest of the cycling club.

'Ha! I don't think so! You might be crazy enough to get out of bed that early, JP, but no one else is going to!'

'Sure they will,' he grinned.

JP is a man of his word and at 6 a.m., on the day of departure, I met a group of ten riders at Hub Coffee Roasters in downtown Reno. I couldn't believe that many people had dragged themselves out of bed to come and say goodbye, or hello and goodbye in some cases. I was humbled to the core and made to feel like a local celebrity. JP gave a short pre-ride briefing to the group, which boiled down to 'ride safe, and don't behave like idiots', and, after fuelling up on cups of deliciously bitter coffee, the Reno Cycling gang and I rode a short way together through the town centre, before stopping for a photo.

'You can't leave without a photo under the famous sign!' JP insisted, as we lined up in the middle of the road against a backdrop of twinkling downtown skyscrapers, Vegas-esque lights and the odd late-night gambler stumbling home. The air was thick and even though the sun was just a faint red glow on the horizon, it was already starting to heat up. I looked around, perplexed by the lack of people out and about in a city at that time of the morning. It was now approaching 7 a.m., but I was learning that Reno was a nocturnal place. It buzzed through the night and rested in the daytime. I was grateful to be passing through it at a time of rest, and the lack of traffic, pedestrian or motorised, meant that we could take over the whole road without the fear of being disturbed. I positioned myself in the middle of the group, directly under the sign and stared up at it: 'Reno – the biggest little city in the world'.

After the group photo shoot, we wound our way out of the city centre. Although I'd originally hoped to leave town alone, I was soon grateful I had an army of escorts and I enjoyed the luxury of not having to worry about navigation. Instead, I busied myself chatting to those within the group, many of whom I hadn't had the chance to speak to until now. For that hour, at least, I became part of a tight-knit, mobile community.

As we rode, I had the chance to chat to JP a little more and learn about his life in more detail. I knew something of his backstory from an article I'd read online. In 2007, he had been working as a teacher, leading an ordinary life, and enjoying weekends spent cycling in the mountains around Reno. All that changed when he had a car accident which involved a head-on collision with a truck. He'd snapped his left upper arm bone clean in two, detached his left triceps and shattered the bones in both of his lower arms. His lower lip was almost torn off in the impact and he also lost much of the tissue surrounding his left eyelid. After six months of being pinned back together, and with the help of an amazing plastic surgeon and some psychological support, JP managed to get back to his favourite hobby, cycling.

Unbelievably, JP then had another collision with an SUV, although this time on his bike. It left his bike in tatters and his body back at accident-crumpled square one. In the space of 24 months, he had had two horrific accidents. And yet, through it all, through all the pain and the suffering, somehow he managed to retain his humour.

'You know, Anna, when my bones had finally healed and it was time for all the pins to come out, I handed them to my mum and asked her to "do something useful" with them. You know what she did?'

'What?' I asked

'Turned 'em into a hanging mobile!' JP grinned again and there was a brief moment of silence. 'That kind of thing, Anna, it makes you take stock of what's important in life.'

I nodded; it was an understatement to say the least.

'So that's how I'm here, doing what I'm doing now. After all of that, I asked myself what it was that I really wanted to be spending my days doing. I mean, being a teacher was great, but what I really love is cycling. So I became a cycling coach.'

JP's accidents had led him to become the lead of the Reno Cycling Club, which, as a result, had led him into my adventure, and for that I was grateful.

It was still early morning as we climbed upwards through Cedar Hill Canyon pass, on the outskirts of the town of Virginia, but I could already feel the heat and humidity start to build. We had been shedding members of the Reno peloton since leaving downtown, and now there were just five of us left, slogging our way up to 2,000 metres above sea level. In need of some respite from the heat, we agreed to stop in the shaded porch of a gigantic fudge factory on the side of the road.

JP and I had been chatting on and off about his life and mine for an hour in the lead up to stopping at the factory, but now he had been silent for a few minutes and seemed preoccupied with something.

'Say, Anna, how far you planning on going today?' he asked.

'Errr, I'm going to do my best to make Fallon.'

There was a long pause again.

'You know what, Anna?'

'What, Mr Pettengil?' I asked.

'I'm going to come all the way with you.'

I nearly fell off my bike seat.

'Really?!' I yelped.

It was 115 miles to Fallon. That'd be like me saying I was going to ride out to Windsor from London, and wind up cycling all the way down to Portsmouth.

'Are you serious?!'

'Yep. I've decided. I mean, we're never going to be here again, are we? You'll never be here again, I mean. So it seems just stupid for me not to make the most of it.'

And with that he got his phone out and began rearranging his afternoon appointments, moving them to days later in the week. He then called his wife, Kristi, and I listened to one half of the conversation.

'Hey Kristi, so I'm gonna ride all the way with Anna today. Uh-huh. Yeah. That'd be great. Okay, thanks.'

He put the phone down and smiled.

'So Kristi's going to pick me up at the other end. She might even take us for some dinner.'

He grinned, and that was us set. My first day into the Nevada desert was now a two-man assault – my mum would be delighted.

JP and I left the remainder of the group resting in the shade of the fudge factory and set off up the road. It fast became apparent that JP was the most perfect riding partner I could have asked for that day. That is, he was perfectly happy with both of us doing our own thing. One of the challenges of riding with others on a long-distance cycle tour is that, for some reason, it was expected that I would always ride at breakneck speed. Most would end up sorely disappointed when they realised I had the steady pace of a fully loaded touring bike.

JP was riding a beautiful little black carbon racing bike, and was a good deal faster than I was. Not to mention he was a cycling coach; knowing how to go fast on a bike was his full-time occupation. His 9-kg shiny steed made Boudica self-conscious about her 30-kg total weight, I could sense it, but I soothed her as we rode and we were all very content – bikes and riders, existing in our own little worlds, side by side. We hit the foot of a small but steep climb and JP looked across at me.

'Fancy swapping bikes?' he asked.

'Do I want to swap? As in, do you want to ride my thirty-kilogram beast up that and I go up on your little carbon thing?!'

'That's exactly what I mean! C'mon – I want to see what it's like!' he squealed, like an excited child.

So we swapped bikes for 10 minutes, giggling, snorting and almost falling off, as neither of us had the right clips on our shoes for the other one's pedals. As much as I had enjoyed the wafer-like weight of JP's bike, I was relieved to be back on Boudica afterwards, because she felt like home. In a landscape that was forever changing, both physically and emotionally, she was my constant.

For the rest of the day, I took much joy in watching JP revel in the adventure. He was like a child who'd just been given permission to go out and play, and the best part was that he had given himself that permission. For the periods when we were riding together, we chatted and played games, one of which was to try to work out how many miles away the small buildings on the hazel horizon were – it turned out to be 16 miles.

I found the road leading to Fallon to be… odd. I couldn't fit it into one stereotype or another. It fell part way between serene desert landscape and industrial park. The buildings that did appear on the horizon were there clearly to perform a function. Some seemed to be farms, others were warehouses, and some had another purpose altogether. As we moved from built-up areas into smaller pockets of towns, I began to notice gentlemen's clubs. The car parks were half full, and that led me to think about who was in there at this time of day. And what they'd told their wife/daughter/neighbour they were doing.

By late afternoon, it started to get really hot and was pushing 35°C. We had agreed to stop roughly every 25 miles at the various gas stations en route, and were taking it in turns to buy one another treats: ice cream, sandwiches, water. JP used my phone to take a picture of me at one of the gas stations while I was eating my fourth ice cream of the day, and when he handed it back to me, I almost didn't recognise the woman in it. My skin was deeply tanned. Strands of hair spouted from beneath my helmet and were bright blonde, bleached by the sun. Wrapped around the stick of the ice cream was my grubby hand, clad in an equally grubby set of white and blue fingerless cycling gloves. Or, at least, I think they were white once. I was looking sideways at the camera and you could see I was tired, but my eyes seemed bluer than they usually were. More alive. As if they had more to them, and more stories to tell.

That afternoon, I was touched when a passing car stopped to hand us two bottles of water. I was actually already carrying more than enough water with me, and didn't really want to take on any more, but JP swooped in and accepted the gifts. Waiting until they'd driven off, he turned to me and said, 'Doesn't matter if you need it or not, Anna. Best take it because they've been kind enough to give it.'

It was just past 5 p.m. when we finally rolled our exhausted bodies into the modest town of Fallon, population 8,606. We'd been riding since 6.30 a.m., covered a hot and hilly 115 miles and only ever stopped briefly. I was knackered, but equally chuffed to have completed the longest day on the bike so far. As promised, JP's wife Kristi was waiting for us in town. We met her at a local fairground, where apparently it was okay for me to pitch my tent for the night. There was no one at the fairground and sadly no big wheel or candy floss stalls, so I stashed my bike behind one of the empty buildings and went on up the road to get some dinner with JP and Kristi.

My ego took great delight in noting over dinner that JP's face was as red as mine. After all the energy he'd given out through the course of the day, he now seemed unusually quiet. I mostly chatted to Kristi as I filled my face with fish tacos, salsa and guacamole and gulped down litres of icy water. When the time came to leave the restaurant, JP and Kristi insisted they picked up the bill. Well, JP waved something from his slumped position and Kristi took the lead. I tried to protest, but then remembered what JP had said to me earlier in the day about letting people give, and so I shut my mouth and graciously accepted.

After a trip to the local supermarket to top up on water and snacks for the following day (which JP and Kristi also insisted on buying for me), we returned to the fairground. Kristi had told us over dinner that a storm was due to roll through the town tonight, but I'd thought nothing of it. These things never seemed real until they were actually upon me, but as I pitched my tent, I couldn't help but notice that the wind was getting stronger. I say I couldn't help but notice because it was attempting to rip the tent clean out of my hands.

JP and Kristi offered to stay longer, but they had a long drive home. And besides, I was eager to be alone now. The longer they stayed the more I felt I was delaying facing the desert alone.

'Are you sure you're going to be okay?' Kristi called, as I wrestled the last tent peg into position. I looked at my flimsy ripstop structure, watching as it flexed and groaned with every gust of wind that passed through it. The poles already looked like they were going to snap and I had a sneaky suspicion that the storm hadn't even got going yet.

'Yeah! I'll be fine!!' I shouted over the now roaring wind, shutting my eyes to avoid the sand getting into them. Kristi was squinting and doing the same.

'Okay!' she shouted back. 'You call us if you need anything though, anything at all. Promise?' She put her outstretched arms on my shoulders.

'Promise,' I said as I moved in to hug her goodbye. I

hugged them once each, and then again together for good measure. I felt a small lump in my throat and tears started to well at the backs of my eyes. The full weight of a ride across the desert, of what I was about to embark on, was sitting just out of reach, a black hole of fear ready to swallow me up, if I even so much as glanced at it. So I shoved it away again. Half of me wanted to scream 'please don't leave me!' but the other half of me knew I had to do this alone.

After JP and Kristi left, I crawled into my tent and winced as the flimsy yellow inner walls flapped around my ears and the storm grew stronger. The noise was deafening, as if someone were repeatedly cracking a whip just centimetres from my ears. Truth be told, I was now caught between being terrified and angry. I was so tired, almost too tired to be terrified, and so the energy required to be terrified was really starting to hack me off. I began to wonder if it would get worse. *What if this just the start of what's to come in the week of crossing the desert?! What if I end up alone out there in an even worse storm and the swirling sand grinds me to cyclist dust?!* Eventually I settled on asking myself the more helpful question of what was the worst that could happen, right at that very moment? This is a trick that always stops my catastrophising dead in its tracks and brings me back to the present. I resolved that the worst that could happen was that all my tent pegs would be ripped from the ground by the wind and that I would wind up cocooned in a tangle of ripstop material, perhaps gasping for air. I concluded that, if said shelter disaster were to actually occur, I would likely have time to make a swift exit from the tent and would not, in fact, suffocate and die alone at the fairground in Fallon. I took a video on my phone which I intended to upload to my followers on social media in the morning.

'When the wind is raging around you on the edge of the desert, there's nothing for it but to crawl in your tent and eat a chocolate bar,' I said, brandishing my favourite coconut and dark chocolate treat to the camera.

The chocolate soothed my nervous belly, while the wind kept me awake – it shook my makeshift home forcibly and continued to make one heck of a racket on the inside. Eventually, I grew weary of being afraid and, alone on the edge of the desert, I fell asleep.

***

In 1986, one of America's more popular publications, Life magazine, declared that the particular section of Route 50 that crosses Nevada is 'the loneliest road in America', stating: 'It's totally empty. There are no points of interest. We don't recommend it. We warn all motorists not to drive there.'

Back in 2011, I'd taken a cycle-touring trip through Scotland and had come across a 50-mile section of road to the town of Lairg in the Highlands with nothing on it except a lodge and a few highland cows. At the time, I had mentally rated it as 'extremely remote'.

That morning, as I packed away my tent in a fairground where calm had been restored after the storm, I was preparing to head across something seven times the length of that road in Scotland, and goodness knows how many times as desolate. And yet, in the cold light of day, buoyed by my efforts with JP the previous day, I was more intrigued than frightened. More nervous than excited. I'd also taken great joy in learning that Nevada's Great Basin is North America's only 'cold desert'. That is, the majority of its annual precipitation falls as snow. How is that even possible?! My mind was blown and the journey across it hadn't even begun.

I loaded up with the 9 litres of water I'd bought in the store the previous night and began to pedal away from Fallon. Nine litres equated to an extra 9 kg of weight – and that was a lot to be carrying on my already heavily loaded frame – but running out of water out 'there' was one of my greatest fears. At least, I think it was one of my fears. There were piles of them in my mind on that first day of cycling alone. I had organised them into little mentally constructed filing cabinets, marked with different labels: boredom, loneliness, death by shooting, death by dehydration, death by sandstorm. Even though I would only be following one road in a straight line for 600 miles that week, there was even a neat little filing cabinet drawer marked 'getting lost'.

As I left the buildings of Fallon behind me, the surrounding landscape grew ever quieter and ever more intriguing. The Great Basin wasted no time in dispelling any expectations I had for it. More alarming was the fact that it didn't conform to images of deserts I had seen in geography textbooks as a kid. There was sand, but it wasn't piled into dunes. Instead, it was lightly dusted over a rocky, almost volcanic ground. Patches of green-brown shrubs lined the sides of the road, which led to a backdrop of small, sharp mountain peaks. I had expected the desert to be lifeless too, but it was far from it. On the first day, I was joined by flocks of small grey birds, watched lizards dart from the sides of the road and under nearby rocks and squealed when I saw a chipmunk scamper across the road in front of me. During a snack stop, I was also gobsmacked to find a patch of small, wild, bright yellow flowers. Flowers?! In the desert?!

I felt so confused that the desert wasn't living up to its stereotype that I wondered whether it was in fact a desert at all. Perhaps I had taken a wrong turn out of town and I wasn't even in the desert?! I later read online that the deserts of the world can be placed into one of four categories or 'desert biomes'. These are hot and dry, semi-arid, coastal and cold. Famous hot and dry deserts include the Sahara and the Mojave, so this is what most people traditionally think of when they hear the word desert. The Great Basin is a semi-arid desert, which means that it gets slightly more annual rainfall than the hot and dry deserts, and this would explain the plant life and the small wildlife. It would also explain the thunderstorm I'd experienced while I was in Fallon and the storms that continued over the next week.

It was 3.30 p.m. and the end of a long day on the bike when I rolled into Cold Springs station. A 'station' I'd worked out by that point referred to one or two buildings, or an outpost of some kind. There was no way you could call it a town, but there would normally be one bar or freestanding shack and an accompanying campsite that was sometimes with, sometimes without, running water. These stations were often in historically significant locations. In years gone by, they'd have been the places where pilgrims and weary travellers stopped to rest, grab a bite to eat and indulge in a rare conversation or two with those passing in the opposite direction.

Cold Springs had a trailer park, one main Wild-West-style saloon building, which housed a bar, a few small one-bedroom huts and a tiny patch of grass for camping. It looked rather odd, a patch of grass in the middle of the desert, but that was to be my home for the night. I spoke briefly to a woman inside the saloon, before returning to the patch of grass to pitch my tent.

Midway through putting up the tent, a man in his early 20s appeared from a nearby trailer and came over. He was slim and tall with sloping shoulders and dark hair. His skin was pitted, presumably from a bout of acne as a teenager, and his blue eyes darted to and fro more rapidly than was normal, as if he were surveying the landscape for any potential signs of danger. He was wearing a scruffy, crinkled off-white shirt, faded jeans and an expression that was halfway between vacancy and intrigue.

'Ain't it a little hot out there to be ridin' a bicycle?' the man asked, his eyes still darting from side to side, but his head now cocked firmly to the left.

'Hello. Oh. It's not too bad.' I smiled. 'Besides, it keeps raining so I'm getting cooled down a bit.' I smiled again and turned my attention back to the tent, assuming he'd walk on. Thirty seconds later, I became aware that the man hadn't moved, but was instead stood still in the same spot, watching. I looked up and smiled again. I felt mildly creeped out, but there was nothing overly alarming about him. He seemed a bit odd, but then again, I was the girl who had just rolled into a station in the middle of nowhere on a pink bike, so perhaps he thought I was odd too and was therefore curious. It did seem awkward to have him just watch me in silence, however, so we started to chat and, as is polite, I asked him about himself.

Hans, as it turned out, was the chef at the station. He earnt $6,000 a year (about £3,500 at the time) and lived there year-round. I paused our chat and looked about. Beyond the boundaries of the station, I knew that there was nothing but vast desert for 60 miles in each direction. Hans told me that it was his day off.

'What do you do on your day off round here? For fun, I mean,' I continued, trying to reel in the note of incredulity in my voice.

'Awww, not much nowadays. You see that fourby over there?' He gestured to a khaki-coloured quad bike sitting next to the back entrance of the bar. 'I used to take that up into those hills… but…'

I looked in the direction he was pointing to. Those hills looked pretty cool, albeit a little barren, and I guessed that the view up there would be spectacular.

'But you don't anymore?'

'Naah. I had an accident. I was giving it a bit too much juice, down the hill, y' know. And well, I guess I overcooked the gas. Came clean off. Smashed up my shoulder… Now the boss won't let me take it ridin' no more.'

'Oh, that's a shame,' I said, thinking how unfortunate it would be to smash up your only source of entertainment in the desert.

'Yeah, it's okay though. I've got a computer, so I just go on that. Although I keep myself off the grid.'

'Off the grid?' I asked.

'Yeah. I know they're watching me, watching all of us, so I try to keep a low profile.'

'Who's they?'

'The government. They know everything I do. You too. And I don't want the president knowing jack shit about my life. So I use this special software. Keeps 'em out. And that's the way I like it.'

There was a long pause. I doubted that the president of

the United States was overly interested in Hans' life, but perhaps that was presumptive. Perhaps there was more to Hans than met the eye.

I'd finished putting up my tent and the conversation with Hans was beginning to wear thin. Sweet as he seemed, it'd been a long day through heat and thunderstorms and I was tired. I'd mentally prepared myself to spend the rest of the evening reading a book and relaxing. Alas, Hans seemed to take the silence as an invitation to make some plans of his own.

'Say, Anna... Can I buy you dinner?' he asked

Oh crikey. I looked around again, just to confirm there was indeed just one bar here. That one bar that I was about to go to and sit in on my own anyway. How could I refuse this one? Instead of a flat 'no', I managed to negotiate the offer down to allowing Hans to buy me a Diet Pepsi. We could have a quick chat for 30 minutes and then I'd make my excuses and go and hide in my tent.

'How long will it take you to get ready?' Hans continued, now seemingly eager at the prospect of a Diet Pepsi desert date.

'Oh, not long – ten minutes?' There were no showers, of course, so it was just a case of how long it'd take me to baby wipe as much of my body as I could be bothered to.

'See you in the bar in ten minutes then,' he said, and I nodded. 'In there, I mean.' He pointed at the bar, just in case

I was under any doubt and was going to go to the bar in the next town. 'Ten minutes,' I repeated. He smiled and turned back toward his trailer. I wondered what he might do with his 10 minutes to spruce himself up. Perhaps a little aftershave? Some Lynx for the pits?

Operation 30-minute-date did not go to plan and two hours later I was still sitting at a round, high table in the bar with one very inebriated Hans. As I'd supped on one Pepsi for the entire two hours, a Pepsi which I insisted on pouring myself, Hans had fixed himself two beers and three cocktails and had become increasingly drunk. Something told me he was harmless, but as a lone female in unfamiliar surroundings, I had to listen to the sensible side of my brain, and Hans' state was beginning to make me feel uncomfortable.

Through the hours of Hans sharing tales from his life, I'd made a conscious decision to tell him as little about my own life as I could. For one, I felt guilty. My life was a world away from his, which I had learned was full of struggle after his mum had left him as a young child and his girlfriend had told him she was pregnant with his child, only for him to bring that child up until the age of five and then discover that his best friend was the real father. You couldn't make this stuff up. In stark contrast to Hans finding himself here at the station in a bid to make ends meet, I was effectively on an adventure jolly. Searching for something to fill the void because my well-paid job in one of the most vibrant cities in the world just didn't quite 'do it' for me. What a princess.

I wasn't entirely confident that I'd figured Hans out just yet. I was trying to work out whether he was one of these harmless types who, for all his quirks, was genuinely kind or whether he was a caged serial killer. If he was the latter, I had found comfort in the fact that there were four other people in the bar, including one female cook who came over to chat to us for a while. If Hans was in any way intending to cause me harm, that would make her part of the elaborate plot too, which seemed unlikely. As the conversation began to draw to a close, I made up a fake boyfriend called Adam (whom I had to call tonight – hence why I would be leaving Hans' company shortly) and stretched the truth a little more about my route once I'd left Nevada, just in case. Just then Hans interrupted me and said, 'Anna.'

'Yeah,' I replied.

'I really appreciate that you're not flirtin' with me.' I nearly spat out the icy remains of my Diet Pepsi. Well, thank God he'd cottoned on to that one! 'Cos, you know, some women, they'll just flirt because they want somethin' from you. But we're friends. And I like that.'

Oh crikey.

As a parting gift, Hans offered to take me on a 'tour' of the station. I didn't really see how there was much to be toured, but he was so insistent – and I didn't want to hurt his feelings –that we went outside. All the while my brain was screaming,

'What the heck are you doing, Anna?!'

Hans and I stood alone together behind the bar and he pointed up into the hills again. 'There's people living up there, you know. They've been there for years.'

'Where?' I squinted in the direction he was pointing. All I could see was red and brown rock face. 'That dark patch, there, you see?'

He moved in closer next to me and pointed ahead. I smelt the alcohol on his breath – it wound its way up my nostrils and into my windpipe like poison. I flinched.

'Oh, yes, I see!' I yelped, leaping away from his side. Did I see anything? Bollocks did I. 'I've been up there to try to find them, you know? But every time I do, they hide from me. It's like someone told them I was coming,' said Hans.

At that moment, the dark clouds in the sky cracked and a thunderstorm began, so we both ducked into a nearby shelter. Now 100 metres from the main bar, hidden from it by a cor-rugated metal sheet, and with the deafening rattle of rain on a tin roof, I suddenly felt vulnerable. Hans continued his tirade about the people living in the hills, sloshing his drink around and spilling parts of it on both of us.

A few minutes later, the rain slowed and I saw my chance – I summoned up the most enormous fake yawn I could muster. 'Aaaawww. I'm really tired. I think I better call Adam, then get an early night. I've got to be up before dawn tomorrow.'

He looked at his watch. 'But it's only six thirty?'

'Yeah, I know. I can sleep for England though!' I said with a smile, already walking away and back towards the bar, Hans trailing behind.

Just as I reached my tent, I turned to face Hans. 'Well, thanks for the drink. I really hope everything works out with your ex-girlfriend and your son. You take care of yourself.'

I leant down, unzipped the front porch of my tent and crawled into my canvas cave, zipping up the door once again and sitting perfectly still. I listened, my heart pounding. I could hear the shuffling of Hans' feet on the gravel outside and his breathing. His feet stopped shuffling and I held my breath.

'Hey… Umm… Anna?'

Gulp. Oh my. Here we go…

'Mmm hmmm,' I replied, not moving a muscle and sat bolt upright, but making it sound like I was already half asleep.

'Can I get your email address?'

I breathed out. Not entirely relaxed but a little relieved. I unzipped the door again, dictated a fake email (I was always 'Anna Scott' to strangers), felt terrible about doing it but resigned that it was for my own safety. I looked up at him from the tent, waiting to see what he'd do next.

'Thanks. It was real nice to meet you.' He held out his hand, shook mine and, with that, disappeared.

With Hans gone, I lay awake, staring up at the ceiling of my tent and thought about the events of the past four hours. As it turned out, Hans was harmless. And with others in the bar nearby, I was perhaps never in any real danger, but it did make me rethink how assertive I'd been. I was always one to assume the best in people and to trust them from the off. But in this instance, I had been so concerned with not hurting Hans' feelings, and in assuming the best in him, that I hadn't put my own sense of unease first. I hadn't made my safety the priority, a fact that made me embarrassed. Even though I was the only person there to note my predicament. I made a firm resolution from then on: safety first, politeness second.

***

As I continued to trace my way along Route 50, I began to enjoy the solitude I'd been so fearful of when JP had left me in Fallon. There wasn't much to do except listen to music or be alone with my thoughts. Each day I wondered what kind of people lived out here – a train of thought that my encounter with Hans had sparked. Those that I'd met so far seemed kind, yet content to keep themselves to themselves.

In one old miners' station, at a small place called Middlegate, it'd taken the lone bartender a good 10 minutes to even notice that I'd walked in the door. Being British, I didn't want to be rude and interrupt his thoughts, but eventually I grew a little tired of waiting so I cleared my throat. He came around from his daydream with a start and seemed surprised to see me there.

After ordering the most disgusting pastrami sandwich I'd ever attempted to eat, Brian the barman explained the history of the building to me. The ceiling was covered with hundreds of dollar bills, some so old and faded that they were barely recognisable as currency. Brian told me that pinning a dollar bill on the ceiling was a tradition. It was from a time when the miners would drink the night away and spend more than they should filling their bellies and drowning their woes with liquor. Before they were too far gone, they'd stick a dollar bill to the ceiling with their name on it. That way, when they emerged from their alcohol-soaked cocoon in the morning, they had enough money to buy breakfast, before heading back out to the mines.

After Brian's stories, I looked around the shack with fresh eyes and imagined the tiny bar bustling with soot-covered men, clinking glasses, and laughing and drinking the night away. I knew one thing, however; after that pastrami sandwich, there was no way I'd be back for breakfast. Nevertheless, I stuck a dollar bill up on the ceiling for good measure.

The drinking traditions weren't the only history I'd un-covered on the journey across Route 50. Every now and then, I would come across a sign that read 'point of historical in-terest' and I would follow a small trail away from the main road to a faded, often barely legible, information board about some piece of local trivia. For example, the Pony Express was a piece of real Route-50 Wild-West history, and one that I was immersing myself in on a daily basis. Back in 1860, it would take weeks, even a whole month, to get a message from the west to the east of the USA. So, a few military types had a bold brainwave to hire young, wiry, preferably orphaned, boys to ride like the wind across most of the US in just 10 days, carrying mail sacks with them. Thus, the Pony Express was born. Orphans were preferred as the long days and nights of riding through landscapes plagued by fierce weather and frequented by bandits was dangerous. With no family, it was assumed there would be less of an uproar if the boys (sometimes those as young as 11 years old) never returned. Despite the expected success, the Pony Express was no money spinner and, after 18 months of running at a loss, and four days before the first West–East telegram was sent, the Express shut down. Years later, Route 50 was built following the original route the Express riders had taken.

It was thoughts of the young solo riders out here alone, in this vast expanse of nothing but sand, scrub, basins and passes that led me to feel a sense of kinship with them. The sense of solitude that I had been so afraid of when JP and Kristi left me in Fallon was something I had grown to love. I was only riding eight hours a day, and on tarmac – how the Express riders managed 12 hours, sometimes longer, on the back of a pony, through all seasons, time and time again, was beyond me.

In the town of Eureka, population 601, I was delighted to

find a store that sold apples. My diet so far that week had largely consisted of meat-like substances with cheese melted on top, or whatever remained at the bottom of my front pannier. I desperately craved something fresh. Large white ulcers had begun to develop on my gums and tongue, and cuts were beginning to form at the sides of my mouth – a sure sign that the heat and wind were wearing me down, but also that I needed more vitamins than I was getting. At the grocery store in Eureka, I bought an enormous bag of apples and some veggies. I stood outside the shop and ate three apples immediately. Then I munched on a raw pepper and three carrots – just because I could. I let the fresh flesh of each remain in my mouth for far longer than was necessary, pushing it into my gums with my tongue, enjoying its cooling sensation against the sores that had developed.

That night, I camped on a small patch of grass which was the local park. It couldn't have been more than 30 metres long by 20 metres wide, and despite sharing it with some of the local youths, I decided it was as good a spot as any to pitch my tent. Even if I did have to put up with the kids whispering, 'That funny cycling lady – she's still here.'

The day I left Eureka was by far the most difficult so far on Route 50. Four passes stood between me and the relative metropolis of Ely (population 1,900), 70 miles down the road. Each pass sapped just that little bit more energy than I had and the wind was relentless. On the third pass, I clocked my speed at 7 mph, going downhill. I was practically being pushed back up it. I stopped to eat in the shelter of a riverbed at the bottom of the pass – the only place I could find out of the wind. I curled up in the small space on the clay bed I'd made for myself, stuffed a tortilla wrap in my mouth and let my eyes rest for 15 minutes. I went for a pee (the safest place to do it without a chance of it ending up blowing all over my legs) and set off again.

Upon leaving the shelter of the riverbed, a thunderstorm began, and it was accompanied by raging crosswinds. I found myself unable to cycle due to laughing out loud at my own attempts to make progress. I took a video on my phone to document the absurdity of the desert winds.

'Just being blown sideways across the plain… Speedo says five miles per hour… The fact that I could walk faster is neither here nor there.'

I decided that strong winds were a wonderful way to train patience. The angrier I got, the more energy I wasted and the slower I went. It was like the wind fed my anger; it grew stronger as I grew weaker. I soon decided to submit to the desert's whims and roll with it. The rain lashed down and the skies crackled violently overhead, but with 20 miles left to Ely, I gritted my teeth and pushed on. The wind got stronger and the rain heavier. I let out a war cry, which in hindsight seemed insane, but in the moment I felt like I was being tested. Just one last test before Route 50 and the Great Basin would release me from its grasp.

'Come on then, come on!' I shouted from my saddle as the rain battered into my cheeks. 'Is that all you've got?!

The wind blew again, this time almost making me lose my grip on the increasingly slippery handlebars. Suddenly, and it really was suddenly, the rain stopped. The wind died away and everything was calm once again. There were now just 10 miles to go. In a unique twist, the road left the wide-open scrubland and plunged into the steep walls of an area called Rabbit Canyon. I found myself sandwiched between walls of reddish orange rock, as the brown-green waters of Gleason Creek appeared to my right. I whooped and hollered so much that my shouts reverberated off the walls around my ears and I pushed harder and harder on the pedals so that I felt as if I was whooshing through the canyon at warp speed. I burst once again into the open scrubland and heard a loud hissing sound as a steam train pulled alongside me. A steam train?! Where had that come from?! It was full to the brim with passengers, passengers who had now spotted me on the road and were waving from the open windows. I returned a wave before turning my attention back to the spinning of the pedals and racing the train into town with a huge grin on my face. I had an inkling the weather would get far worse than it had that day, but for the time being at least, I'd claimed a victory.

That night I posted on my Facebook page: 'Errr NEWS-FLASH – it's thunderstorm season in the desert. Google says the 'cloud storms' usually last for 30 minutes. Not the one I cycled in today – it was me against the world for most of it.

Following some *Braveheart*-esque war cries, I'm going to put it out there that I won. I shall prep the blue face paint for round 2 tomorrow. They can take my tailwind, but they shan't take my freeedooommmm!'

The number of people following me online was still minimal to say the least, but those who were watching the journey unfold knew me well. I smiled as a string of comments appeared from old work colleagues. One was from a guy called Doug, whom I used to go cycling with – he apologised that he and his mates weren't there to protect me as part of a peloton from the weather. Another comment was from JP: 'Just watch where you put your broad sword! Stay Tuff Chick!' Just seeing these posts and words of encouragement made me feel at times like this journey wasn't a solo one at all, but that I had a whole adventure army behind me, cheering me on when the going got tough.

The following day things became easier, and I found myself riding in a tailwind. I was zooming along, heading for the town of Baker, assisted by a gradual downhill that had joined the tailwind to make things even more enjoyable. I spotted a silhouette on the horizon and could have sworn it was someone riding a bike coming towards me, although it looked too tall and upright to be a cyclist. *Perhaps they are on a unicycle?!* I thought, although the desert was an odd place to take a unicycle for a ride. As the figure got closer, I could see that it was indeed a cyclist, and he was far from your average tourer. A scrawny looking man in an open-chested Hawaiian shirt and loose khaki shorts sat on top of a very upright, Dutch-looking bike – some might call it a beach cruiser. He had long, straggly hair that might have touched his shoulders had the wind not been blowing it out behind him like a flag on a pole. I crossed the road so that I was on his side and waited to greet this 'desert cruiser'. His face looked pained and ashen as he pulled on the brakes and came to a stop just in front of me.

'Thank God!' he said, slumping over his Harley Davidson-style handlebars and looking up at me. 'I haven't seen anyone all day. There's nothing out here, and this wind is just killing me!'

I felt for the guy. I was getting all the wind's assistance, and he just got the resistance.

'Oh, you're doing great!' I chirped. 'Where are you headed?'

'Los Angeles, man.'

'LA?! Woah. That's a long way!'

I took a guess that LA was 600 miles from where we were. This guy looked like he was just on a little pedal down the road, so fair play to him if he was riding that thing all the way to LA. I looked past him to the back of the bike and noticed he didn't have any panniers or bags, but he did have a yellow plastic crate, the kind you might keep oranges in. The plastic looked heavily faded by the sun and matched the man's jaded appearance. I looked down at his feet and noticed that he was in flip flops. It looked like someone had picked this man up from the beach and plonked him in the desert. He was completely out of place. Rather than think him silly, he actually made *me* feel silly. How could this dude cope out here in storms, rain and wind, and in clothes like that – and here I was, well-equipped, battling with the elements.

'My name's Kit,' he said, extending a tanned, leathery looking hand over his handlebars. I smiled, introduced myself and shook his hand.

'So why the big ride?'

Kit shrugged. 'I dunno really. I lived in LA for a while, then I went to visit some family in Virginia, and I found this beach cruiser at a garage sale. It says "Venice Beach" on the side, see?' Kit pointed to some sparkly purple script-style writing, which was just about readable against the chipped pale-blue paintwork on the bike. I nodded. 'So, I decided that I'd take the bike home – to its home, I mean, Venice Beach in LA. Sort of like a pilgrimage, you know?'

I was impressed. Virginia was on the East Coast, and around 3,000 miles from where we were.

'So you've ridden that all the way from Virginia?!'

'Yeah. It's been cool. I've seen a lot of things, but this last stretch is killing me, man. There's no people!'

We chatted for a further five minutes about our respective trips, before turning my attention to the crate on the back of the bike.

'You've packed pretty light?' I said, thinking about the fact that I had four large panniers to hold everything I needed for a ride through the states.

'Oh, yeah, I don't need much, you know. I've got a sleeping bag and tent, but mostly I just sleep in this gear,' he said, tugging at his shirt. 'Or I just pick up stuff from charity stores along the way.'

Fair play to the guy – he'd got the efficiency of packing minimal kit down to a tee. In some ways I envied him, although I wouldn't be swapping my bags for the crate any time soon. Intrigued, I then asked Kit what he did for a living.

'Oh, you know, this and that,' he said. 'Picking things, fixing things, some music, some chillin'. I just go wherever this takes me,' he said, patting his chest above his heart.

'Well, Kit,' I said. 'I think you're just a little bit awesome.' I dismounted my bike and gave him a hug. 'Take that for the rest of the day – it's a bit breezy out here.'

Kit hugged me back. He briefly readjusted the faded plastic crate across his rear pannier rack, smiled, placed his flip flops on the pedals once again and started to ride off.

'Thanks, Anna, you take care now – you've got a long way to go too. Keep it real out there!' he called, his words being carried away on the wind. I didn't quite know what 'keeping it real' entailed, but in Kit's honour, I was going to try.

As I rode away from Kit, I thought about what I admired in his story. There seemed to be a freedom and spontaneity to his life that was enviable, especially to anyone tied to a daily routine. It'd taken a year to plan my own journey, and Kit had planned his within an afternoon, or not at all, it seemed. And yet both of us had wound up in the same place, physically at least.

After seven days of riding, I approached the outer edge of the Great Basin National Park. I knew that on the other side of the park my journey across Route 50 would come to an end. The desert had been a roller-coaster ride in every sense. In between the wind and the rain, and the characters, there was a simple silence. A quiet and calm like nothing I had ever experienced.

I'd been repeatedly told by friends, strangers and locals that the desert would be a scary place. It was a point that had been made so many times that I'd begun to question if these 'others' knew more than I did. According to them, there was a high risk that I would be attacked, murdered or would run out of water – or all of these things at once. Nearing the end of a journey across it, I couldn't help but feel a sense of triumph. It was a feeling that bubbled in the pit of my stomach for a brief moment, before being absorbed into the rest of my body, adding another layer to my suit of life-armour. Not only had I 'survived' the desert, I had adored it. It was one of the most serene and beautiful weeks of my existence. It was more than a memory, it was a set of feelings that no one could take away from me. There was an anonymity in the desert. It didn't care who you were. It battered you just the same; it welcomed you just the same. And I liked that. At the end of the final day, I spotted something I hadn't seen in over a week – a major junction. I turned right onto SR 487 and left Route 50 behind, as I headed for the Utah state line.

THE FOUR CORNERS

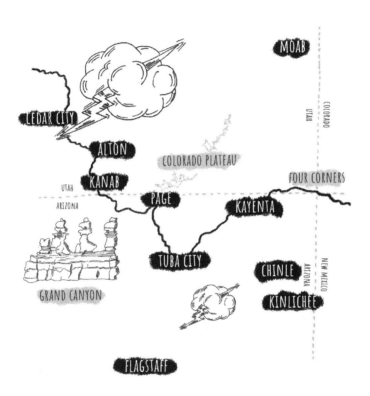

MOAB

LEDAR CITY

ALTON

COLORADO PLATEAU

FOUR CORNERS

KANAB

UTAH
COLORADO

UTAH

ARIZONA

PAGE

KAYENTA

TUBA CITY

CHINLE

ARIZONA
NEW MEXICO

KINLICHEE

GRAND CANYON

FLAGSTAFF

7

A Rim with a View

Distanced Cycled: 2,545 miles
States Completed: 6

I spent my first night in Utah in Cedar City. Given the size of the desert towns, Cedar City was a relative metropolis with a population of 29,000 people. It took a few hours of readjusting to get used to being surrounded by people, cars and steady streams of traffic again. I had been amused crossing the Nevada–Utah state border line, to find that the tarmac changed from cracked grey to smooth pitch-black, precisely at the interstate border. The Utah state government had resurfaced the road right up to the border line, and they clearly weren't going an inch over their 'patch'. At times, the United States seemed a little less than united and tarmac was clearly a dividing point. I'd taken great joy in posing next to the Utah state sign and was beginning to gather these state sign photos like trinkets. It read, 'Welcome to Utah. Life. Elevated.' I hadn't been paying much attention to the elevation, except for the passes I was going up and over in the Great Basin, but a quick google had told me that Utah has an average elevation of 1,859 metres above sea level. I would officially be living the high life from here on in.

The following day, 30 minutes out of Cedar City, the landscape began to change. It was as if an artist had dragged her acrylic-laden paintbrush along the horizon, leaving streaks of colour where dusty rocks gave way to the vibrant reds of the hills. The mountains on either side of the road became taller and the colours became ever sharper, as if someone was fine-tuning the TV of life.

I'd expected this kind of scenery in Utah, although I had imagined the rocks would be more orange than they were red. The red rocks were dotted with patches of bright green shrubs – as if someone had splattered them across the hills with a shrubbery machine gun. What I liked most of all in the land-scape I was looking out on was that it was the buildings, the roads and the cars that looked out of place. The rocks and plants looked like they very much belonged.

I was fast learning that if I didn't have many miles to cycle in a day, I would engage in the following routine: I'd promise myself that I would be on the road before 9 a.m., so that I might miss the worst of the late-afternoon August heat, and have an 'early' finish (and bathe in a smug sea of glory with hours of daylight the other end). In reality, I would wake up, faff, faff some more, tell myself I'd leave soon, and finally roll out of town somewhere between 11 a.m. and 1 p.m. It would then become a sticky and humid race to make it to my des-tination before the sun went down, and as buckets of sweat dripped from my brow and elbows onto Boudica's frame, I would curse myself continually for the final hour for not having left earlier. Today was no exception to the rule.

I only had 60 miles to ride to Zion National Park from Cedar City. Before the trip, that would have seemed like a long way but now I knew that I could smash that out in four hours if I really wanted to. So, in usual fashion, I didn't leave town until 11 a.m., by which time it was starting to get really hot. The temperature pushed 35°C and the air was soup-like as I gulped at it greedily, trying to extract as much oxygen from it as I could. Gone were the wide-open spaces of the Great Basin Desert. Towns were now more frequent and there seemed less space in every sense of the word. I found there to be less space in my mind too; to think and to breathe. The midday heat mingled with the fumes of the cars, creating a toxic cocktail of dirt which settled on my forearms.

After stopping for an 'emergency' ice lolly in the town of Virgin, I slogged my way up and over the final climb of the day. When I rounded the bend at the top of the climb, the view that greeted me was breathtaking. To my left were towering haphazard red and peach cliffs with broken edges, overhangs and ledges – as if Mother Nature had been chipping away at a sculpture over time and not quite finished it yet. Lining both sides of the road were bright green trees set in sandy coloured fields. It was bizarre to see things so seemingly lush in a landscape which looked arid, and I wondered how much of it occurred naturally, and how much of it was maintained by those who lived on the outskirts of the park. Where I could see small homesteads next to the road, their gardens were surrounded by white fences – the kind of fences you might see in a farmyard set given to a child. And beyond the tops of the green trees and the little white fences to the right of the road was a large red, jagged mountain. The tarmac beneath my wheels changed from its usual grey to a deep shade of orange, marking the entrance to the grounds of Zion National Park.

There were a million and one things whizzing through my mind as I struggled to get to grips with the visual feast in front of me, but the one overriding thought was this: how is this the same planet that I have lived on my whole life? How have I gone 28 years and not seen anything like this?! I felt humbled. Grateful and head over heels in love with planet earth all over again.

I made a base for myself at a cosy lodge in Springdale, a town at the gateway to the park. Shoving open the door to the air-conditioned bedroom, I took one look at the crisp white sheets on the marshmallowy soft bed and gave a little squeal. After many nights spent spread out on top of my sleeping mat naked, sweating buckets and attempting to sleep, that air-conditioned bedroom was paradise. Beyond the lodge, I soon discovered that Springdale was a very pleasant place to spend some time and seemed to be a perfect example of how to exist in the shadow of nature. It was tidy but relaxed, bustling but not overrun. In fact, I concluded that Springdale was like Sweden; everything just worked. On the first night at Springdale lodge, I had to be honest with myself that there were a few things going on with my body that were really starting to bother me. Being in constant pain from my dodgy knee was not only a source of irritation, it was sucking the lifeblood out of my energy levels. It was official; my knee was stealing my mojo.

As well as my knee injury, two sizeable cracks had now formed at the sides of my mouth – like paper cuts. They would heal up overnight and then split open again each morning when I took a bite of breakfast or smiled. I knew from experience that these slits meant I was run-down and needed a rest. And then there were my fingers. I'd noticed that I was starting to lose grip strength on my left hand and could no longer clip up the fasteners on my pannier bags. I'd suffered from numb fingers since Portland in Oregon, but this was taking the numbness to a new level and I was getting concerned. After consulting Doctor Google, I discovered that I was suffering from 'cyclist's palsy' – which is when the nerves in your wrist become damaged from all the bouncing around of your hands on the handlebars. All in all, I was a mess. So rather than take just one day off the bike, I opted to take two full days of 'rest'. I used the term rest loosely, of course, because I would have gone nuts just sitting in the lodge doing nothing, so I went in for active rest instead, and decided to spend one of those days hiking in Zion National Park and (after rave reviews from another cycle tourist) the following day over at nearby Bryce Canyon National Park.

After a leisurely and mildly terrifying jaunt along the famous Angels Landing Trail in Zion on day one, I woke up the next morning and hitched a ride to Bryce Canyon National Park. There, I immersed myself among haphazard spires of orange and white layered rocks or 'hoodoos', to give them an official name. The hoodoos were a sight to behold. They looked like knobbly walking sticks, or giant cheese puffs, stacked upright in the land. They were wider at their base and then thinned out towards the top, almost as if they had run out of energy to be fabulous by the time they reached the sky. Each one changed in colour as it rose from the ground; bright orange, white, peach, back to white and then a salmon pink. I struggled to grasp how something that could so easily appear in a child's drawing had been created naturally and, in short, I decided that hangin' with the hoodoos was the closest I would ever get to feeling like Alice in Wonderland. I later got my Google geek on and read that the hoodoos are formed because rainwater seeps into the rocks then freezes, shattering the surrounding fragile rock into the sharp formations. If ever I needed a reminder that nature was a law unto itself, the hoodoos were it. If only all geography lessons at school had involved a hike through the hoodoos of Bryce Canyon National Park, I might have paid a little more attention.

After those two days of hiking, my legs craved the monotony of circular motion once more, so I climbed back on top of Boudica and headed for Grand Canyon National Park in Arizona. There was something so familiar about being in Boudica's saddle, I felt guilty leaving her to one side, even for a day or two – like I was being unfaithful by choosing to walk instead of ride. I was drawn back to her because being on Boudica made me feel like the best version of myself. Boudica brought out the best in me, even though she never said a word. After passing the small dusty town of Kanab, I crossed the Arizona state line and waved goodbye to Utah. My mind and body felt refreshed, and I could at least now smile again without fear that the sides of my mouth would split into a full-blown joker's smile. I had reclaimed some of my stolen mojo from my knee, but I was sad to be leaving Utah after such a short visit to a state that had blown any expectations I had for it clear out of the water. I made a vow to Utah that I would come back to visit her one day.

From various Google sessions and time spent on geology websites, I had learnt a huge amount about what was called the Grand Staircase Area of America. In order for my normal brain to comprehend what was quite a complicated explanation of rock formations, I had simplified things into a framework that made sense. As I saw it, 2,000 million years ago, layers of sediment were deposited gradually on the earth, one on top of the other, like a heavily loaded beef burger. You had the sesame bun, then the lettuce, the beef patty, the special sauce, cheese, lettuce, pickle and another sesame bun. In reality, these layers translate to the pink, grey, white, vermillion and chocolate cliffs of the Grand Staircase. The Grand Canyon (Arizona), Zion and Bryce National Parks (Utah) reveal these cliff layers to varying extents. And so, with each park, you are seeing a different weathered slice of the earth's history.

***

The decision to visit the North Rim of the Grand Canyon in Arizona was a tricky one because it meant a 90-mile off-route detour. I would need to follow a road down to the canyon then turn back on myself to come back to the main highway. But I had long since made the decision – there was no way I could pass through Arizona without visiting one of the wonders of the natural world. It would be adventure sacrilege! I'll level with you that I had to play a few mind games on the ride down to the canyon. I was pedalling 45 miles in the 'wrong direction', after all. I chose to pretend that I would not be cycling 45 miles back again the following day. Instead, I soaked up every morsel of scenery as if it would be the last time I would ever see it. Denial is a wonderful tool in the armoury of any long-distance cyclist, and on that day to the canyon, I used it in spades.

At 2,500 metres above sea level, the North Rim of the Grand Canyon sits 300 metres higher than the South Rim, and (largely because it's more difficult to get to by road) gets just a quarter of the number of visitors each year. I turned onto the road leading to the canyon and found myself pedalling under bright blue skies, past open pastures of long grass and evergreens. I'm not quite sure what I was expecting of the landscape on the approach to the rim of the Grand Canyon, but the scene in front of me was vastly different from anything I had in mind. I climbed steadily to a high point on the road at the Kaibab Plateau at 3,000 metres and noticed that the sky had begun to darken. It was too early for the sun to be going down, and I realised that it was being blocked by grey and black clouds forming above my head.

Alone on the road under thunderous skies and on a high plateau, my overactive imagination began to conjure up images of being struck by a stray bolt of lightning and frazzled to a McCrisp. I shoved those thoughts down into my toes and pushed hard on the pedals, hoping and willing that I could make it to the campsite at the North Rim before a thunderstorm hit. Closer to the canyon, I began to pass lightning-singed trees, stumps turned grey and black from their own dances with lightning-death, and, just then, with 5 miles left to go, the dark clouds overhead made good on their promise. All of a sudden, the heavens opened, lightning crackled overhead and thunder boomed as I pumped my thighs as hard as I could and made a final bid for the campground.

By the time I arrived at the campground, I was drenched. Shaking slightly, and struggling to sign my registration slip, I smiled and chatted to the park ranger who checked me in and took the princely sum of $6 from my sodden palms. Dennis the ranger directed me to a special area of the site, reserved for those who arrived on foot or by bike and told me to pick whatever spot I fancied. The camping area was dotted with trees and shrouded in thick cloud, so I decided that any old pitch would do. I had gotten my tent-assembly skills down to a mean seven minutes by this point in the journey, but that evening I wrestled with it for the following 20 minutes, locked in a battle with what felt like a mass of green seaweed. The downpour was torrential as I raced, slipping and sliding on my shoe cleats in the surrounding mud, in a desperate attempt to get my home for the night up as quickly as possible so that I could crawl inside and get warm. As I was putting the final peg into place, the rain stopped. The clouds around the site began to clear and I looked up towards the canyon. My hair was plastered to my face, drops of icy rain dripping from my nose, but my eyes were wide open. In the cover of the rain cloud, I hadn't quite grasped where I was, but now I could see it. There, just 3 metres in front of me was an edge. It was *the* edge. I was camped just a stone's throw from the North Rim of the Grand Canyon! Mother Hubbard! I walked over to the edge and peered tentatively out beyond the rim. Although the clouds were clearing above me, I still couldn't see much beyond where I stood, as between the walls of the canyon, various remaining clouds were gently parting and fusing in what looked like nature's very own witches' cauldron. I was starting to shiver now and it was beginning to get dark, so I returned to the home I had so painstakingly put up, set about cooking up dinner and hoped for a better view in the morning.

The following day I woke at 5.30 a.m. and leapt out of my tent, excited at the prospect of the clouds having cleared and getting my first proper look at the canyon. To my delight, and as far as I could see in the partial darkness, there wasn't a cloud in sight. I brewed up a cup of fresh coffee and took a stroll along the rim trail in my Superman pyjamas. There was no one up and about at that hour and I had the trail entirely to myself. I rested a while on one of the viewpoint benches along the trail, coffee cup nestled in palm, listening to the gentle rustle of leaves from the forest behind me, and the rush of wind through the canyon below. Sitting watching the sun slowly creep its way up over the horizon, I drew in a long deep breath of cold morning air and exhaled. Shards of dawn light caught the formations of rock in a way that made it appear as if they were waking up too.

There just aren't enough adjectives in the English language to describe the feeling that I had in that moment. I had visited the South Rim of the Canyon when I was nine years old, but I didn't remember much of it, other than it was huge. Standing here on the North Rim almost 20 years later, I felt ready to appreciate the sheer scale of what was in front of me. The one thing that kept spinning through my mind was 'how?!' I found so much beauty in the haphazard nature of the canyon's formation. From the main canyon, dozens of smaller ones branched out, reaching like great fiery red and orange fingers across the horizon. The layering was imperfectly perfect.

Sandy coloured bases led into oranges with streaks of white and each ridge was topped with red rock. It was like looking at a pile of cake slices. Layers of multicoloured sponge and splashes of whipped cream running through the middle. It looked inviting and terrifying all at once. I felt like I could leap from my bench and make the other side, but the sensible side of my brain told me that it must be at least a mile across, and that I should stay right here, sitting in my PJs with my coffee in hand.

Later that morning, as I cycled away from my rim with a view, I got the full benefit of having been up on a high plateau. It had been a brief yet beautiful fling with the canyon, yet I promised myself that I would come back one day to hike down into it and explore it more. I glided steadily back to the junction at the main road past Jacob Lake, before continuing on the main highway and enjoying 50 miles of gradual downhill, beautifully smooth, tarmacked cycling. Lightning storms rolled in and out throughout the day as I wound my way down to the bed of the Colorado River. The final 20 miles of the ride were the most spectacular yet, as I pedalled adjacent to the vermillion cliffs, the layers of white and orange rock set in stark contrast against a backdrop of thunderous grey cloud. It was now early September, but the summer heat was still in full swing in northern Arizona.

For the next three days, I followed Route 160 across northern Arizona, tracking just below the Utah–Arizona state line and through the Navajo (Nava-ho) Nation Reservation. A key trip revelation had been the discovery of Native American reservations. I knew they existed, but I had no idea just how many there were, and how large. In Arizona, I spent two days cycling through Navajo land, which spans over 24,000 square miles. At one junction near a spot called Marble Canyon, there were roadworks underway and traffic was taking it in turns to filter through a single lane of road as several women were holding manual stop signs. There were two women at my end of the construction wearing high-vis vests, and I could see a couple of others 100 metres or so down the road. They were young girls, in their late teens or possibly early 20s, and seemed to be having a whale of a time controlling the flow of traffic, chatting and laughing among themselves over their walkie-talkies in a language I didn't recognise. As I was at the front of the traffic line (I say line – there were two cars), I asked one of the two dark-haired women close by what language they were speaking.

'Me and my sisters?' she asked. I nodded. 'We're speaking in Navajo.'

I'd never heard anyone speaking Navajo before, and I felt ignorant to not have ever even considered that I would encounter languages other than English in my journey through the States. As I waited for the 'STOP' sign to spin to 'GO', I asked her a few questions about the Navajo Reservation – how big it was, how many people lived there, that kind of thing.

'Do you have a lot of strong traditions?' I asked, thinking back to whatever I'd learned in school about Native American culture, which mostly revolved around names relating to animals, tipis and powwows. I listened hard through my embarrassment at knowing so little.

'Some,' she said. 'Family is important, you know, really

important to us.'

'And you get to work and hang out with your sisters all day here – so that's a good thing then?!' I said.

'Ha, yep, it is!' she laughed. 'We love it! Although our parents don't love it so much. They'd rather we were at home with them, but we've got to earn some money. So here we are.' She smiled and gestured to the surrounding landscape.

'Well, it looks like you're having fun and I'm sure your parents would approve of that!' I said, and she nodded.

I didn't want to distract her from the task at hand, so when the 'STOP' sign turned, I waved the nice Navajo lady goodbye and pedalled off, getting an equally warm reception from her sisters at the other end of the construction, as I whizzed by.

Intrigued by my brief encounter with the Navajo ladies, that night in my tent, I read more about the Native Americans online. I learned that the Navajo Reservation in Arizona even has a different time zone to the rest of the state. Native reservations in the US are sovereign states, which means they have their own laws. This explains why you'll find a lot of casinos on reservations in states where gambling is illegal (like California) and large firework shops in states where the purchase of fireworks is illegal too (like Colorado). Aside from Navajo, the Cherokee, Sioux, Chippewa and Apache are just a few of the other major tribes living on one of the 326 reservations across the US. I wondered how many I would get to pass through on the rest of my journey, and whether I would get a window into their languages, as I had with the Navajos today.

Riding on through Arizona, I found myself frequently alone on the road, with just bright red and orange boulders for company against an otherwise flat horizon. The shapes on the landscape looked like an assortment of once-square chocolates, left out to melt in the sun. Each time I saw these structures standing tall and proud (or square and proud in many cases), it seemed like time itself had granted them permission to be there. Although I was riding just south of Utah's famous Monument Valley, I was being treated to my own fair share of impressive rocks – including Shiprock, which, much as the description would suggest, appeared like a ghostly ship-shaped rock, sailing its way towards me from the horizon.

My marvelling at Shiprock, which went on for a good hour as I pedalled towards it, was at last disturbed by a new, exciting prospect on the horizon – the chance to stand in four American states at once, and two new states on the journey. I stopped briefly and waited for an appropriate moment when the Four Corners Monument was free of visiting tourists and launched into a backwards crab across all four corners. It was like an inverse game of Twister; left hand Utah, right hand Arizona, left foot New Mexico and right foot in state number nine, Colorado. I was pretty sure that was the only time I'd get to hang out in four states at once, and even more sure that it was the only time I'd make it into a backwards crab over the course of the trip (I discovered I wasn't as flexible as I used to be). My left foot and right foot had helped me tick off two more states, and that brought a real sense of satisfaction to my day. I was now officially nine states down, with just 41 to go. Almost time for a sprint finish, I'd say...

ROCKY MOUNTAINS

WYOMING

COLORADO

FORT COLINS

DENVER

DELTA

MONTROSE   GUNNISON   SALIDA

$ 3,500
REWARD

DURANGO

COLORADO

NEW MEXICO

FARMINGTON

8

The Thousand-Year Flood

Distance Cycled: 3,497 miles

States Completed: 9

I didn't really know much about New Mexico. I mean, it had featured heavily in episodes of *Breaking Bad*, and I knew, given its name, that it would perhaps have a location close to the border of Mexico, but that was where knowledge of the state stopped. Because New Mexico was a relative stranger-state to me, it had meant that during the hashing and rehashing of the route, there was no one, or rather no part of my mind, fighting its corner. It had become a casualty of the shortened route and I resolved to spend just one brief night in the city of Farmington before pedalling north across the state border and into Colorado. I can firmly report that the 70 miles of tarmac Boudica and I travelled over in New Mexico were hot, dusty and not unpleasant. I'm sure the rest of New Mexico is wonderful, but I'd have to come back again one day to find that out.

Now with almost 3,500 miles under my belt, I had a concrete route plan for Colorado. I would arrive in the state via its south-west corner. From there I'd head north, into the Rocky Mountains via Durango, and on to Telluride, via Montrose, then Gunnison and Buena Vista, before making a beeline north-east for Denver. Just south of Denver in a suburb called Highlands Ranch, I was due to spend a few days hanging out with a long-lost friend called Cindy, whom I'd met on a swimming trip to the British Virgin Islands a few years previously. I would like to say that I hang out in the BVIs all the time, but I will hasten to add that the trip to the BVIs was put on a credit card, which took me five years to pay off. But it was worth every dime, because I saw sharks and turtles, and I met Cindy, and Cindy was a total doll.

I was apprehensive about heading into the Rocky Mountains. I mean, they are the Rockies – the Granddaddy of Mountain Ranges, the Tony Soprano of the Mountain Mafia, the Papa of all the Peaks. They straddle the site of one of the greatest tectonic-plate showdowns in history – where the humongous North American tectonic plates (blue corner) ran headlong into the fists of the gigantic Pacific plates (red corner). It was a fierce and long-fought battle that lasted 110 million years, and neither one of the plates fancied backing down. The result was a clash of earth, a lot of crumpling and an uprising of a mountain range where there was no mountain range before. In riding through the Rockies, I knew that I'd be taking on passes as high as 3,650 metres above sea level, and what concerned me the most about that was getting dumped on with snow. Yet what I had failed to consider in my snow-dump anxiety is that after Florida, Colorado is the lightning capital of the USA, and I was entering the state in a prime season to watch the show.

It was late into the evening and beginning to rain when I arrived at Priest Gulch campground. Rain was no big deal; of course I could handle rain. But the rain soon turned into a full-blown thunderstorm, with lightning directly overhead. I couldn't see any other tents and was surrounded by camper vans, where I assumed, quite sensibly, that everyone else was sheltering. I quickly put up my tent, tied Boudica to the guy ropes and crawled inside.

The noise of the growing storm was deafening. I made several attempts to count the seconds between the lightning and the thunder to see how far away the storm was, before accepting that there were no seconds to count. The storm was directly overhead.

I'm not ashamed to admit that I reached about an 8.0 on the poop-my-pants-ometer that night. Storms had been plentiful on the trip, but never in all my days have I heard thunder that loud. I lay awake in my tent as the storm raged around me for the next hour, too frightened to move in case my own 'static energy' attracted lightning (this was clearly a train of rational thought). Just when I thought things couldn't get any creepier, my tent began to light up, as if I were at a disco. After googling 'can tent be struck by lightning' (I always google before taking action), I decided that there were enough scare stories online to warrant making a dash for the campground toilet block. There I sat for the next hour with only an inquisitive moth for company (I can only assume that the moth had been googling too). At last, the skies calmed themselves down, and I returned to my tent to grab some shut-eye.

The morning after the storm, I got chatting to a nice man named Bob. He had spent the night in the camper van adjacent to my tent, and had had a solid night's sleep through the storm, on account of being indoors 'n' all. After chatting for 30 minutes, we'd exchanged all the crucial information about life goals, friends, families and favourite local fishing spots (okay, Bob just talked to me about that one). All of a sudden, Bob stopped the conversation and said,

'You're a brave girl, you know that, Anna?'

I shuffled my feet a little and looked down. 'Ah, thanks, Bob. I think I'm more stupid than brave.'

'No, no, you're a brave one,' he said.

Leaving Priest Gulch and Bob behind the following morning, I began a long and steady climb to the 3,054-metre-high Lizard Head Pass. Because this was my first ever Rocky Mountain pass, I had a fizz of nerves in my belly. As had been the case with the desert, I had many strangers say to me 'you're not riding over the Rockies, are you?' Well, of course I would be riding over the Rockies. I liked mountains. In my mind, they were mountains and I had wheels. That was as complicated as things got. And, besides, there was something about the size and scale of giant lumps of rock that humbled me and made a little piece of my soul quieten down. But the more people asked me how I'd cope with the altitude (this was something I hadn't thought about) and whether I was fit enough, the more I began to question my nonchalant approach to a journey through the mountains.

When the worries of whether I had underestimated a challenge overwhelmed me, I always found that distraction and daydreaming were the finest tools you can have in your armoury. My campground friend Bob had told me that my route would take me past Ralph Lauren's ranch. Yes, *the* Ralph Lauren, of Polo fame. Bob said that on reaching the crest of the pass, if I turned to the left, I would be looking out over Ralph's land. Inevitably, this nugget of information laid the foundation for an elaborate daydream, which went as follows: as I neared the top of the pass, growing weary and oxygen-deprived, Ralph would emerge from the oversized entrance to his ranch in an understated truck (I'd recognise him because of the cameo he made in the sitcom *Friends* – the one where Rachel allegedly got it on with him in the copy room). Ralph would stop his truck and lean out the window to politely inquire where I'd come from and where I was going (just as everyone else does). He'd then invite me to his ranch for a spot of luncheon. I'd politely refuse, then accept. He'd love my Britishness, he'd love me, my aims to speak to schoolkids across the country, and he'd put in a call to the president for me – who would naturally then agree to meet me when I got to Washington DC. It was a ridiculous daydream, but one that kept my mind occupied for much of the 13-mile slog to the top of the pass. I was just reflecting on how far-fetched my day-dream had been when, nearing the crest of the pass, I heard a truck approaching. It tooted its horn and I heard a shout from the window.

'Woooo! Go, Anna!'

Was it? Could it be?! Ralph?! Had he found me, heard my story and come out to see me?! I flicked my head sideways just as the truck rolled by. It was Bob. Leaning out of the window whooping and hollering. I laughed. Just Bob.

'Thanks Bob!' I yelled back, taking one hand off the handlebars to give him a hearty wave.

Descending from Lizard Head Pass, I entered into the first of what were to be many achingly hip towns in eastern Colorado. Telluride was an early contender for the cream of the cool-town crop. Home to a host of international music and film festivals, it's the kind of place where, instead of returning your smile with a wave, locals deliver a 'hang ten' or 'rock hand'. (This actually happened several times on my stroll through the town.) In a night spent at the campground on the outskirts of town, I learned that hipster Telluride is heavily into its beer and bikes and has an even hipper history.

Once a gateway to the San Juan mines, Telluride was famous for its abundance of brothels and saloons. It was this lucrative seedy underbelly that kept the place booming for almost half a century, as the local government even learnt to rely on the brothel fines as a source of income. Telluride's wealth reached such dizzying heights that in 1889, Butch Cassidy targeted it and stole $24,000 from the town bank. It was a real Wild West kind of a place.

**

After Telluride, the next order of business for Boudica and me was to weave our way up and over the Dallas Divide. It took three hours of huffing and puffing, and several loops of albums by the band Train that I had uploaded onto my iPod, but eventually we made it to the top of the 2,783-metre pass. There, I promptly stopped for a celebratory bottle of chocolate milk, which I had deemed was a worthy thing to lug all the way to the top, purely for the moment it first hit my lips. Sadly, the milky chocolate goodness didn't ease the discomfort caused by riding 90 miles that day. By the time I made a campground for the night in the small town of Cimarron, my knee was in agony and I had run clean out of energy. Yet, as I cooked up a noodle surprise in near darkness and watched a beautiful purple-orange sunset go off into the hills, the pain seemed to matter far less.

In a bid to be more sensible, I dropped my daily mileage down to distances that wouldn't leave me a total blubbering wreck at the end of each day, and with that change in tactic, I actually began to look forward to every pass. As I climbed, grinding myself into a satisfying rhythm, all around me were peaks covered in evergreens. Every now and then I would spot a patch of land that wasn't coated green, but was instead a golden field, rolling gently off down the valley. I could see mountain-bike trails snaking their way along neighbouring mountains, cars on roads in the distance, little collections of buildings here and there, and the odd ski lift too. I decided that the Rockies were 'good mountains'. They were perfectly formed, heading skyward in neat little peaks that you might see appear in the drawing of a young child. The ascents were long and winding, and often I couldn't see where the road went beyond the next corner, so I simply took each section of road, one bit at a time.

At the top of the 3,447-metre Monarch Pass, I was clapped and cheered into the car park by an elderly couple who flung open their camper-van door to offer me fresh pears and butter pecan fudge from the cafe shop – fudge so good, you'd sell your own mother for a bite. Things were definitely on the up. There was a predictability about climbing mountains that I have always loved, and so here among them, now fuelled by fudge, I felt a veil lift. My knee seemed more manageable and easier to deal with rather than a trip-stopping injury. I enjoyed the cool mountain air and found that Colorado had by far the most comfortable riding temperature of the trip yet. For the first time since Washington, I wasn't caked in thick layers of sludge and sweat every evening. With each pass of the Rockies, I grew in confidence, and on my fourth day through the Rockies, I wrote in my diary: 'Tired. Chilled. In love with life.'

Aside from the mountains, the celebs and the free fudge,

there were a lot of things I had begun to love about Colorado. After chats with Bob and other locals, I learnt that Colorado boasts the lowest adult obesity rate of all US states. Living in Colorado and not embracing an active, outdoor lifestyle would be like going to a sushi bar and not ordering fish. Winters are filled with Nordic skiing, snowboarding, snow-tubing or sledding. Summer sees residents swap boards for wheels, as they career on bikes up and down the very same mountains. Coloradans simply excel in enjoying every inch of what the good earth planted on their doorstep.

On the final day of the Rocky rampage, I switch-backed my way to the top of Loveland Pass before piling on as many clothes as I could muster and enjoying a glorious three-hour descent from 3,655 metres high, towards the city of Denver, which sits at a mere 1,600 metres above sea level. The first section of the return from the clouds was a joy. Gliding from one small town to the next, I stopped briefly in Georgetown to settle my chattering teeth and replenish coffee and pancake levels within my bloodstream. But, as is always the case, the closer I got to the city itself, the uglier things got. More cars, more houses, more noise, more people, all the honking and the bumper dodging, growing in intensity until it seemed there was no more space to fit anything else in. Boudica didn't much care for the new, more urban surroundings either, showing her disdain by picking up three punctures in the final two hours. Then it started to tip down with rain, and navigation on my now soggy phone became impossible. Google maps showed me that there was a network of bike paths to follow, but in the fading light I often missed the exit to them, and instead found myself on a busy main road, separated from the paths by a concrete wall. On those big roads, in the pouring rain and near darkness, I felt like a sitting duck. I was being honked at left, right and centre, and I could understand why. These roads were no place for a cyclist to be. I'd probably honk at me too if I were the drivers. At one intersection, I stopped to take the British flag off my rear pannier rack, because I felt like all I was doing out there on the road was making everyone angrier at Britain. It was 8 p.m. and long after dark by the time I extracted myself from the suburban Denver maze and skidded into my new home from home at Highlands Ranch.

When I swung into the driveway, Cindy Glen was waiting for me and, despite me not having seen her in four years, she greeted me like a long-lost daughter. In fact, her first words were 'we were starting to get worried about where you'd got to!' – motherly love, right there. Within an hour, I was warm, clean, dry and sitting around the dinner table with the rest of the Glen family.

Dinner was followed by a soak in the hot tub on the balcony and a good old catch up on life. Cindy is a flight attendant and never fails to make me laugh with her stories of 20 years in the skies. I could always imagine her in the air – the perfect mix of hospitable and assertive. I knew she wouldn't take any crap from disruptive passengers. Not on Glen Airways. I told her that she would have to write a book about her experiences one day, and she told me she'd have to change some names to do that.

That night, as I snuggled into a big bed at the Glen home, I was battling a headache. It took me some time to work out why I would have a headache, and then I remembered... I was at altitude! I had been at altitude, nipping up and over passes without a second thought that I might have needed to allow some time to acclimatise. I looked back over the route I'd taken through Colorado so far. I'd climbed 14,500 metres over five Rocky mountain passes, covering 530 miles in six days – a fact that could explain why I was perhaps a little tired. I was sad that the Rockies were over, but all at once a little relieved.

I spent the following three days resting and hanging with Cindy, her sister-in-law, Cathleen, and mother-in-law, Carol-Anne. I had intended to spend just a day or two with the Glens, but I was there or thereabouts on track with my overall schedule, so I figured that Cindy's home was a great place to spend an extra day of rest. Besides, having not seen her in four years, we had a fair bit of catching up to do. The Glen sisters and I quickly formed a close-knit lady-clique and enjoyed large breakfasts, hot-tub sessions, big lunches, even bigger dinners, art-gallery visits and painting classes. It was as if I had been picked up from the life of a smelly adventurer and plonked onto the set of *Sex in the City*.

In those three days, I had a total blast. I got oodles of sleep and felt fully recovered and ready to rock by the end of it. But on the final morning at the Glen household, I awoke with a fuzzy feeling in my stomach. I focused my attention on the feeling and found it to be a mixture of sadness and excitement. On the one hand, I'd stopped longer than intended and was therefore itching to get going. On the other hand, I'd become so comfortable and such a part of Cindy's family life that I really didn't want to leave. This seemed to be the delicate balance of a life on the road: the stops were needed to refuel mind and body, but stop for too long and I would remember what it was like to feel comfortable. With Cindy, everything had been easy – she had gone out of her way to make everything as easy as possible for me. Our capacity for giving as humans is extraordinary, and Cindy's family had given more than most.

I dragged my heels as usual that morning. I spent far too long having a pancake breakfast with Cindy (I'm pretty sure it was classified as lunch by the time we'd finished). I checked some emails, began writing a blog post and, before I knew it, it was 1 p.m. I was planning on riding 75 miles that day, which, all being well, should have still been possible, but I needed to get a wriggle on.

Cindy had one of those houses with a combined open-plan kitchen and living room, so over breakfast I'd been able to hear the news coming from the TV in the living room. For the past four days, Colorado had been experiencing one of the worst floods to hit the state in over 40 years. They were calling it the 'thousand-year flood' and it had torn through and caused landslides in many parts of what's called the Front

Range of the Rocky Mountains. During my stay at Cindy's house, I'd tuned in every now and then but, admittedly, I'd not taken too much notice of what was going on. I'd been so consumed with the business of having a nice time that I had failed to grasp the gravity of the situation.

But now, as I clipped shut the final few clasps on my panniers, I started to listen in properly. I stopped packing up and paced a few steps closer to the television. It was a full-blown natural disaster. I noted a fizzing sensation in my stomach – what did this mean for my ride out? And how had I not thought about it sooner? The worst of the flooding seemed to be happening to the north-west of Denver, which was slightly west of my intended route, but close enough to give me cause for concern. I watched videos of landslides, listened to reports of those who had gone missing in the course of the past 48 hours. Thankfully, the news reports were saying that the worst of the flooding was over – so I made the call to hit the road.

After fond goodbyes with all the Glen family, I hugged Cindy goodbye last. With arms wrapped around me, she whispered in my ear, 'I've left you a little something in your purse.' She released me from the hug and grinned.

'Cindy! You didn't need to…'

'I know, I know,' she interrupted my protest. 'I've got to look after you, girl – like I would want someone else to look after my girl. Get yourself a nice hotel or something one night.'

I nodded and hugged her a little tighter, before clambering

back onto Boudica and riding off down the road. I raised an arm to wave one last time and looked back at the Glen family, all five of them standing on the driveway, arms linked and waving back. The image looked like the kind of prized family photo you might find on a mantelpiece.

Not wanting to make the same mistake I'd made on my way into Denver, I had taken some advice from the Glen family and opted for a quieter, yet slightly lengthier route into the city. At the upper limit of Denver's urban sprawl, I pulled into a cafe for a final caffeine pick-me-up and to reconsider whether the mileage I'd set for the day was perhaps a little ambitious. I was in a bit of a funny mood, readjusting to being back on the road and also slightly frustrated at the slow pace of moving through a city full of cars and people. Still slightly scarred from the ride into the city in the dark, I made the sensible call to cut it short and make up the miles the next morning instead. I looked at the map, and then at my watch – it was now 4 p.m. I'd originally intended to make it to Loveland (what a lovely name for a place), but tracing my finger backwards from Loveland, I spotted that there was a campground at Longmont, just 10 miles down the road from where I was sitting.

Turning off the main highway, I started down County Road 7. The light was really beginning to fade now, and away from the hum of the main highway, this road seemed unusually calm. I began to feel increasingly uncomfortable with how dark it was and I chastised myself for leaving so late. The skies were turning a gentle shade of purple and I could see the moon more clearly. Dusk had well and truly arrived, but it was only three more miles to the campground, so I pushed on, legs pumping, lungs burning, as fast as I could.

A mile further on, I came across a barricade, which read 'Road Closed: HAZARD AHEAD'. I stopped momentarily at the sign and looked around, considering my options. If I didn't take this road, I'd have to go back to the highway and ride along it in the fading light to the next turn off. I had lights, but even with them on I hated riding in the dark, and I definitely hated riding in the dark on a busy highway.

I thought back to the report on the news from the past few days. I knew the sign was likely due to the flooding, but I was also of the firm opinion that authorities tended to be over-cautious. I'd wriggled through a dozen closed-road signs in the US so far, and usually was able to manoeuvre my bike around whatever it was that was blocking the flow of motorised traffic. I squinted behind the flimsy plastic sign and concluded that if this was a flood-disaster zone, there would have been more 'action' going on. That's what happened on the telly anyway. But in front of me there was no one – not a soul in sight.

After wheeling Boudica past the barricade, I fixed my torch onto my helmet, switched on my back lights, hopped back onto her and began pedalling slowly onwards. Two hundred metres down the road, I could begin to see the problem; there was running water covering the road. It stretched out like a lake in front of me – the purple haze of the sky was reflected in fragments across the water's surface, which bubbled and flexed as it parted around small pieces of debris also scattered on the road.

I rode into the water until my wheels were 5-cm deep in it and stopped. Was I concerned? Nope. I'd ridden through flooding many times in the UK, sometimes on weekend rides with friends, and enjoyed the thrill of having to find a way through. Usually it involved taking shoes and socks off and carrying my bike over my shoulder but, given Boudica's weight, that wasn't an option this time around.

Everything on the road was deathly quiet. There was a mild breeze which made the surrounding trees rustle. I could still hear the distant hum of the highway and an eerie trickle of water beneath my wheels as I pedalled on slowly but, beyond that, there was nothing. After a further 200 metres I passed a detached farm house. It stood like an island in what was now a field of water. The blood in my veins started to tingle, as I began to feel decidedly uneasy. I checked the map. It was now only 1.75 miles to the campground. I'm not sure why it didn't occur to me that the campground could also be underwater, but seeing how close I was to it distracted me from the increasingly uncomfortable situation I seemed to have put myself in, so I concluded that once I made it through this area, I'd be there in 10 minutes.

But then things began to transition from the mildly unnerving to the really creepy. At first it was just a gradual increase in the amount of debris on the road. A piece of broken wood here, a shard of jagged metal there. I flicked my head from left to right, directing the torch on my helmet, and doing my best to avoid the obstacles in my path. At the side of the road, the houses were all now half underwater and I could see brightly coloured plastic children's toys floating in what presumably once were front yards. A few pedal strokes further on and I passed a car in a ditch by the side of the road, its bonnet crumpled and its windshield smashed… a result of having been forced against its will into the lamppost it now lay dormant under. That had to be some surge of water to move a car into a lamppost, I thought. Perhaps I was riding through the immediate flood aftermath of yesterday's events? Five more minutes, I told myself, five more minutes and I'd be out the other side…

Fifty metres further on, the surface water on the road disappeared and the tarmac became fully visible again, as a large shape loomed into view. It was a tree lying across the middle of the road. A full-sized tree with its roots and branches still attached. My legs slowed as the cogs in my brain turned at an equal pace. This definitely didn't feel safe. It was blatantly clear that this wasn't the site of a flood that had subsided but one very much still in progress. My body was still on autopilot, however, and I couldn't seem to stop moving forwards. I had skirted around the tree and was manoeuvring slowly past a big white and yellow water tank, another gift from the flood, deposited in the centre of the road. I fixated on the tank, looking sideways at it and not at the road ahead. It was then I became aware of a new element of background noise, one that sounded out of place on a road. I snapped my head forwards and slammed on my brakes, heart pounding, eyes wide. What on earth?!

The road in front of me could no longer be classed as a road. It was missing a huge chunk, as if a bulldozer had driven across it from left to right and ripped out an entire section of the tarmac. Only, it wasn't a bulldozer that had removed the tarmac, it was flood water. Between where I stood on the edge of the crumbled road and where it continued some 10 metres away was a full-blown river. I'd never seen anything like it. Holy shit! I dismounted, propping Boudica on her stand. I stood stock-still for 30 seconds or so and, once over the initial shock, began to feel nauseous. This definitely wasn't fun anymore, nor was it remotely cool. I was a complete idiot tourist somewhere I really shouldn't be. I turned the bike around in haste and placed a foot on the pedal to move off.

Just then I heard another new noise and saw headlights coming towards me. It was a car – a large silver 4x4 and it was hurtling down the road. They'll stop in a moment, I thought, wondering how they had made it down here and knowing that they would have had to manoeuvre past the tree and the gas tank in the road too. It was then I realised that the car wasn't stopping; in fact, the car was speeding up. It was now coming towards me at breakneck speed. I began shouting and waving my arms wildly, desperately.

'Stop, stop, stop!'

The 4x4 flew past me, passing a metre from my left-hand side, and everything went into slow motion. I watched in horror as its front right wheel skidded off the edge of the crumbled road. There was a sickening crunch as the undercarriage of the car made contact with the edge of the tarmac and then a deep hum as all four tyres lost contact with the road and the car flipped onto its side and dropped into the water below.

My mind raced. I began shouting, 'No, no, no!' as I threw my leg back over my bike, dropped Boudica to the ground and started running towards where the car had left the road. They had to be dead, I thought. I had surely just seen someone die. I heard the car engine rev, as the wheels on the driver's side spun around in the air and I could hear muffled cries from inside the wreck as I ran towards the edge. I was overwhelmed, and surprisingly so, with concern for my own safety. I thought immediately of my parents, and how I'd promised that I'd return safe and sound, and then of the countless first-aid courses where it'd been drummed into me that you're no good to anyone if you wind up in danger too.

I shouted at the car, 'Are you okay?! Are you okay?! Hang on, just hang on. I'm coming!' The car was lying in the water on the passenger's side. The belly of it was sitting about 2 feet away from the crumbled edge of the road. I looked down to make sure I was safe on the fragile edge and reached for the driver's door. I could hear movement from within the car, and the door began to move too. Once, twice – someone was trying to open it. I jammed my hand under the rim on the second attempt and began to lift it.

I'm not sure if you've ever tried to lift a car door open whilst it's on its side in a river, but it was heavy. Somehow I managed to lever the door to the fully open position. The whimpers from the car were now more audible. Abs shaking, arms like jelly, I held the door there as a grey-haired man poked his head up. He was round-faced, heavy set and looked completely dazed. He was struggling to get out, his arm was reaching for mine. I have no idea what I was thinking, it must have been instinct, because I took one arm off of the door and attempted to hold it open with one hand, as I pulled the man out with the other.

It was a ridiculous idea. There was no way I could manage the weight of both the door and the 14-stone man. Strength gone, I dropped the door. It fell straight across the bridge of the man's nose and shoved him back inside the car as it slammed shut.

'Shit!' I exclaimed. 'You idiot, Anna!' *You're supposed to be saving this man, not killing him!*

I braced my abs again and wrenched the door back to its fully open position. The man appeared, and he was now sporting a cut across the bridge of his nose and looked twice as dazed as before. Keeping both hands on the door this time, I made sure he was out of the vehicle and standing on the edge of it, before I let the door slam shut again and helped him back onto the road.

'Is there anyone else in there?' I asked.

The man ignored me and walked off, shaking his head. The bottom of the car was level with my eye line, so I couldn't see in. I tried again and followed him. 'Is there anyone else?!'

Just then I heard another call from the car. I wrenched the door open and a woman appeared from inside, shaking. I held the door (this time taking care not to inflict collateral damage) as the woman clambered onto the side of the car. I dropped the door back down, and with the man now at my side we helped her from where she was balanced on the back wheel, and onto the safety of the road. The couple embraced, and the woman began crying.

I stood and watched as the couple touched one another's faces, then arms, as if they were checking for injuries. They stopped, looked one another in the eyes and embraced again. It felt strange to see two people, so raw, so fragile, so grateful that one another was unharmed. With both of them out of the car, I began to think ahead, and was now thinking very clearly. Thanks to volunteering to be the qualified office first-aider at work, I'd done enough first-aid courses to know that they would probably go into a state of shock and I felt a duty to keep them safe.

'Come away from the edge,' I said. They appeared to ignore me, and instead wandered back to the edge of the road, close to where the car was. I used my arms to gesture for added impact and slowed my speech. 'Come away, come over here and sit down. I'm going to call the police,' I said.

I managed to get them both to move away from the edge and take a seat in the middle of the road while I used my mobile phone to call 911. Luckily, I knew exactly where we were, and exactly how far we were from the junction with the main highway up ahead.

'You've dialled 911, what is your emergency?'

'Hi, I'm with a couple, a man and a woman. They just flipped their car off the road. They're okay, I think. But it's in the water. In the flood.'

I relayed the particulars to the female officer on the other end of the line. I guessed the couple were in their mid 50s and noted that they seemed in an okay condition but were starting to show signs of shock and weren't being very responsive to my questions.

Out of the corner of my eye, while on the phone, I could see that the couple had returned to the edge of the crumbling road. I motioned to them again as I spoke to the emergency services. 'Come away!' I said, but they didn't seem to be listening to me. The officer on the other end of the line told me that she'd be sending out some units, and to hang tight until they arrived. I hung up, just as the man appeared at my side and began typing on his phone and pointing at the screen. I read what he'd typed. 'We're deaf,' it read.

It all made sense! He typed again. 'Why wasn't the road closed?'

I shook my head and said, 'I don't know.'

I feigned ignorance but the road *was* marked as closed in the direction I'd come from at least. I'd snuck through it. How they'd not seen the barriers was a mystery.

I typed back. 'It was closed further down but perhaps they missed this part?' The man looked confused. I carried on writing. 'The police are on their way. They say they'll be here in fifteen minutes. Are you okay?'

'Yes. Okay. Thank you for being here,' he typed.

Five more minutes passed and I felt like a lemon. I wasn't able to fully communicate with the couple, and they were naturally more interested in one another anyway, so I left them to it. At last I heard sirens and then saw police cars appear, but they were on the road across the river! My phone rang and I answered it right away.

'Hello. Is that Anna?'

'Yes, this is Anna.'

'This is the police. We're trying to find you – where exactly are you?'

'We're on County Road seven,' I repeated the information I'd relayed earlier. 'Four hundred yards south of the junction with the ninety-one.'

'Which junction?!' the officer asked.

'The ninety-one,' I repeated. 'We're about four hundred yards from the junction with the ninety-one.'

'Are you sure? You can't be there. There's a huge hole in the road.'

Mother above! I thought.

'Yes! That's where the car is, in that hole! Are you on the other side?'

'Yes – we think we can see you.'

I began holding my flashlight out and putting my hand in front of it to make a signal.

'That flashing light, you see it? That's us.'

'Ah, okay, ma'am. We're coming round. We'll be there in five minutes.'

Sure enough, five minutes later, a convoy of flashing lights appeared down the road, this time on the correct side of the newly formed river. I managed to herd the still wayward couple towards a line of police cars. I counted eight cars on the scene, which seemed a little excessive, but better to have too many than too few police, I thought. As we walked towards the line of cars, the officers began turning off their engines and emerging from within them.

'Is this the couple who are hurt?' said one officer, who'd just got out of the second car in the line. I nodded, and he led the couple away from me, towards an ambulance at the back of the line. I stayed put, not quite sure what to do.

The next 10 minutes were very surreal. People fussed around, moving from cop car to cop car, between groups of gathered officers, jotting things down in notepads, chatting on radios and walking back to where the car had crashed into the river. I didn't want any attention, but I felt like a ghost in the scene unfolding around me. I was now seemingly invisible.

Eventually, an officer came over with a statement clipboard. 'You the girl who made the 911 call?' he asked, and I nodded. He then asked me to detail what had happened in a statement. I had now been holding it together for a good hour since the crash, and it all got too much. I sat down on the road in the headlights of the nearest police car, with the clipboard on my lap and began to sob. The officer next to me now looked uncomfortable. 'Umm… ma'am… are you… are you okay?'

'No, I'm not okay!' I wailed. 'I just, I mean. This isn't normal. This doesn't happen all the time!'

After a 30-second outburst I calmed down a little, and dutifully recorded the events, a tear dropping onto the page every now and then, leaving smudges in my statement.

The couple were taken by ambulance to the hospital, and it was only after they'd gone that I realised I didn't have the chance to get any of their details before they left. I was struggling to string together any kind of coherent thought at this point, but I knew they'd be alright now at least – they were in safe hands.

I should have insisted that the police officers give me a ride to the nearest motel. I had sort of just assumed that they would, but now I felt embarrassed to ask so I asked for directions instead. The officers debated amongst themselves which route I could take that wasn't underwater. I waited for them to come to a sensible conclusion, and then pedalled off, taking the turning they'd said would offer me a safe passage. It was pitch-black, and half a mile down the road I came across another sign saying, 'road closed'. This way was flooded too. I felt so angry, let down and alone. I turned back and cycled a further 15 miles taking turning after turning, sobbing away in the darkness, until I made it to a motel in the small town of Firestone. I said very little to the clerk on the check-in desk, went up to my room and was worried I wouldn't sleep at all, but I was so exhausted that I passed out as soon as my head hit the pillow.

***

I spent the following two days at the motel. Watching the floods unfold on the news brought home just how ignorant I'd been over the past week, and what little notice I had taken of a natural disaster which was destroying people's homes and turning their lives upside down. At breakfast, I was surrounded by a full room of people and caught glimpses of their sombre conversations.

'It's gone, there's nothing there. Completely gone,' one woman said.

'They won't let us back in, I just want to see what's left. But they won't let us back,' said another man.

I spent all day in my room, watching the weather channel and trying to process the events of the previous night. I didn't want to speak to anyone. I felt brittle. As if I might shatter into a tiny thousand pieces if I was spoken to. I was a chipped windshield. The tiniest bit of pressure, a wrong word, an unwelcome emotion and I would crack and crumble. I would become useless.

I felt pity. I was pitying myself, but I refused those thoughts. How could I pity myself when I was not the one who had come to any harm? I had lost nothing. In light of the loss that others at the motel were experiencing, I had so much to be thankful for. I felt foolish and all at once confused.

I'm not religious, although I do believe in some order of the universe, and so I spent much of the day trying to work out why I was there on the road that night. Was I there to help those people, I wondered? I'm sure they'd have made it out on their own eventually. Who knows? Was I there to remind myself to be grateful? Was I there to be reminded that bad things happen in the world, and that perhaps my little bubble of bliss needed to be burst? My sunny view of the world had been smacked way out of kilter, and I just couldn't understand why. It seemed a very human thing to do to search for meaning in seemingly random events, but then again, maybe there was no reason at all. Maybe last night just… was. That was a very plausible explanation too.

**

The following day, it took a fair amount of wiggling to avoid closed roads, collapsed bridges and blocks north of Denver. Passing through Fort Collins, I stopped to take in the scene around me. The town was a wreck. Whole paving slabs had been unearthed by the power of the flood waters and 20-ft-high ballpark fences buckled under the weight of trees dragged through the town.

I pushed on for another hour, feeling increasingly relieved as I neared the Colorado–Wyoming state border. I'd originally been headed for Cheyenne, but after bridge collapses and road closures, I'd now diverted to take the 287 all the way to the town of Laramie instead. I did my best to reflect on the events of the past 48 hours, but they passed like a bullet train through my mind. It was all a blur. The harder I tried to recall the details of the crash, the more confusing they became. Fragments of memory played out like video clips through my mind: the car coming towards me, the sickening crunch of the metal meeting tarmac, the couple embracing, the lights and sirens of the police cars. I was feeling a whole range of things, but the two overwhelming sensations were of numbness and embarrassment. *Was it possible to* feel *numb?* I wondered. Surely that was a contradiction in itself? And, of course, the remembering of any details only made me sadder and even more confused, so what was the point in thinking about it at all? I resolved that there was no rush to make sense of what had happened. Perhaps, with a little time, and a little distance too, everything would become clearer.

Highway 287 to Laramie was a long old slog, but I soon ground into a steady rhythm and found the wide-open landscapes of Wyoming to be the perfect antidote for such a busy and crowded mind. I'd been feeling empty all day, as if someone had put cotton wool in my head, but when I crossed the Wyoming state line, I felt like I could breathe again. That state line was physical, but it drew a metaphorical line under the recent events in my mind too. Whatever had happened, and whatever conclusions I made about the crash in the weeks to come, it was all behind me now. I was 4,000 miles into the journey and into state number 10.

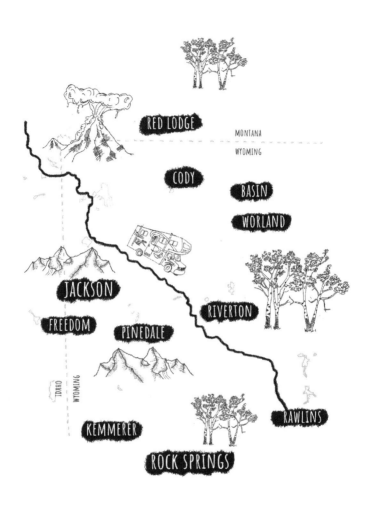

RED LODGE

MONTANA
WYOMING

CODY

BASIN

WORLAND

JACKSON

RIVERTON

FREEDOM

PINEDALE

IDAHO
WYOMING

KEMMERER

RAWLINS

ROCK SPRINGS

WYOMING

9

The Dream Dumper

Distance Cycled: 4,118 miles
States Completed: 10

The vast plains of Wyoming stretched out in front of me for an eternity. There was so much sky. I don't think I'd ever seen that much sky before. Patches of clouds were smeared across it, like paint smudges left from the work of a hasty artist on a canvas of blue. I followed the road with my eyes – it was laid out like a pale grey ribbon stretching from my feet and not stopping until it reached a hazy horizon. The surrounding land was a carpet of straw-coloured scrub. Ankle-high bushes covered the earth – it looked like they were doing their best to grow, but there wasn't much out here to help them out. In fact, there wasn't much out here at all except the odd flock of birds and, on one occasion, a small pack of wild horses that galloped alongside me for a couple of miles on my first morning in the state, making me feel for a few precious moments as if I were as wild and free as they were.

In Wyoming, I was no longer using the 'official' Adventure Cycling Association routes to help me navigate; instead, I was using a basic state map and wrote down the town names I needed to head for on a scrap of paper. As the directions usually boiled down to 'carry straight on for 80 miles then turn left', there really wasn't much to it.

Although the navigation was straightforward, if you had looked at the route I was taking you wouldn't be mistaken in thinking I'd got lost. The most direct route from Cheyenne would have been to head straight north and into Montana, before making an eastward bid to cross the northern states, but that route would mean missing out on Yellowstone National Park. Having seen vibrant images in National Geographic of its rainbow lake and steaming geysers, Yellowstone National Park was one of the reasons for me deciding to do a journey in the USA in the first place, and it was somewhere I just *had* to visit. So instead of taking the most direct route, I would take a wigglier diagonal line across the state, eastwards through Grand Teton and Yellowstone National Parks, before ducking into Montana and heading west again. It was a route that would add 500 miles to the journey, but 500 miles was a small price to pay for the chance to see a rainbow lake.

I wasn't taking any notice of the names of the roads in Wyoming, only the road numbers. Now looking at the map, I could see that the road I was on was called Snowy Range Road, a name which perhaps indicated that I would indeed be heading up a mountain. For the next few hours, my pedals turned slowly as I embraced 14 miles of steady climbing to the summit of Snowy Range Road. The air was cold as it passed my cheeks and nose, but the sun was shining, and so I was in good spirits as I once again settled into a steady upwards motion.

One pedal turn after another, my mind was lost in thought and my thoughts were lost in the mountains.

I was surrounded by aspen trees with leaves that were just starting to turn. Aspen trees are one of my favourite kind of tree. They have white beech-like bark and thousands of tiny teardrop-shaped leaves suspended from narrow branches. One side of the leaves is green, and the other side is white, so when the wind blows, the leaves flutter and switch between white and green, making it seem as if the whole tree is a sparkling freestanding glitter ball. Now that the leaves were on the turn for autumn, I was seeing sparkles of greens, reds and yellows as I continued to climb.

I reached the top of the pass at 3,300 metres high as it started to rain. Pulling on my rain jacket, I glided down the other side just as dusk began to fall. It was night-time when I made it to the town of Saratoga, and I was feeling blissfully happy. Another day done, another mountain climbed, another step closer to feeling a little bit more like myself.

***

It is a well-known fact that Wyoming is the windiest place on earth. Okay, perhaps there are areas of Antarctica or Chile's Atacama Desert that could give it a run for its money, but if there were a wind Olympics, Wyoming would be tipped for a podium position. I defy you to find a place more willing to commit an air-assault on your entire body, hour after hour, day after day.

The Adventure Cycling Association summed things up rather accurately in their notes by saying that 'Winds in southwest Wyoming are often between 40–60 miles per hour. Expect the wind to be against you at all times.' If you google, 'why is Wyoming so windy' (something which I did as I left Saratoga), you will find some marvellous theories about high-altitude prairies, broad ridges, longitude and general arrangement of the surrounding land. Whatever – it's windy. There are, of course, pluses to battling in such a wind. Firstly, I acquired an attractive new facial feature – a weather-burnt upper lip that left me looking like Charlie Chaplin's love child. And secondly, anything that was not a direct headwind felt like I was flying.

The first 20 miles of the day towards the town of Rawlins passed in a flash. More than a flash, in fact; I had covered those 20 miles in just one hour. I had a sneaky suspicion that perhaps I was being assisted by a tailwind, and my suspicions were confirmed when I turned 90 degrees and onto the I-80. It was like riding into a brick wall – my speedo plummeted and I wrestled with the handlebars on the bike in what was now a strong cross-headwind. For the hours that followed, I flitted between overwhelming feelings of frustration and manic laughter. At one point, I hit a downhill section and felt like I was flying. Oh, joy of joys! The wind was in my hair once again! I looked down at my speedo - it read a blistering 7 mph.

I decided it was high time to pull into a truckers' stop and enjoy some weak diner coffee and a Philly cheese and steak sandwich – so that's just what I did. With a belly full of food again, things seemed a little brighter back out on the road. Thirty minutes after leaving the truckers' stop, I spotted a sign by the side of the highway that said 'Strong winds possible'. I smiled a wry smile, now rather enjoying the novelty of it all, and propped Boudica up next to the sign. I stepped ten paces backwards to take a photo. A strong gust of wind blew Boudica off her stand and onto the ground.

I battled on all day, riding the bipolar waves of exhilaration and exhaustion until finally rolling into the town of Rawlins at 5 p.m. I'd battled just 46 miles in the wind since leaving at 8 a.m. and I was utterly pooped. I knew that there was a posh campground somewhere towards the back of town, and still feeling a little fragile from recent events, I decided that I would treat myself to a couple of nights there.

Eight months earlier, before I'd even left the UK, I'd sent an email to a teacher called Harmony Davidson at Sinclair Elementary School. I'd found her contact details on the school website and, after working out that I might be taking a rest day near Rawlins, I'd emailed her to ask if I could speak at her school on my way through. When I send emails of this kind, part of me thinks, 'Why would the teacher say no?!' And the other part thinks, 'Why on earth would they agree to a total stranger from another country coming in to speak to their kids?! And on a date that's eight months away at that.' But Harmony was just the right kind of person for my email to land on, and her response was marvellous.

'Hi Anna, that sounds incredible! I teach at a school of about 40–50 students so we usually do everything together. I think bike safety (we don't even have motorcycle helmet laws in this state, it drives me crazy) with some tales from the road would be great. We're not sure of scheduling for next year yet but I think we could rearrange things for a special presentation. Thanks so much, I'm excited to hear more.'

After settling into camp at 6 p.m., I made a quick call to Harmony to confirm the plan for tomorrow.

'And you know where we are?' Harmony asked.

'Oh, sort of – not really? Are you far from the centre of town?' I enquired.

'Which town is that?'

'Umm… Rawlins?'

'Oh, we're actually in Sinclair.'

I paused while I racked my brains as to why Sinclair sounded so familiar, and then I realised I had ridden through Sinclair 7 miles back. It was not far from the truckers' stop where I had enjoyed the world's most satisfying cheese and steak sandwich. Sinclair was on the way into Rawlins.

'Oh, of course,' I said. 'Silly me,' I continued, trying to remain nonchalant about the situation and the prospect of riding 7 miles back in the wrong direction, in the winds. 'What time would you like me there in the morning?'

'8.30 a.m.?'

'Perfect. See you then.'

I hung up and breathed a deep sigh. I was an idiot. But this idiot had a school full of children to speak to in the morning, and there was no time to waste. I found that maps really helped kids to put things into context, so I threw some clothes in the laundry and whizzed into a local supermarket for map-making supplies. There I picked up a giant piece of cardboard, some coloured pens and glue. That evening, I drew, cut and stuck together a map of the USA, complete with my route drawn on it. I sat back and admired my handiwork, before rolling it into a tube and setting it aside, ready for the ride back to Sinclair in the morning.

I then set my alarm for 5 a.m. and had a fitful night's sleep – something I found to be customary when you know you have to get up early. I set five alarms on my phone 'just in case', and of course I woke up at the first alarm, because I'd only actually fallen asleep an hour before it. Funny that.

The ride back to Sinclair was an unexpected joy. Having left the bulk of my gear at the campground in Rawlins, Boudica was boasting a far lighter load. In fact, all she was carrying was me and the giant roll of card which displayed the make-shift map. It was below freezing when I set off, teeth chattering in the biting morning air and under the silver light of full moon. By the time I rolled into town at 7 a.m., the skies were beginning to glow in the most wonderful shade of indigo. I was way ahead of schedule and as cool as a cucumber, and so sat in the local park for the following hour, watching the squirrels dance around beneath tall oak trees, and doing my best to stay warm.

Harmony had set aside a whole hour for me with her kindergarten and year one classes, and I was nervous. *An hour?!* That seemed like a long time to talk for, but then I remembered – I really do like to talk.

'Come on, McNuff, you've got this – they're kids,' I muttered to myself as I took a deep breath and stepped up in front of the 50-strong roster of students, and the five teachers.

Within five minutes, I'd hit my speaker's stride; the kids were up and doing tasks with me and the bike, pointing out areas on the map, and I was loving it. Thankfully, my enthusiasm for the task at hand was matched by the kids, who blasted me with question after question over the course of the hour. I was truly buoyed to see them so intrigued by the route, the bike and all my equipment. There were the standard logistical enquiries, like: 'What happens when you need to go tinkle?'; a safety conscious query: 'How do you not die when you're going downhill?'; and general observational statements: 'You sound like you're from *Harry Potter*' – big thanks to J. K. Rowling for putting my accent on the map.

After countless hugs with each and every student, and one particular set of girls that didn't want to leave my side, I rolled out of the school gates and pedalled towards Rawlins. I was back in town by 10.15 a.m. and absolutely buzzing. I spent the rest of the day celebrating with a stack of pancakes from Penny's Pancake Diner and catching up on admin. I'd been putting off writing any kind of blog about the experience in Colorado but, fuelled by the energy from my visit to Sinclair Primary School, I was now ready to write. I turned on my iPad and started tapping away on a blank page.

***

In the days that followed my visit to Sinclair School, I covered big distances. I camped behind an abandoned building one night, with cows nearby, and had vivid dreams about being trampled by giant cow-beasts. I passed through the Wind River Indian Reservation and looked on, saddened by the brash casinos, which disturbed an otherwise picture-perfect landscape. I trucked on, eager to make the Teton and Yellowstone National Parks as soon as possible, and to get some miles under my belt before the weather turned colder.

Nearing the end of a long day through the windswept yellow landscape, I realised I had run out of energy beans entirely. I began to look for somewhere to pull over at the side of the road, when a black jeep passed me in the opposite direction. I hadn't seen many cars that day, so I always took note of any kind of vehicle, but in this instance I was acutely aware of the man in the driver's seat staring at me as he passed. I looked across, smiled, and thought no more of it. Five minutes later, I found a gravel verge, just big enough to pull over on, and reached into my bag for a packet of emergency Skittles.

I was midway through eating all my favourite green-coloured Skittles first, when the same black jeep appeared on the horizon – only, this time, it was on my side of the road. I considered it a little odd and pulled my puffy jacket a little tighter around me to combat the growing desert wind. I watched as the jeep pulled over at the side of the road some 20 metres from me, and the man got out. I recognised his face – it was definitely the same jeep and the same man that'd passed me a few minutes earlier.

He was walking towards me in exaggeratedly slow footsteps, almost as if he had just landed on the moon. His arms were outstretched in front of him, palms towards me and fingers fully splayed, as if he were Fox Mulder and I were some kind of alien life form. Bemused, I looked behind me, just to check there wasn't a bear or something equally terrifying nearby, anything that could explain the trepidation in his approach. He stopped just a few metres from me, still with outstretched arms, and opened his mouth to speak.

'Hello, woman!' he yelled over the wind. Did he actually just call me woman?! Oh my.

'Ummmm, hello,' I said, staying firmly put on the gravel and cramming another handful of Skittles into my mouth. Chewing them slowly, I wondered what he planned to do next.

'Are you okay? Can I get you anything, water or something?' he asked, taking a few steps closer, but still seemingly too frightened to get too close.

Oh! How nice of him, I thought. He's come back to see if I'm alright. What a fine fella.

'Oh no, I'm okay. Thank you though. I just got a little tired so I've pulled over for something to eat.' I pointed at the now almost-empty packet of Skittles.

'I passed you back there. About five minutes or so,' the man continued.

'Oh, did you?' I replied, trying to make out that I hadn't clocked him staring at me from the seat of his jeep.

'And I, well... I just had to go ahead and turn my car around, and come back to tell you what a beautiful creature you are. And I mean that in a respectful way.' He stepped back a pace and held up both hands outspread in a sort of 'Woah there, I mean no harm gesture'.

Crikey. I nearly choked on the final mouthful of Skittles. I looked down at my grubby legs and then at my salt-encrusted shorts. I noted how the salt from my sweat had formed a perfect white ring around my crotch. Was this some kind of mating call I was inadvertently putting out? I didn't really know what to say, but I remembered that you should thank people when they pay you a compliment and so I did just that.

'Oh, thank you. That's very kind of you. I'm Anna.'

I decided that such a show of bravery at least warranted me getting up from the floor and shaking the man's hand. I generally always assumed the best in people and, although it paid to be savvy as a solo female traveller, I always trusted my gut. Although the man's initial comment had thrown me slightly off guard, I could tell by his general demeanour that he was a nice man. I took his overly cautious approach as his way of trying to make sure I didn't feel threatened, all alone out here in the middle of the Wyoming plains, being complimented on my natural, sweat-encrusted beauty.

We chatted for five minutes and the man introduced himself as Luke. Although he didn't reveal his age, I guessed he was in his late 40s. He did take pride in telling me he was a lawyer from New York – the Big Apple. I didn't find him in the slightest bit attractive, which was a small shame as I started to think that this could have been a fairy-tale beginning to a movie-worthy love story. 'Tell us how you met?' people would ask. 'Well, it was approaching dusk on the plains of Wyoming…' I would begin.

Luke said he'd been hiking in the hills for the past week and that he flew to the West Coast frequently from the city to 'get away from it all'. The conversation started to come to a natural end, and so I began to thank Luke for his kindness and the compliments.

'Well, it's been lovely,' I said. 'I better get going and make these final miles before it gets dar–'

'So, can I take you to dinner?' Luke blurted, cutting off the end of my sentence. 'In town, or something?'

'Oh! No!' I blurted immediately back, shock exploding from every letter of every word that had left my mouth before I had had a chance to think about their delivery. 'I mean, no, no thank you. That's very kind, Luke, but I'm not going to get in until late, and I'm um…' I racked my brains for a good excuse. 'I'm actually meeting up with a friend in town.'

Who the hell would I be meeting in Dubois, Wyoming?! Still, it worked. He accepted my refusal graciously, and we parted ways. I cycled off, flattered, but mostly bemused. I was 4,500 miles into the trip and had had two requests for dates so far. *How many more would my sweat-encrusted shorts and I receive in the 6,500 miles left to ride?* I wondered.

The following morning, I was woken abruptly from my sleep in a Dubois campground by a low and terrifying rumble. It sounded like someone had submerged a jet engine into the earth, just next to my tent. The vibrations reached my stomach, where they danced a little with the contents, and then, just as fast as the noise had appeared, it was gone. What on earth was that?! I turned on my phone and looked at the time; it was 6.30 a.m.

I decided that I would get out of my tent to investigate, but I was so exhausted from the 115 miles ridden yesterday that I fell straight back to sleep. I am clearly not the best person to be around in a disaster. At 9 a.m. I was awake again and had made my way to the kitchen of the modest campground. One half of the couple who owned the campground came in and smiled at me as she made her way to what looked like a utility cupboard at the back of the room.

'Did you feel it this morning, deary?' she asked.

'Feel what…' and then I remembered that the jet-engine experience wasn't just an odd dream. 'Yes! Yes, I did. What was that?!'

'Oh, just an earthquake,' she said, nonchalantly, moving bottles of bleach and buckets out from the cupboard and into the room.

'An earthquake?!'

'Yeah, we get 'em all the time out here. A side effect of living near the park.'

I was speechless. I'd never been woken by an earthquake before.

'Is everyone okay? I mean, it wasn't bad, right?!'

'Yeah, it was quite a big un – a four-point-six – but all we got is a few bust pipes here.' She motioned to the cupboard, which I could now see housed a spaghetti junction of plumbing.

I pedalled away from the campground at 11 a.m., feeling satisfied if a little bemused to have experienced my first-ever earthquake. I thought it'd make a great story for the grandkids, one which began with 'There was a terrifying roar!' and ended with 'So, I mostly slept through it.'

I crossed out of the Shoshone National Forest and into the Bridger–Teton National Forest, heading for the day's challenge: Togwotee Pass. Continuing along Route 26, I wound my way up on a gradual 32-mile climb to the top of the pass, which towered over the landscape at 2,944 metres high. Luckily, Dubois was already 2,000 metres above sea level, so the 900-metre climb up to the top of Togwotee Pass wasn't too much of a tall order. That said, after yesterday's over-enthusiastic mileage attempt, my legs creaked and groaned and I was certainly glad to reach the top. The previous night at the campground, I'd read a little about Togwotee Pass, and had discovered that it was named after Togwotee, the sub-chief of Chief Washakie, who was the chief of the 'sheep-eater tribe'. Yikes. I pondered on the name of the sheep-eater tribe – *did they exclusively eat sheep?* I wondered. *Or did they branch out to other forms of meat? And was there a cow-eater tribe, a bison-eater tribe and a chicken-eater tribe living in the surrounding areas way back then?* I considered what tribe I would fit into. Given that I had only recently given up 22 years of vegetarianism, I concluded that I would have been the sub-chief of the tofu-eater tribe. My mum would, of course, have been the Chief.

By lunchtime, I had made the top of the pass and was enjoying the view from the western side. Where I stood, astride Boudica, I was sandwiched between Two Ocean Mountain to my left and Breccia Peak to my right. The fact that it was called Two Ocean Mountain intrigued me somewhat – it seemed greedy for a mountain to be named after more than one ocean, after all. A quick Google search later that day told me that I wasn't far from The Parting of the Waters – a unique hydrologic site at the Continental Divide where a river called Two Ocean Creek splits into two smaller tributaries, Pacific Creek and Atlantic Creek. These creeks then eventually run into the Pacific and Atlantic oceans. Wowsers. Geography as a subject was so much more fun when it was brought to life in front of your very eyes. Looking away from the Parting of the Waters and back in the direction I was headed, I could see a set of grey jagged peaks, which rose from the ground and sat side by side like the bottom row of a set of giant's teeth. These were the Tetons, and I decided then and there that they were some of the most majestic looking mountains I'd ever seen.

Over the course of the next few hours, I became transfixed, unable to take my eyes off the Tetons, following the road closer and closer, past green fields with grazing horses, patches of aspen and pine forest, ablaze with the colours of autumn, until there was nothing between me and them except the dark green Snake River. They were huge, reaching 4,200 metres into the clouds, and now I was close enough to see all the details that distance had made fuzzy from the top of Togwotee Pass. It was getting late in the afternoon and the sun had dipped behind the peaks, making their triangle hat-like tops glow, and fragments of golden light were being caught and held hostage by clusters of jagged rocks. I followed the great fissures in the grey rocks up from the riverbed and spotted a series of narrow, now partially frozen waterfalls, suspended in time, mid fall, waiting patiently for the seasons to change.

I wanted to spend as long as possible in close proximity to the Tetons, so I took a 10-mile detour along the road towards the town of Jackson, with the Tetons at my side. I was in my own little world as I pedalled enthusiastically along the flat road, enjoying the dull throb of weary legs. I began to think about just how much I was actually enjoying the gentle level of pain in my quad muscles, when I noticed that there was something missing. My knee! Well, not that my knee was missing, but there was no pain! In fact, I tried to think back to the last time it had hurt and it was the day that I rolled into Highlands Ranch and met Cindy. In all the madness with the car wreck and getting out of Colorado, I hadn't given the tendonitis in my knee a second thought, and it had now miraculously disappeared. I daren't touch it for fear that I would bring the pain back and so instead I just smiled a gigantic grin! No more pain!

Riding on my new pain-free high and having had my fill of the Tetons, I turned around and began heading away from Jackson, back to the junction which would take me to Yellowstone National Park. I was revelling in the silence and calm of early evening, when I spotted a cyclist coming towards me on the road ahead. His bike looked heavily laden, with large panniers and extra bags laid over the top. I wasn't entirely sure if I was in the mood for a chat – it was getting late in the day and I should have really pushed on to pitch my tent – but cycle-touring etiquette dictates that you should stop for at least a hello, no matter how brief. I checked the road behind me for cars and crossed over to the other side to greet the cyclist. He was of a medium build, and had dark skin and dark hair. I put him in his mid 40s. From afar, his body language told me he was a relaxed sort, hands resting gently on his front handlebars as he waited for me to arrive at his bike.

'Hi there!' I said, pulling on my brakes and smiling.

'Oh, hey,' the man replied.

'That's some load you've got. Where are you headed?' I asked, now getting a closer look at what must have been 40 kg of kit strapped to his bike, taking up every scrap of surface of his bike frame.

'Oh, nowhere,' he replied.

'Oh, I mean – where are you going today?' I clarified my question.

'I don't know. Maybe that way, maybe this way…' He gestured into the air in each direction. 'I really don't like to plan – I just like to go with it.'

'Oh… cool. Well, I'm Anna,' I said, leaning over the front of my handlebars and extending a hand for a handshake. He looked at my outreached hand but didn't move.

'I'm Cheveyo,' he said, and there was a pause before he continued. 'It means spirit warrior.'

'Oh, that's cool. Is that your real name?' I withdrew my hand.

'No, but I adopted it. It's what I go by these days.'

'Oh, right – what's your real nam–'

'Where in Australia are you from?' he interrupted.

'Oh, I'm actually from England.'

'Really? Huh. You sound Australian.'

'Ha, um… well, I'm definitely from England.'

'Huh,' he said again. 'I could swear you sound Australian.'

I chatted with the spirit warrior (who, I began to have suspicions, was really called Dave) for a further five minutes. He was American-born, from Idaho, and had been touring the world for 15 years. Three years into his trip, in Thailand, he'd split up with his wife and travelling partner. She'd gone home and he'd carried on alone. He explained how he had no intention to stop travelling any time soon and how he really hated plans. He didn't seem to be keen to accept that I was from England, and after several more times of him insisting that I was Australian, I began to get irritated and decided to change the subject.

'So, I'm cycling the fifty states,' I said. I wasn't one to tell everyone that, but I really fancied getting off the topic of my accent and where I was from.

'Huh,' he replied.

'Yeah, I think it'll take me another four months. I've been going for two and a half months so far.'

'Huh. That's some plan you've got there,' he said.

'Ha! Yes, it is. I'm ten states down and still really excited about the forty states left to go.'

'I hate plans,' Cheveyo-Dave said.

'Well, I suppose it's not everyone's cup of tea… But it suits me!' I said, in as chipper a manner as I could, but secretly considering how much longer I wanted to spend talking to this man. His energy was toxic.

'And what's your route?' he asked.

I went ahead and described the route I'd made so far, and explained that after hitting Montana, I'd be starting to head east to Maine.

'You're going across the North?!'

'Yes, indeed I am.' I smiled, already getting excited at the prospect of reaching Maine and the Atlantic Ocean.

Cheveyo-Dave sighed and smiled at me, his eyes wide with pity, as if I were a foolish child. He then spoke slowly and said, 'You know we have this stuff called "black ice" here in the US? You slip on that and you'll be in trouble.'

I bit my lip, hard. I knew full well what black ice was, funnily enough we had it in the UK too. I took a deep breath, channelling my inner Dali Lama and searching for the elusive thing called patience, as Cheveyo-Dave continued.

'You'll never make it. You do know that, right?' I stayed silent. Letting my patience fly out the window for a moment, I wondered if cycle etiquette extended to punching a stranger square in the face.

'You should do what I do and head south. Down to southern California. We call it So-Cal down there, you know?'

'Well…' I said, starting to make a move to leave. 'I'm going to give it a go, and I reckon I'll make it,' I said, looking him square in the eyes, and breathing deeply as my whole body began to shake with anger.

'Okay, okay – I'm telling you now that you won't make it, but I suppose you can always just stop when it gets too cold,' he continued, holding his hands up.

My blood was beginning to boil. I was all for friendly conversations, but this guy had just tipped the balance. He had listened to my dream, turned around, pulled his pants down and (metaphorically) taken a dump on that dream. A big, steaming, free-spirited dump. That made me angry. Not just for me, but for all the other people he might have done that to in his 15 years on the road. I knew I needed to extract myself from his company and fast. I gritted my teeth, thanked him for his concern, and began to pedal off down the road.

'Say!' he yelled after me as I pedalled off. 'Maybe I'll look you up if I ever find myself in Australia?!'

'Oh yes, great!' I shouted back, before muttering, much more quietly. 'Good luck finding me in Australia when I live in ENGLAND!'

I rode on for the rest of the day engulfed in a cloud of rage. I kept trying to calm myself down, and then I would replay a portion of my conversation with Cheveyo-Dave and my anger would flare up all over again. I ranted and raved alone on the bike, shoving harder on the pedals and muttering, 'Black ice… ?! Black ice?!' under my breath.

By the time the sun began to slide from view that evening, I was feeling calmer. I resolved that, ultimately, Cheveyo's words reflected a belief in his own capabilities. It was sad that he felt the need to pass them on to me. I reasoned further that I should let it wash over me, like water off a duck's back. But it rocked me to my core, and I just couldn't let it go. It's hard enough to convince ourselves to do things that frighten us, that scare us, that stretch our capabilities but the last thing we need is others telling us we can't. And so I made a little kingdom in my mind where all the Dream Dumpers of the world could live happily together – merrily taking dumps from great heights on one another's dreams at every opportunity – and leave the rest of us in peace. It would be called Dumpville. From that day, I made a promise to myself that I would live my life a very, very long way away from the gates of Dumpville.

***

I had just about recovered from my rage induced by Cheveyo the Dream Dumper, as I crossed the threshold into Yellowstone National Park. Then suddenly all rage was gone and excitement reigned supreme. I deliberately didn't read too much about Yellowstone National Park before the trip, so, aside from seeing some very cool pictures, my knowledge of what lay within it was limited to having watched a lot of *Yogi Bear* cartoons as a kid. Yogi lives in the fictitious Jellystone National Park, which is a play on Yellowstone. If Yogi was there, there had to be more bears, which explained the mix of nerves and excitement in my tummy. Yellowstone, it turned out, was indeed prime bear territory, and despite my encounters in Alaska with the furry friends, I was a still a little nervous. It didn't help that as I entered the park someone had taken the care and time to spray paint in red letters on the road 'Grizzlies eat people'. Lovely.

Right from the off, the Yellowstone scenery lived up to everything I had hoped it would be. Dramatic grey canyons gave way to cascades and wide-open riverbeds scattered with logs and surrounded by rainbow patches of native forest. Alive with yellows and reds of the early autumn, the explosion of colour was breathtaking, and I stopped repeatedly to take it all in. With every bend I turned, a new, different vista came into view – each one like a picture-perfect postcard.

It was a busy day on the roads in the park. After spending so much time alone with little to no passing traffic, it made me nervous to be among vehicles again. Having grown up in London I was comfortable riding in densely packed urban conditions, where the traffic moves slowly and you must weave your way among it. But out here, the trucks and cars moved so much faster, and that scared me. More than that, in Yellowstone, visiting tourists could rent giant camper vans to explore the park, many of them with little experience of ever having driven something that size, and even less experience about what a safe passing distance for a cyclist is, which is at least 1.5 metres. That's a lot of space to give cyclists when you're driving on a narrow, winding, single-lane highway in Yellowstone.

It was approaching midday and I was heading up and over the Continental Divide for the third time in two days, when I heard an especially large rumble of tyres behind me. There it was, bright purple and covered in two-tone glitter with a silver wave down the side of it. It was half camper van, half truck – and it was enormous. I yelped and my pulse raced, but I had heard it too late and the van was already upon me. I was engulfed in a whirlwind of glitter and purple as the camper van just missed the edges of my rear pannier racks. The front wheels had passed me now, but I felt the wheels of the bike being sucked sideways as the main body of the camper created a vacuum and dragged me towards it. I gripped the handlebars tightly in blind panic and, for a moment, was convinced I was going under the back wheels. The grip of the vacuum was so strong, it had taken me by surprise. I was helpless to its pull. At the last minute, the vacuum released me with a 'pop!' and I struggled to get the bike back on a straight line, heart pounding. It was then that I realised that grizzlies and any danger nature could throw at me were not the problem. I'd take a wrestle with a bear over another glitter-ball camper van any day. My heart was pounding and I was in total shock. That was close, far too close.

Although I wouldn't go so far as to say that Yellowstone was worth dying for, it was certainly a fascinating and unique place and the awe-inspiring scenery made up for the near-death camper-van experiences. The entire park sits on top of the largest active volcano on earth, and as a result it is full of bubbling mud pools, asymmetric sulphur-encrusted grottos and shimmering oases in every colour imaginable.

During my short visit, I learnt that Yellowstone is 3,468 square miles in size, with five entrances and seven campgrounds, over an area contained within a 142-mile circular ring road. Although many campgrounds were now closed for the season, there were still a few that were open, but, unfortunately, they were fully booked. Without a reserved camp spot, and with winter growing ever closer each day, I had no choice but to try to 'see' as many of the main attractions as I could in an afternoon.

The main attraction is Old Faithful – the largest, most predictable geyser in the park. Every 35–120 minutes, Old Faithful erupts, shooting up to 32,000 litres of boiling hot water into the air, much to the delight of the awaiting crowd. After locking up my bike next to the Old Faithful Inn, I wandered over to the viewing area and watched two of the geyser's cycles, discovering that the crowd was almost as fascinating as the eruption itself. Fifteen minutes before the predicted eruption, hundreds gathered in horseshoe formation, a safe distance from the geyser, shrouded in library-esque silence. Everyone held their cameras, poised and ready, arms outstretched with their fingers tentatively balanced on the trigger, and then 'Whooooosh!' – a huge jet would shoot skyward from the earth, creating one of the most magical natural spectacles known to man. The jet then carried on for almost three minutes, spluttering and fading at points, but all the while expelling boiling water from the earth. By minute number two, the fickle crowd, having got what they came for and with dopamine levels now returning to baseline, began to leave. Out of respect, I waited for Old Faithful to finish her display.

Largely thanks to a desire to try out the lunch menu at the inn, I'd stopped cycling for an hour longer than I'd intended to. It was coming up to 4 p.m. and I figured that I had just 90 minutes of daylight left. Although all of the attractions I intended to see were within walking distance of the inn, I still had 32 miles left to ride to the town of West Yellowstone, where I intended to camp for the night.

Leaving my bike locked up next to the inn, I spent the next two hours dashing around on foot to see everything I could before the sunlight faded. First, I visited the Grand Geyser, which was much like Old Faithful's slightly smaller cousin –

a cousin which spat out boiling water a little more regularly. I then moved on to Castle Geyser, which resembled a giant salt-encrusted egg cup. Having had my geyser fill, I moved on to the pools in the surrounding area. My first visit was to Sapphire Pool, which was an oasis swimming with every shade of blue the human eye is capable of seeing. I was mesmerised. Pale blues at the shallow edges nudged into deeper shades of turquoise and aquamarine, until the ground dropped steeply away and gave way to a crescendo of bright royal blue in the centre of the pool. It was beautiful! Oh, how I wanted to get naked and cannonball into the pool at that very moment. Instead, I stole myself away for a visit to the final attraction: the Grand Prismatic Spring. The Grand Prismatic Spring is a posh name for what I had called 'the rainbow lake'. I'd seen images of it a thousand times in geographers' magazines and assumed that the images were modified in some way, the colours enhanced. I was wrong. A ring of fiery orange steaming volcanic ground surrounded a near perfect circle of water. As the water of the pool deepened, the orange earth changed to a lighter peach, then a lemon yellow, into jade green, turquoise and finally to royal blue at the centre of the pool. Steam rose from the water's surface, so that I could never quite catch all of the colours at once, only glimpses of them between the mist. Oh, planet earth, I thought. How you rock my world!

It was 5 p.m. by the time I hopped back on my bike and gunned it out of the park, lights turned on and hammering on the pedals as hard as I could to avoid riding in total darkness.

As I panted and pedalled, I had an icky feeling in my stomach. I was leaving the park desperately wanting to spend another day there. I had considered for a moment that I might just give in or at least stay in West Yellowstone that night and come back into the park the next day, but with rumours of snow on its way and 40 states still to go, I felt that I had to keep moving. As darkness fell, I crossed the Wyoming state line, and entered into the tourist mecca of West Yellowstone, Montana. I looked at my speedo. I'd covered 97 miles that day, and what a day it'd been.

It had started to get cold that night, and I was pleased to make West Yellowstone, but as I searched for a place to stay in town, I began to reflect on how frantic everything had felt that day. For the first time, I questioned the way in which I'd planned the trip. *Should adventure travel always be this rushed?* I wondered. *Surely I had come on this adventure to give myself time, not to rob myself of it.* I vowed to come back one day, hopefully with my yet-to-be-created kids, and to share with them one of the most truly remarkable places in the world.

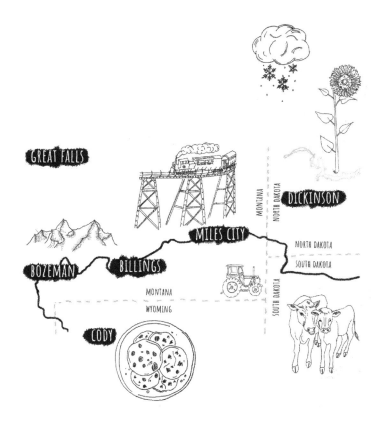

GREAT FALLS

DICKINSON

MONTANA | NORTH DAKOTA

MILES CITY

NORTH DAKOTA

BOZEMAN

BILLINGS

SOUTH DAKOTA

MONTANA

SOUTH DAKOTA

MONTANA
WYOMING

CODY

Montana

10

The Weichmanns

Distance Cycled: 4,636 miles
States Completed: 11

I made two attempts to leave West Yellowstone. On the morning following my visit to the park itself, I had ridden out of the bustling town bound for the solitude of the mountains once again. Alas, 5 miles down the road my rear wheel emitted a loud twang, and I turned around to discover a broken spoke flapping left and right, making the kind of noise that a child might make if dragging a coat hanger along a set of railings. It was 80 miles from where the spoke gave way to the next sizeable town, so I gave a loud sigh and made the sensible call to turn around and take the bike back into West Yellowstone. It was frustrating to have made the decision not to spend an extra day in the park (on account of trying to stick to the schedule) only to end up delayed anyway by the broken spoke. I wondered if the adventure gods were trying to tell me what they thought of my schedule. By the time I made Yellowstone Cycles, my back wheel was shaped like a banana, lunging left and right with every rotation.

The following morning, my wheel was fixed and I was on the road again. It'd been chilly when I'd set out from West

Yellowstone two hours earlier, but now the temperature had plummeted close to zero. I hadn't dropped much in altitude since leaving Colorado, so I had expected it might be a little chilly – but it seemed bitterly cold for late September. My cheeks stung in the icy air, my nose ran constantly and there were small icicles of snot beginning to form on my upper lip. I am unaware as to the official name for such snot-sculptures, so I shall refer to them as 'snotstacles'. The snotstacles were breaking off at intervals and making the area around them red and raw. My toes, feeling like they were missing out on the icicle action, had also decided to go numb. Still, having already ridden 25 miles that day, it was now only 60 miles to the town of Ennis, Montana, and I decided that 60 miles of cold, dry riding would be perfectly doable. I wiped the last of the snotstacles from my face, pushed a fraction harder on the pedals, and with the resulting rise in body temperature, willed it to reach my toes as soon as possible.

I wound my way north-east, deeper into Montana, and then across the state line to make an obligatory dip into state number 12, Idaho. Poor Idaho. I spent approximately 15 miles within its confines before crossing back into Montana, and for that I felt a little guilty. Second only to New Mexico, it was the shortest time I had spent in a state so far. I wished there had been some kind of official Idaho state board I could have called to apologise for such a brief visit, but my visa just wouldn't sanction the time to give each state the love it duly deserved.

The road was undulating but the inclines were mere pimples compared to the Rockies, and so the miles passed easily enough. After 20 miles, my toes had gone entirely numb and I was struggling to keep any sensation in my fingers too. I decided things were going just the wrong side of comfortable so I decided to pull into a rest area next to a river. I could see a brick-built toilet, intended for use by those fishing from this spot, and I had to do something, anything, to get out of the cold wind and get some blood back into my extremities.

I put the bike on its stand, heaved open the heavy metal door and squeezed inside. It was everything you would imagine a public toilet to be. The strong stench of urine made me gag and there were all kinds of nondescript smudges on the cream tiled wall, as well as cobwebs in the top corners near the roofing and scraps of toilet paper and several beer cans scattered across the floor. I chanced a look down the toilet itself (no, I'm not sure why either) and was rewarded by the skid marks of fishermen from weeks gone by. Still, the toilet block was large enough to stand inside and be, for just a little time, warmer than being on the bike. Perhaps I had the leftover heat from all the urine to thank for that.

I stood for 15 minutes in the bog-palace, too afraid to touch anything but letting the blood return to my toes and fingers, and feeling them come slowly back to life. I winced my way through the wave of excruciating pain that is unavoidable after toe-and-finger freezing, and was finally satisfied when I could wiggle all of them again freely once more. When the 15 minutes were up, I took a deep breath, coughed at having inhaled so much stale air, shoved the metal door back open and dashed over to Boudica. I swung my leg over her, kicked up the stand and pedalled off out of the car park as hard and as fast as I could in a bid to keep the newly returned blood pumping around my extremities.

Spurred on by the need to stay warm, I made great time, and by mid-afternoon I was only 20 miles from the town of Ennis, and my campground spot for the night. I thought I was almost home and dry, until a crackle of thunder overhead told me otherwise. Large droplets of cold rain began to plop onto the arms of my rain jacket. The droplets turned into a full-blown downpour and an hour later the rain was still going strong. I was soaked to the skin and freezing. However, I wasn't bothered by the painful sensation in my fingers and toes anymore, because they now had as much feeling as the rest of my body – which was no feeling at all.

You'll be warm and dry in an hour, I told myself, playing the words like a record on repeat through my head. The mantra was a superb distraction from the discomfort, and I cruised through the main section of town, passing tempting motel after tempting motel, before arriving at Ennis Campground and RV Park. Dismounting the bike, I shuffled my way to the reception building, looking like an Antarctic penguin, and approached the front desk. Behind the desk was a grey-haired woman who looked to be in her early 60s. She glanced up from the paperwork she was filling out, and a look of concern spread across her face.

'Oh my!' she said. 'Would you look at you, all wet. Isn't it cold out there?'

'Yep, it's not the warmest,' I said matter-of-factly. 'But I'm here now. And I'll be warm and dry in a few minutes.' I chirped, already feeling better that my mantra was coming true so soon. With numb, trembling fingers, I struggled to sign the payment bill for my camping pitch as the lady talked me through the various grass spots available. She paused and looked at me. 'You do know there's a storm coming in, don't you? Tonight, they say.'

'Oh, yes, I had heard that, but I guess you don't know until it happens,' I replied. Someone had mentioned a snowstorm was due, but I figured that I'd be able to make it through somehow. 'And I'll be warm enough. I have a hat and everything,' I continued, doing my best to sound convincing.

The woman behind the counter looked sceptical. 'Okay… as you like…' she trailed off and continued with the run-through of facilities. 'There's a drying room for your clothes, and there's a shower room round the back. If you want somewhere warm and dry to sit, there's a community room over there. You can sit in there as long as you like.' She smiled again. That warm, homely smile.

'Thank you,' I said, smiling back as best I could, willing my cheeks to move just a little more than they were able.

Heading back outside, I quickly threw down my bike and tent in my allotted pitch and ran straight to the showers. I didn't even bother to pitch my tent. I figured that was best done once I could feel my hands again. My body was starting to shake and I couldn't stop my teeth from chattering, so I turned the shower up to scalding hot and got in, still in all my clothes. They were wet anyway, and I was planning to stick them in the dryer, so a little warm water on them would probably do the world of good. And besides, I couldn't close my hands enough to grasp the material on my leggings to get them off. After five minutes I felt brave enough to peel the sopping mess away from my skin. Once naked and now decidedly warmer, I spent a further 10 minutes bathing in the steaming glory of the shower.

When I emerged, once again clothed in warm and dry gear, the lady from the desk came into the shower room.

'Feeling better?' she asked.

'So much better! Thank you!' I beamed back.

She seemed to genuinely care and I got such a kind energy from her. I decided that the lady behind the counter was a good egg.

'Listen…' she started. 'I've checked and that storm is definitely coming in, they say there could be up to 4 feet of snow. I mean it could be nothing, but it's the first storm of the season and you just never know.'

I started to launch into my usual, well-rehearsed, terribly British 'Oh, I'll be okay' reply, but the woman interrupted me. 'I don't normally do this…' she said. 'But why don't you just come home with me? To me and my husband. I finish in an hour and I could take you back home. We have a spare room. It'll be warm and dry. And if there's no snow in the morning, you can just be on your way.'

I thought for a moment… a cold tent… or a nice warm bed with the nice kind lady from behind the counter. I was blown away.

'Are you sure?' I asked, watching her face closely to check that she wasn't just being polite.

'I am very sure,' she smiled.

'Oh, then I would love that! Thank you, thanks so much.'

'Okay then, you go dry your clothes and wait in the community room. I'll come by and fetch you at 6 p.m.'

'Great!'

The woman turned to leave, and then spun back around.

'My name is Susan, by the way.'

'Hi Susan, I'm Anna,' I replied. 'Very nice to meet you.'

An hour later, I was being driven round the corner to Susan's house, and getting her life story as we drove. As it turned out she and her husband had managed the campground here for over a decade. They'd spent several years travelling around the US in a motorhome, and now were finally settled in Ennis. On the way home, we stopped by a neighbour's house to pick up a fresh apple pie that had been baked for Susan, and we continued the journey with a steaming pie on my lap, letting the wafts of steam pass up my nostrils.

Susan's home was set all on one level, clad in wooden slats and with a large veranda. I made my way up the front steps onto the porch and followed Susan through the front door into a large kitchen/living room. Two dogs went nuts as I entered, jumping, licking, barking – I think they were more excited to be there than I was. I later learned that they were called Lexie and Brandy. Her husband was heading out for the evening, but on hearing Susan was bringing a guest home for tea, he had got dinner ready and on the table. I hoovered down bowls of steaming soup, complete with pasta and vegetables, and slathered disgusting amounts of butter onto white crusty bread, which I then dunked in the soup, before cramming it most unladylike into my mouth. Naturally, this was followed up with double helpings of freshly baked apple pie and cream.

'Would you like to watch something on the TV?' Susan asked, clearing away the plates. I nodded heartily, plonking myself down on the sofa.

'Oooo, we like this one!' she said, flicking on ITV's *Lark Rise to Candleford*.

And so there I sat, in a stranger's home, a belly full of home-cooked food, snuggled deep into an oversized brown leather sofa, surrounded by photos of grandchildren, Susan's quilting pieces (her hobby), Brandy the dog snoring happily on my lap and watching a good old ITV drama. I felt almost as warm on the inside as I did on the outside.

***

I loved everything about Montana. Despite flurries of snow, a biting wind and the likelihood of my being able to feel my toes sitting at an even 20%, I was completely head over heels in love with the Big Sky state. Vast blue skies and crisp wintry air kept me awake and feeling alive through the long days in the saddle that followed my departure from Susan's. In a bid to keep moving as much as I could, and to stay warm, I was regularly pushing out 90-mile days – surrounded by snow-capped peaks and white-dusted evergreens.

Montana is sparsely populated and 400 miles across – which to many people is 400 miles of not much to stop off and see. Bar a few exceptions around the country, it's illegal to cycle on Interstate Highways in the USA, including on Montana's speed-limit-less I-90, which was a good thing: Montana is the only state in America which doesn't have a speed limit on its interstates, perhaps because people want to get across the state as fast as possible. But that wasn't the case for me. I would be revelling in everything Montana had to offer for those 400 miles and looking to take a more scenic route. Sometimes there were 'frontage roads' running alongside the main highway, which would have been old highways. These were perfect to ride along and had a decent level of tarmac. However, as the state wore on, I began to realise that these frontage roads were few and far between. Quite often, they would just lead back onto the Interstate, and I'd have to turn around and backtrack on myself. I discovered that the only option was to pick my way along a network of unnamed gravel farm tracks.

In the week that followed, I went back to navigational basics. After taking a few wrong turns on the maze of tracks, I worked out that so long as I could see either the Yellowstone River, or the freight railway line, I was still on track and heading across the state. To make sure that I wasn't heading in the wrong direction across the state (it may sound stupid but it is surprisingly easily done), I used the position of the sun. With so much sky in Montana and nothing on the horizon, I chased it as it rose in the east in the morning, and made sure it was positioned directly behind me in the evening. It was a week of serenity and good old-fashioned adventure riding. It made me appreciate a decent tarmac surface more than I would do usually and realise that when push comes to shove, there is more common sense in my brain than I gave it credit for.

I camped my way merrily along the south of Montana, mostly finding campgrounds on the outskirts of the small towns I passed through. Well, I say merrily, I did have one not-so-nice experience when a campground owner with enough pent-up anger to power New York City slung me off his land and threatened to call the cops on me due to the campground being 'closed for the season'. On that occasion, still mildly concerned about the presence of Montana bears, I wild-camped in a bush between the Interstate and the freight railway line. I spent the night trying to fall asleep to the sound of traffic moving along to no speed limit at all, and the ground being shaken every two hours as a freight train passed, blaring its horn. I had nightmares about rogue cars whizzing off the road through the crash barriers and squashing my tent, and the train being derailed and doing the same, but there was no way a bear was coming anywhere near me here, and so I took that as a triumph.

Continuing to follow the path of the Yellowstone River and the railway line for the next few days, I skirted the northern boundary of the Cheyenne Indian Reservation until I made the modest mecca of Miles city, where I crossed the I-94 and turned onto County Road 12, headed for the south-west tip of North Dakota.

North Dakota immediately seemed a whole different ball game to Montana. There were no mountains and the landscape displayed acres of sunflower fields against a backdrop of bright blue sky. The temperature seemed to have risen a little too, and I was glad to be in state number 13.

'Lucky number 13!' I yelled, as I spotted the 'Welcome to North Dakota' sign and stopped for a picture next to it. Interstate 90 had now dropped away to the south, the gravel roads were gone, as were the Yellowstone River and the railway line, and I was back to following small tarmac roads. It was an all-too brief 2.5-hour pedal through North Dakota, and for that I was sad. Now when I think of the state all I can see are those sunflowers – with their yellow petals and lush green stalks – waving me on, swaying in the breeze as I headed south and over the border into state number 14, South Dakota.

***

That cold October day when I met the Weichmann family was the worst I'd had in three months on the road. Two days earlier, I had been warned via text from a member of Reno Cycling Club about the course of a record-breaking blizzard. As a result, I had taken evasive action and tried to head east across South Dakota as fast as possible, instead of south. Pedalling east had led me along a sparsely populated, minor back-country road. A relentless South Dakotan crosswind had nudged me back and forth for 80 miles, and in the midst of an attempt to out-cycle the blizzard, I'd now been riding for almost two weeks without a break. By the time I rolled into the tiny town of Bison, population 342, I was in a real slump. I was tired, run down, and on the verge of cracking out the emergency Tom Hanks-inspired volleyball and naming it Wilson.

Bison wasn't much larger in real life than the dot on the map. Two large cylindrical metal grain stores poked up from the landscape and were surrounded by modest one-storey farm buildings – a sight that had become familiar in the American

Midwest. I was just preparing to turn right down the main street when a rusty grey estate car appeared alongside me. I'd only been passed by two cars that day and so this in itself was a monumental event. At first, I kept my gaze fixed forward, waiting for the car to pass, but it seemed to be moving unusually slowly. Turning my head to the left, I looked into the car. In the driver's seat was a young girl, and she was waving so enthusiastically that I feared her whole right arm might just detach and fly off into the windscreen.

I looked back to the road ahead, thinking perhaps I had imagined the whole scene – I was exhausted after all. I blinked and then looked left again. There she was – still waving, still smiling, and madly so. Being the dignified lady I am, I responded with a wave of equal magnitude, coupled with a gigantic grin. The grin 'n' wave combo must have had an impact on the girl because a little further on, in the centre of town, she pulled off the road and into a gravel car park, and leapt swiftly from the car. When I entered the car park myself, she was still breathless from her speedy car exit.

'Where… are… you from?!' she panted excitedly.

I squeezed on the brakes and ground to a halt, dismounted my beautiful pink touring bicycle and kicked out the stand.

'Oh! I'm, um, from England,' I replied, upping my BBC British accent a little more than usual. The girl clasped her hands together under her chin, balled them into a fist, smiled broadly and squealed – the kind of high-pitched squeal that only dogs might be able to hear. 'Ooook! I've never met any-one from England!' she exclaimed, her eyes ablaze. 'We don't get many visitors here. What are you doing in Bison?!'

We proceeded to indulge in a mutual exchange of whos, whys, whens and wheres. This girl's excitement was infectious, and so both of our voices became increasingly high-pitched. Imagine two overexcited puppies meeting in a park, minus the butt-sniffing. During the exchange I learned that the sweet girl standing in front of me was 21-year-old Katie Weichmann. She had mousy brown hair tied in a high loose ponytail and hazel eyes and was dressed in grey tracksuit bottoms and a pink hoodie. Katie was a shot glass full of sunshine, and the energy she exuded transfused itself into my weary veins.

'Well, you've just gotta come back to our farm. It's just up the road,' said Katie in an accent that resembled those I'd only ever heard in the film *Fargo*. 'You know that blizzard is due, and we'd love to have you visit with us for a few days. My sister would just love to meet you! And Auntie, oh auntie would adore you!' She stared at me and blinked. Her soft voice had all the innocence of a child, and her eyes were wide, like a Disney princess's.

I was a little taken aback by her offer. I hadn't expected to meet anyone that day, let alone be invited for tea.

'Oh, that's so kind… um… where's your farm?' I asked, thinking that 'just up the road' didn't sound like too far to cycle.

'Eleven miles back that-a-way.' She grinned and pointed over her shoulder and back in the direction I'd just come from. And then she stared and blinked at me again with those eyes. Eleven miles back? This girl was sweet, but I was really tired. I didn't fancy an extra 22-mile cycle to her home and back again in the morning. I really needed to get some decent sleep and just get on my way.

'Oh, thank you, thanks so much, but it's okay. I'll just stay here in town. I've got to be on the road early tomorrow.'

Her expression shifted from bright and breezy to confused, and her mouth drooped a little. 'But, but – there's a blizzard coming?'

'Yeah, yeah – I'm going to try to, err… out-pedal it…' I could hear how ridiculous it sounded as the words left my mouth, but I couldn't take them back.

I could see that Katie was just about to protest some more, when a truck pulled into the car park.

'Oook, look! My brother!' she squealed. 'Come meet his kids!'

I went over and chatted for a few minutes with some of the other Weichmann family, but as everyone was engaged in conversation, I took this as a chance to make a polite exit. I told Katie that it was lovely to meet her, and pedalled off down the road, following the original plan and heading for the motel.

Cycling off, I couldn't help but feel – for want of a better word – icky. Something in the pit of my stomach felt distinctly odd. What was I doing?! That girl had just extended me the greatest kindness, and I had declined it for a night on my own in a motel. I didn't even like motels. They mostly smelt of boiled cabbage and came with other people's pubic hair scattered around the toilet seat. My refusal of Katie's offer felt wrong. I thought back to what JP had told me in the desert, when he accepted the gift of water, and wondered if I'd learned anything at all since then. I stopped to look back to the car park, and for a brief moment considered turning around. Katie was laughing and throwing the young blonde-haired kids around in the air. I couldn't go back now, she was enjoying time with her family and I didn't want to be a burden, so I continued on and checked into the motel.

An hour later, I was surrounded by a recently exploded kit-bomb. My tent, bike tools, panniers and food were strewn across the room. Cycling clothes dripped from every available surface like a Salvador Dali painting. I was just removing my sleeping bag from its case to give it a good overnight airing, when I heard a knocking sound. I dismissed it as a knock for the people in the room opposite, and turned my attention back to unpacking my musty sleeping cocoon. But there it was again, knock, knock, knock… and I could swear it was my door. I moved to the other side of the room and tentatively opened it. Standing on the other side was Katie.

'Hey! I, um… thought I'd come visit!' she chirped, holding out her arms for a hug, which I enveloped her in immediately.

Her innocence was just adorable. I ushered her inside and, sitting on beds opposite one another, we picked up our chatting where we had left off before her family arrived at the car park. Just then her phone rang.

'Ooook, it's my sister! Hang on… y'ello Dorena. Uh huh…. yees… mmm huh… oh, I'm just with her now…'

Katie dropped the phone away from her ear and looked at me. 'Are you sure you won't come back to the farm? Dorena says she'd just love to visit with you.'

I had learned that Americans liked you to 'visit with them'. That meant 'spend some time with you'. That was it, I didn't need asking twice! I nodded and Katie squealed.

'Yes! She said yes. See you soon, D'rena!'

Despite having paid for the motel room, I crammed all of my stuff back into my bags and, as I flung the key back into the hands of the bemused receptionist, yelled, 'I'm… errr… going with Katie!'

We stashed Boudica in the local church so I could collect her the following day, and Katie drove me back to the family farm. Turning off the main road at a large oak tree, we bounced down a rocky half-mile-long track. We pulled into the farm and a single-storey blue house with white window frames came into view. It was slightly raised off the ground on stilts and there was a ramp leading up to the front door. The outside was clad in wooden slats, and in the front yard were an assortment of hay bales and a big red tractor. To the left-hand side of the house was a long, white static trailer.

'So here it is!' said Katie, turning the key to kill the car engine. 'That's our home.' She pointed to the blue house. 'I live there with Dorena and Grannie and Auntie. And that…' (she pointed to the white trailer) 'that's where my brother Ethan lives. Not the one you met earlier, that was our oldest brother. Ethan is a bit younger, you'll meet him, his wife Amber and little Christopher. Oh, you'll love Christopher!'

'Lovely,' I said, almost to myself – already feeling glad to be here and not at the motel. 'Do your parents live here too?' I asked.

'Oh no, they live about forty-five minutes up the ways. We look after Grannie and Auntie.'

'Oh. How old are Grannie and Auntie?'

'Ooook now, well, let me see…' Katie bit her bottom lip and stared at the floor. 'Grannie just turned 88, and Auntie… well, Auntie would be 98!'

'And you look after them. Just you and Dorena?!'

Katie nodded and gave a simple, distracted, 'Mmmm hmm.' As if it were the most normal thing in the world. 'Oook, look! There's Dorena!'

The door to the blue house was now open and a young woman was standing in the doorway. It had started to get dark and so Dorena was lit by a soft orange glow coming from the kitchen behind her. She waved almost as enthusiastically as her younger sister had done earlier that afternoon, and I waved right back.

Sitting inside at the kitchen table, with a girl I'd known for only three hours, and her older sister whom I'd known for even fewer, I felt strangely at home. It was gone 8 p.m., but Dorena insisted on cooking up a feast for us all. I troughed down pizza, hot chocolate, marshmallows and ice cream, as we three chatted into the wee hours: about religion, family, boys and life growing up in small-town Bison. At 27 years old, Dorena had all the kindness of her little sister, but the air of a mother goose about her. She made it very clear that I could stay with them just as long as I wanted to. At last, something in my heart gave way and I relented. My trip schedule was no match for the kindness of these two. Regardless of whether the blizzard hit tomorrow, I decided that I would spend the following day getting to know the Weichmann sisters a little better. There was a magic about them and their home that filled a void. It nourished me from the inside out. After 92 days on the road, I craved attention, company and genuine affection, and this family was offering it all.

I was up at 6.30 a.m. the following morning and ambled bleary eyed into the kitchen to find Dorena humming and busying herself: chopping fruit and stirring oatmeal on the stove. She spotted me in the hallway and lit up.

'Morning!' she cooed, immediately coming over to give

me a hug. 'How did you sleep?' 'Like a baby,' I replied, emerging from her monster embrace, and it was true. I'd passed out before my head had hit the pillow and woken up dehydrated, without a clue where I was.

That morning I was introduced to the girls' grandma, who joined us for breakfast. I was also led into a bedroom to meet Grandma's older sister, whom the girls called 'Auntie'. After completing the full family introductions, the breakfast chat turned to the weather.

'Is it normal to have a blizzard come through this early in the year?' I asked Dorena. I'd done a lot of research for the trip and thought long and hard about how to weave through the States without being in places where snow was likely to stop progress or make riding dangerous. And yet here I was preparing to hunker down for a blizzard in early October.

'Oh, no,' Dorena replied. 'It's a month or so early. I can't remember the last time we had a blizzard this early in the year. Still. Those winds have blown you here too, so I'm grateful for that.' She grinned.

Did she just actually say that?! This girl was so nice! If there was a way to put the words that came out of Dorena's mouth into a little app on my phone, and play them back to myself on days when I felt lonely and down in the dumps, I would pay good money for that app.

According to the most up-to-date local forecast, snow wasn't due until later in the day, and so we had all agreed that there was more than enough time for me to make a trip into town to talk to kids at the local school about my bike ride through the 50 states. I said I'd pick up some food supplies while in town (it was the least I could do) and the Weichmann sisters kindly offered the use of their car, which I accepted. After the obligatory turning on of the headlights instead of windscreen wipers (high beam, of course), over-revving the engine and trying to drive off with the car in park mode, I eventually got on my way. I dropped into the school for an hour and chatted to the eleventh-grade kids. They were aloof at first, as teenagers tend to be, but eventually I used the two most powerful tools at my disposal to break down the barriers: a strong British accent and disgusting amounts of energy and enthusiasm. Once they opened up, there were the usual, although notably more mature, barrage of questions, plus a few specials – like 'Do you know Bear Grylls?' 'Not personally, no,' I explained and they went on to ask: 'Didn't he row down the River Thames? Naked in a bath tub?' I said that I couldn't be sure if that one was on his list of accomplishments.

When I emerged from the school at 10 a.m., the kids were being sent home early because the blizzard was in its early stages and the skies were already putting in a big snow-shift. I made my way over to the grocery store to pick up the food for the ranch, when Dorena 'big sis' Weichmann called. She was concerned about me making it the 11 miles home safely in the snow, but I assured her that I would drive slowly. She offered some last-ditch advice: 'If you start to slide, don't brake, just slide, okay?' Yikes! I loaded up the car with the food and began the drive back at 20 mph, much to the despair of other motorists, thundering along behind me in their sensible big-tyre trucks.

All was going well(ish) on the drive home. I was starting to lose visibility out of the windscreen, but that didn't matter because I was almost at the big oak tree and the turn off to the ranch. Only, as it happens, trying to find an unfamiliar, unmarked dirt road off a highway when everything is covered in white isn't easy.

'Come on tree, where are you? I know you're here somewhere…' I said aloud, straining to see through the snow-covered windscreen. Five minutes later, my senses kicked in at last, and I knew I'd gone too far. Dammit! I pulled into the nearest layby, from where I proceeded to hail a plethora of other passing road users, including a busload of school kids, who seemed to find my plight rather entertaining. After explaining, 'I'm staying with the Weichmanns', no one could accurately describe where I needed to be, largely because I had no idea where that was, and of course to make matters worse, my phone battery had now died and I couldn't call Dorena, who would no doubt be worried about me by now. I decided that letting Dorena know I was safe was the priority, so I flagged down another passing truck. When it stopped, I saw that it was full of teenagers. They looked far too young to be out and about on their own, and in a blizzard too, but the snow was coming down thick and fast and I didn't have time to start questioning their driving credentials.

'Do any of you have a phone I could borrow?' I shouted, leaning in through the open window to keep my head out of the falling snow and finding five young bemused faces staring back at me.

'Yeah sure, here!' said a dark-haired boy on the back seat, reaching forwards and handing me his phone.

'Perfect, thanks!' I replied, almost snatching it from him. I was a woman on a mission now, and I wanted to get back to the ranch. It was only then that I realised I had no idea what Dorena's number was. But wait! I had the number in my phone! Oh yes, the phone that had run out of battery.

'Idiot!' I said aloud, and the teenagers looked shocked.

'Me, not you! Sorry, it's just… I'm staying with the Weichmanns, but I've missed the turn off to their ranch. Do any of you happen to know where it is?'

'Dorena Weichmann?' came a call from a blonde-haired boy in the back.

'That's the one!' I shouted.

'I think my grandma knows them. Follow us in your car to my grandma's and she'll be able to direct you.'

So I got back in the car and followed them slowly to Grandma's house. The boy was right, and his grandma explained the location of the Weichmann ranch in relation to where I currently was, which was, of course, nowhere near where I had started, and a long way from where I needed to be.

I had reached my limit. I was well and truly done. In the hour since flagging the kids down, the snow had thickened just that bit past sensible (when was this ever sensible?!) and there was no way I was getting back behind the wheel. Instead, I abandoned the car in Grandma's driveway, hoping that someone could come and collect it once the storm had passed, and accepted a ride home from two 14-year-old boys (after discovering that it's legal to drive from 14 in South Dakota). Shopping intact, but with my dignity in tatters, I finally made it 'home' to the Weichmann ranch. By the time I walked through the door, it seemed that the whole Bison community knew there was a girl from London lost in the snow. My face grew redder and redder as Dorena relayed just how many people had been involved in trying to track me down and get me home safely.

As the days rolled by at the Weichmann ranch, the weather showed little sign of letting up. It turned out that the blizzard I was trying to out-pedal was a record-breaker. Four feet of snow fell in just 24 hours and I watched from the living-room window that afternoon as the world around me slowly turned completely white. Through a mixture of visits from icicle-encrusted neighbours, and phone calls and texts from the girls' friends, we learnt that the blizzard had left 22,000 people across the state without power. There were now only two houses in the town of Bison that still had power and, out of sheer luck it seemed, I was sitting in one of them.

An impending power cut was something that really worried the girls. Dorena told me that 98-year-old Auntie relied on an oxygen machine to help her breathe, and that if they lost power they could hook up the emergency oxygen bottle, but that bottle would only last 24 hours. The roads were so thick with snow that making the two-hour drive to collect a new bottle was now an impossibility. Dorena relayed the information to me so matter-of-factly that I marvelled at how calm she was. She just took everything in her stride. At 27 years old, she was without a doubt the head of the family on that ranch, a role she fulfilled with a wisdom beyond her years.

At times, when Auntie came out of her room to perch on the sofa, led by the two sisters, with her oxygen machine trailing behind, I felt uneasy, guilty even. It put the trivial nature of my own journey into stark perspective. Here I was, a fit and healthy, middle-class Londoner, placing an added strain on a family who had a terminally ill 98-year-old to look after. I grappled with the guilt before reminding myself what my mum always told me: 'You know that you're the only one that can make you feel guilty, don't you, Anna?' So I switched my thinking, and reasoned that perhaps I was providing a welcome distraction for the girls at a testing time.

The blizzard raged on for days, and it soon became apparent that the health of their elderly relatives wasn't the girls' only concern. The cattle the family owned were the

Weichmanns' livelihood, and so I soon learned that keeping them safe was a top priority, a priority that I could offer little assistance in, it seemed. As it turned out, I was as useful as a chocolate teapot. Partly because I had no idea how to look after or indeed hunt for escapologist cows, and partly because I slept for most of the first two days. My back ached, I had waves of headaches and sometimes I would be so tired in the afternoons that I'd fall asleep where I was sitting. Often it takes being forced to be still to realise just how exhausted you are. And I was exhausted. Still, in between my bouts of adventure-induced narcolepsy, I did my best to help out by adopting the role of babysitter-in-residence for the littlest member of the family, 18-month-old Christopher. For days I excelled in the fine art of cooing, throwing myself on the floor, and playing peek-a-boo.

Around babysitting duties and sleeping, I spent my days at the ranch catching up on blog writing, watching old movies and trying to arrange the next set of school talks in the states that would follow South Dakota. Being so relaxed and so still, with the storm unfolding around me, I had time to really observe what life was like for Dorena, who was quite the real-life cow girl.

On one particular day, I woke from an afternoon nap to hear Katie on the phone in the kitchen.

'Well, okay. You take care now… no, no, Auntie's fine. You just stay warm out there.' She hung up just as I came into the kitchen.

'Everything okay?' I asked.

'Oh! Anna! Yes, yes, all fine!' she said, spinning around and delivering a hug. 'The tractor just broke down that's all. Dorena and Ethan were out looking for some of the cows that escaped – one of the other farmers said he saw several of ours out on the road this morning. He even said he saw one in the crik!'

'Oh… that's not good. Errr, what's a crik?' I asked, and Katie looked confused.

'You know, a crik. Where the water goes…'

'Like a type of rain-funnel device?' I said, now imagining that a cow had fallen into some kind of metal contraption designed to collect rain water on the farm.

'No, no… a crik – like a river?' Katie said.

'Oh, you mean a creek?!'

'Sure! That's what I said, the cow's fallen in the crik!'

I still couldn't get used to their thick South Dakotan accents, and I laughed. I'm not sure Katie knew what I was laughing at, but she smiled anyway, as usual.

'Well, they've got a three-mile hike home through the snow now. It'll be a while before they're back, I'll bet,' she continued.

That was the first of two occasions when Dorena and

Ethan had to abandon a vehicle in the snow and hike the remaining miles home. Cold, dehydrated and famished, Dorena would tumble through the door and, following a three-minute sit-down, promptly begin cooking dinner, doing the washing and checking on Auntie and Grannie. When Dorena was at home during the day, a new smell would waft from the stove every few hours: potato soup, pulled pork, roast chicken, home-baked bread, cookies. I never went hungry and not once did I see the girls stop smiling. I began to wonder if they were putting on a brave face for me, but I came to realise that their default was to smile and carry on. The Weichmanns' home managed to maintain power through the storm, and despite it claiming the lives of 14,000 cattle across the state, thanks to their dedication, Ethan and the girls only lost one of theirs.

On the evening of my fourth day at the ranch, I was rested but restless. The snow had stopped falling at last, and so I trudged the half mile up to the main highway to check on the state of the roads. Although the white stuff was still piled well over head-height at the sides of the highway, I found what I was looking for: tarmac. The snow ploughs had made it out and I now had a clear passage out of town.

I was treated to one final dinner at the Weichmann ranch, and by this point the girls really felt like sisters to me. I'd never had a sister, after all. Well, when I was growing up I tried to claim that my beloved black cat Smokey was my sister, but I'm not sure that really counted. She was a little furrier than sisters should be.

Over a meal of steaming bowls of stew and potatoes, the girls told me about a church mission trip they'd once taken to India. They said that it'd been a dream of theirs to go, and that members of the Bison community had clubbed together to pay for the remaining cost of tickets. It was the trip of a lifetime, Dorena said. I got an overwhelming sense that the Weichmann sisters would never take more from the world than they felt they deserved. The trip to India had brought them so much happiness that it would be someone else in the community's turn to travel now, and they would support them too.

The following morning, I filled up on pancakes, sausages, porridge and fruit at the breakfast table. I repacked my panniers and threw in a small bag of home-baked cookies before turning to hug the Weichmann sisters one last time.

'Dorena,' I said. 'You are an angel. Thanks for feeding me up. I think I'm a few kilos heavier you know! Look after yourself and let me know when you make it to London.' I then turned to her sister.

'Katie – keep smiling and keep stopping strangers from Britain and inviting them home for tea,' I said. She nodded.

I thanked them again then looked past them at the ranch, at the dogs playing out the front, and Grannie standing in the doorway. I looked at the snow still covering every surface and little Christopher in Katie's arms. I wheeled slowly away with a lump in my throat and an empty feeling in the pit of my stomach. The reality was that I might never see this family again. And even if I did, it'd be years from now. The relief to be on the move again was coupled with deep sadness and an overwhelming sense of gratitude. The Weichmanns truly felt like my family – only a family could still accept someone who would abandon their car, eat them out of house and home and sleep all the hours god sent. Wasn't life grand? Just when I'd needed it most, the world had thrown the Weichmanns in my path.

NORTH DAKOTA

MINNESOTA

MINNESOTA

WISCONSIN

MICHIGAN

NORTH DAKOTA

SOUTH DAKOTA

SAINT CLOUD

MINNEAPOLIS

ROCHESTER

SOUTH DAKOTA

NEBRASKA

SIOUX FALLS

MILWAUKE

SIOUX CITY

CHICAGO

OMAHA

IOWA
ILLINOIS

IOWA

MISSOURI

KEARNEY

NEBRASKA

KANSAS

THE MIDWEST

11
Adventure's Revolving Door

Distance Cycled: 5,378 miles
States Completed: 14

I flicked open my phone and pulled up a text from Dorena, which read: 'Ron and Elaine live in a brown wooden house with decking out front. There are only three houses in the town. You should be able to find them.'

I had ridden 40 miles east since leaving the Weichmann ranch in Bison, and had now arrived on the outskirts of the small town of Glad Valley (although considering that Dorena had said it was a town with only three houses, I wondered if it was 'allowed' to be called a town? Perhaps a townette would be more fitting). The blizzard had long since passed now and the skies were the most brilliant shade of blue, but still I had decided to take it easy on my first day back on the road.

Every part of my head was telling me to get going and crack out the miles early on and to get ahead of the game while the weather was good. But my gut and heart had other ideas. I was a rolling stone that had come to a halt in Bison. I was overcome with a sense that I didn't want to move too quickly away from the Weichmann family, for fear that I might tear the fragile memories made there, and that they would be lost forever. In reality, I knew it would take me a bit of time to get going again, so I decided that a stop-off with some friends of the Weichmanns in Glad Valley was a nice way to ease my mind and body back into life on the road. And besides, how could I pass up an opportunity to find out what life was like in a townette with three houses?!

Wheeling on into the townette, I passed a white building on my left and spotted a brown wooden house. I pulled on my brakes and stood astride my bike at the end of the rough gravelled driveway of that house and surveyed the scene, trying to match what was in front of me with Dorena's description. The house was two storey, but wide like a bungalow, with decking running all along the front and a split-level staircase to the right-hand side. To the left of the house were two barns. One was larger with grey corrugated doors that were shut, and the other was an open barn, where I could see hay bales stacked up high and odds and ends of farming equipment. Next to the smaller barn was a sty surrounded by metal railings with a Jersey cow inside, merrily going about her business. This had to be the spot.

I set off down the gravel driveway towards the house, walking my bike alongside me, and was greeted by a barking, bounding Labrador. He dashed from the house and began going nuts as only dogs can do at the arrival of a stranger. He bounced around like a pinball in an arcade game, from me, to the floor, to the railings of the sty, back to me. I heard the front door to the house swing open and I looked up to see a man with a grey beard standing on the decking. He was clad in black welly boots, beige corduroy trousers and a blue top.

'Beau! Beau! Calm down, calm down. It's our guest!' the man hollered, addressing the dog and doing his best to calm the Labrador tornado I was now encased in. He needn't have worried. Beau and I had by now formed a strong bond. I bent down and let him sniff me for a moment, and we progressed to face-licking. It was official; I was in. I stood upright again, my face now coated in slobber, and smiled at the man.

'You must be Anna,' he chuckled, enveloping me in a hug.

'And you must be Ron,' I grinned, hugging him back before following him up the stairs and inside.

Before long I was inside, sitting on the sofa, chatting to Ron and Elaine about how they once ran an organic grocery business in Ohio.

'So what happened to the grocery store?' I asked Elaine.

'Oh, we sold it and decided to move to the middle of nowhere,' she grinned. 'Do you know how much this place cost?' she continued.

I looked around. It was such a lovely home. Although the property had to be a little better value out here, way up in 'the boonies', as they called it, I needed to make a more informed decision.

'How many bedrooms are there?' I asked.

'Just two.'

'Bathrooms?'

'Two.'

'Garage?'

'Space for one car and a tractor.' Elaine grinned.

'How far is it to the nearest shop?'

'Fifty miles.'

Hmmmm. I thought a little before offering, 'Sixty thousand dollars?'

'A little less,' Elaine replied, smiling.

'Fifty thousand?'

'Less.'

'Forty thousand?'

'Less.'

'Thirty thousand?'

Elaine shook her head.

'Twenty thousand?'

She smiled again and motioned downwards with her finger.

'Less?!' I asked, now incredulous at this never-ending game of Bruce Forsyth's *Play Your Cards Right*.

'Eight thousand dollars,' said Elaine at last, and I nearly fell off of the couch.

'You bought this house for eight thousand dollars?!'

'We did indeed. Although it wasn't quite so nice when we bought it. A wreck of place, really…'

Elaine went on to explain that she hadn't even seen the house before they bought it. She had seen it for sale online, and knew her son was due to pass through South Dakota on business, so she had asked him to go and check it out for her.

'He called me when he was at the house and I said to him, "Go and give the walls a good hard kick. From the outside. And tell me if the house is still standing when you're done?!" The house was still standing when he was done, so that was that. I said we'd take it and one month later we packed up from Ohio and moved out here.'

I was still in awe of the couple's spontaneity and deep in thought as to whether I would do such a thing, when Ron announced that he needed to go out and tend to his property business for the afternoon. I remained sitting on the sofa, chatting with Elaine. We drank tea and spoke about their quiet life in Glad Valley.

'Is Glad Valley famous for anything?' I asked on the off-chance, keen to learn a little more about the history of the place.

'Hmm, not really…' Elaine started to reply, before

seemingly remembering something important. 'Oh, now then, actually, come to think of it – I do know this: it is the town in the entire lower forty-eight states that is the furthest, in distance, from a McDonald's.'

I nearly spat out my tea.

'Really?! That is a fantastic claim! Isn't that something?!'

Now she mentioned it, I hadn't seen a McDonald's for at least five days on the ride here, and that was a revelation.

Elaine talked to me about her plans to start an organic farming blog, but also how, before she could do that, she needed her study moved back upstairs, and all the pantry moved downstairs. She said Ron would get to it, just as soon as he had the time. It was at times like this that I hated having imposed the 50-state challenge and a six-month visa restriction upon myself. I wished I could have stayed a day longer and helped Elaine move her study upstairs, and soak up their wisdom, but I still had a long way to go and the visa clock was ticking.

As I loaded my panniers onto the bike the following morning, I gave Ron and Beau the last hugs goodbye. I rattled off goodbyes to the wild barn cats one by one and turned to wave at Elaine in the doorway.

'Say, Anna, won't you come back some day? We'd teach you how to ride a tractor, become a real cowgirl,' she called to me.

'I would absolutely love that,' I called back, beaming from

ear to ear. And I meant it.

I hoped that one day I'd be like Ron and Elaine and have the guts to go in search of life at a slower place. I envied them for the simple and rewarding life they'd chosen. For having the balls to say 'thanks but no thanks' to the city rat race. I wondered if I would go back to London and be brave enough to make the decision to do that too. I didn't think I was there yet. I was certainly ready to own ten cats and live a long way from a McDonald's, but I couldn't be entirely sure that I'd cope without at least a corner shop somewhere nearby.

***

It was a crisp, clear October morning when I rolled out of Glad Valley. The vast expanse of sky on the road ahead was bright blue, the sun was shining and there were just the faintest smudges of clouds on the horizon. If it weren't for the piles of snow still lining the highway, I might have thought that the blizzard was something I'd imagined entirely. That morning over breakfast, I'd picked up a message from the local newspaper in the neighbouring town of Isabel. They asked if I would swing by for an interview and a chat, so I popped into the modest press office on my way through. After leaving the interview, I went across the road to the post office to send a letter back home to the UK. Spotting the cycling helmet in my hand, and after surveying my Lycra-clad frame, the lady behind the counter asked, 'Oh, are you that young girl from

London, on a bicycle? We've heard all about you here! I hear you stayed with the Weichmanns through the blizzard?'

I was stopped by several others as I left Isabel, asking for pictures of the girl from London on her 50-state ride. It seems that news of my presence in the state had spread faster than the ABC on *Sesame Street*. The following day Ron and Elaine sent me a picture of the local newspaper – I had made the front page.

It was then that I realised my journey through South Dakota had begun to take on a life of its own. I was no longer dragging myself through the long days on lonely windswept roads, but instead I was being propelled from one sunset to the next. I came to realise that my stay at the Weichmann ranch had caused something about the rhythm and flow of the 50-state journey to change at a fundamental level. In that blizzard, there had been a cosmic shift in the bicycle universe and everything now felt different, somehow. As I continued to pedal east, the Weichmanns continued to call ahead of me, finding hosts to take me in from the cold for the night, and those hosts began to do the same too. They had set off a chain reaction, one that was entirely out of my control, but I was game for the ride.

In a house overlooking the mighty Missouri River in Mobridge, I stayed with Darrell and Francis, before being passed to more friends of the Weichmanns in the town of St Pierre. There I enjoyed an evening with Maggie and Jerry. And when Jerry got out his pet rattlesnake for me to touch, I almost soiled myself with fear. From there, I moved on to Chamberlain, where I visited adventurous single mum Jess.

The following day I was bound for the town of Mitchell, battling 60-mph crosswinds, which caused me to weave and swerve down the shoulder of the highway. I decided to pull into a roadside diner and eat a stack of pancakes in a bid to weigh me down and make me immovable in the wind (it was the only logical solution). When I set off again, the headwind had swung around to a tailwind and I was catapulted towards the town of Mitchell at breakneck speed.

In Mitchell, I was hosted by wine connoisseur, bicycle enthusiast and grandpa-cum-bachelor Jim – a gentle giant of a man who oozed charisma, had a twinkle in his eye and knew all the names of the local waitresses. During my time with Jim, we talked about previous guests he'd had stay with him over the years and I wondered what tale Jim would tell others of me when I was gone. He asked if it bothered me that I was female and staying in a single man's home, and went on to tell me that the last lone female he hosted promptly informed him that she slept with a can of mace. I told him I had a can of mace too, but that I wasn't really getting the vibe that he was a serial killer, so I was feeling okay. We laughed and chatted long into the night.

I pedalled out of Mitchell, marvelling at the glory of the world-famous Mitchell corn palace (a giant palace, covered in coloured corn) before dropping across the border line to cycle through state number 15, Nebraska, for a whopping 30 minutes. I had originally intended to be in Nebraska for longer, but due to the new route I'd taken to try to out-cycle the blizzard, there was only time for a brief hello and goodbye with the state. Closely rivalling the 37 minutes spent in Idaho, Nebraska became a contender for the shortest time spent in any of the states. Crossing back into South Dakota for a final night, I was hosted by Jim's friends Lee and Mary Ore, who fed me pizza, taught me the complex rules of American football and made me an honorary Minnesota Vikings fan. They showered me with gifts in the team's colours of purple, white and yellow and gave me a Viking pendant to make it official.

I pushed on for the next 100 miles and crossed into state number 16, Iowa, pedalling in strong gusts of crosswind past rows and rows (and rows) of cornfields. I was made acutely aware that I had never really thought about where the world's corn comes from, until now. It had to be Iowa. Whenever someone asks me what I remember about Iowa, it is mostly the cornfields. They were a source of mind-numbing frustration that week, but there was also something strangely meditative about being among them. The landscape rarely changed. There was nothing to look at, nothing to see and so it was just me, my thoughts and the corn for most of it. I also discovered that cornfields are very practical places to go for a pee, the corn providing a very nice coat stand to hang my clothing on while I did my business.

***

Over the course of that week, the temperature began to plummet and, having not yet picked up my winter clothing (which was waiting for me in Chicago), I battled with the elements as I danced eastwards along the border that separates Iowa from Minnesota to the north. One day, I set out planning to ride 120 miles in freezing rain and ended up soaked to the skin and verging on hypothermic, before locating a hotel just across the Minnesotan border to take some respite after 50 miles. I vowed never to let myself get in such a state again.

Just nine days after leaving the Weichmanns in South Dakota, I had clocked up 800 miles on Boudica and passed through three states. Now I found myself back in Iowa, on the shores of a living, breathing part of American history: the Mississippi River. I have always considered the Mississippi to be synonymous with adventure. Even trying to spell it transports me to the most far-flung corners of my brain as I grapple with Ps and Is and an abundance of Ss. At the mere mention of its name, my mind floods with childhood follies, thoughts of *Huckleberry Finn* and Mark Twain's colourful depiction of the characters that line its shores. To see it that day for the first time felt like meeting an old friend. There was a familiarity about the Mississippi, coupled with excitement at seeing it in the flesh. I knew that this encounter with the mighty Mississippi would be brief – I was only crossing it after all – but I also knew that I would get a chance to see it again as I pedalled across the southern states, later in the year. For the time being, however, I was determined to soak up every last detail of the river, so I stopped for a while on the bridge, just outside the town of Marquette.

Fall was in full swing and the Mississippi looked glorious. Her meandering banks were dripping with colour – the most spectacular golds, oranges, yellows and reds, tripping over one another, scrambling and tumbling down bluffs into the waters below. I was struck by how brown the water was – I'd always thought that the Mississippi might be a very green river, but that day it was definitely brown. A sea of brown, broken only by swirls of white where the current was strong. The bridge passed over an island in the middle, clad in more autumn colours and flanked by sandy shores leading to the river. I knew that I was seeing a part of the Mississippi that was relatively narrow compared to its width further south in Louisiana, but still it seemed so violent and wild.

Across the other side of the Mississippi River, in the next state of Wisconsin, I spent a few nights in the city of Madison, where I stayed with local bike enthusiast Sally, who was a member of the WarmShowers cycle-touring hosting network. Over dinner at a local restaurant, she told me that I was her first WarmShowers guest. I felt honoured, but I also had a sense of duty to show her that we travelling cyclists were a decent sort. Sally and I got on like a house on fire and, over a veggie burger, we chatted and laughed, talking about her own past adventures in Africa and the importance of following dreams. We high-fived across the table, much to the delight of our waitress. On the walk home, Sally casually dropped in that she'd be going away for the weekend, but I needn't worry. She said that she'd just leave me a key, and that I should make myself right at home. I did just that. I took a day off to give a talk to a group of teenagers at a local bike store – they were kids from tough backgrounds who were being trained up as store mechanics in the hope that it might change the direction of their future. It was a talk which I'd arranged with the store six months before leaving the UK. The kids were brilliant – bright, funny, inquisitive – and the store owner was surprised that I'd managed to arrive on the precise date and time that I'd said I would. It was moments like these which filled me with a deep sense of satisfaction. It went some way towards justifying all those days when I'd had to move swiftly on, or cut the 50-state route shorter, just to make sure I stayed on schedule.

After the morning talk, I spent much of that afternoon ambling around the grid-like streets of Madison. I wandered across town, from the shores of Lake Mendota to Lake Monona, stopping to look at the dome of the Wisconsin State Capitol building, which marks the halfway point between the two lakes, and the centre of the city. I took the time to explore the many local independent coffee shops, getting gradually more caffeinated as late afternoon gave way to early evening. I sat on benches on the shores of the first and then the second lake, each time with a coffee in hand, enjoying the autumnal colours – a patchwork of orange, yellow and green dancing across the blue-green waters. With no worry of where I would be staying that night (Sally had taken care of that one), I was out way past my usual bedtime, watching the greens and golds of the trees turn to purples, reds and blues as the city lights were cast across the water.

After leaving Madison, I spent my final night in the state of Wisconsin with the nephew of a family friend from back home. They said they had an extra special treat for me, and onto the dinner table came mashed potato, sausages, gravy and Yorkshire puddings – real big, fat, gravy-boat-style Yorkshires – all of which was washed down with a can of thick, syrupy Guinness. After four months away from England's green and pleasant land, I reflected on how strange it was when the journey became peppered with moments like these – moments in which I became just a normal dinner guest around a table on an average Friday night.

As I pedalled away from the Yorkshire puddings and towards the Illinois border, I thought about all the people I'd met since leaving the Weichmann ranch two weeks earlier. All that home-hopping from one new house to another seemed a world away from the deserted roads of Nevada and the vast open plains of Wyoming. People, faces, families entered and exited through adventure's revolving door. Time passed slowly when I was with each family, immersed in the normality of their daily life. Small talk went out the window and we skipped straight to the good stuff. Hopes, dreams, values, beliefs – we talked about things that were important to us, we spoke human to human. It felt like I had known each of them for a lifetime, but before too long they were leaving my life again, our time together that much more precious because it was so brief.

My thoughts turned to the type of landscapes that lay ahead, and I thought about the big cities of Chicago, Boston, New York and Washington DC still to come. I realised that the west of the USA was about the wide-open spaces. It centred on the beauty of the national parks, mountain ranges, the small towns and strange characters. Having been hosted by different families for 13 of the 14 nights since leaving the Weichmanns, I was starting to get a sense that the east of the US would be more about the people.

PART II

CHICAGO

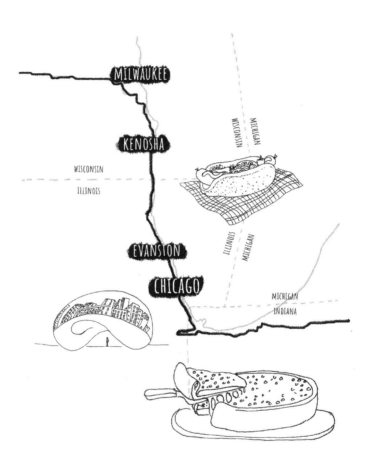

MILWAUKEE

KENOSHA

WISCONSIN
ILLINOIS

MICHIGAN
WISCONSIN

EVANSTON

CHICAGO

ILLINOIS
MICHIGAN

MICHIGAN
INDIANA

12

A Week in the Windy City

Distance Cycled: 6,390 miles
States Completed: 18

It is a truth universally acknowledged that if you find yourself within a 40-mile radius of the city of Chicago, you must eat nothing but deep-dish pizza. The phenomenon I began to call 'deep-dish radius' began as far out as the small suburb of Lake Forest. Here I stopped for a few nights to pay a visit to the local elementary school, stay with a friend of a friend from home and have my first taste of deep-dish pizza.

This local speciality is characterised by a thick doughy base with inch-high crusts that surround a gooey mozzarella centre, resembling something like a freestanding back-garden swimming pool. And the mozzarella is just the start, for a Chicago-style pizza is one in which the tomato sauce is liberated. No longer cowering under a blanket of cheese, it spreads itself proudly on top. Yes, *on top* of the cheese. The result is a sculpture more akin to a baked Camembert than a pizza, and from the moment its soft, melty, salty, tomatoey melange touched my lips, I was in love.

Full of deep dish and with calories to burn, I set off in search of my next fix. I briefly nipped down to the town of

New Lenox to spend an evening with US Olympic cycling legend John Vande Velde and his son Christian, who had just retired from 15 years spent as a pro on the world tour circuit – no big deal. I'd been put in touch with John thanks to a friend of a friend, and I couldn't quite believe that he'd agreed to meet me, let alone have me stay with him for a night. They fed me up on more deep-dish pizza and set my energy levels at an all-time high, preparing me for a few days of culture in the city.

I was grateful for the chance to be stationary for a few days in Chicago, although I had found that periods of rest on the journey so far were a double-edged sword. There always seemed to be an inexplicable unease about being still, hanging over me like a haze.

'You haven't made it yet, Anna. It's not over. Don't relax too much,' a soft voice would whisper as I tried to take afternoon naps, sleep in and do nothing much at all. Oh, how I longed to dispense with those thoughts and just be able to relax, but I accepted that they were a cross to bear. Part and parcel of taking on a large challenge, with the path to success not always being in your control.

Beyond these thoughts, there was something more physical that bugged me when I took a few days off the bike, and that is I felt terrible. I mean, truly awful. When I stopped cycling for more than a day, I'd wake up with pounding headaches and a raspy throat. Despite having not drunk a drop of alcohol, I would feel hungover and spend much of the day trying to keep my eyes open. Still, I knew I needed a rest in Chicago, and so I stored thoughts of the challenge and the anxieties that came with it in the garage along with Boudica, and I set about seeing what Chicago had to offer me.

On my first day in the city, I met a girlfriend who was flying in from New York. Well, I say girlfriend; she is more like a sister. She is my brother's wife's sister. It's complicated, I know. We need a diagram. Let's just say she's my sister-from-another-mister, and she's called Annabel-Zoe. I met Annabel-Zoe in a small downtown café, and together we spent three days resting, sight-seeing and celebrating my 28th birthday – a momentous occasion which had actually fallen the previous week. Initially, it took a while to settle into the hustle and bustle of city life. It felt strange to be sitting in the window of a coffee shop, watching the hordes of people stream by and knowing that just a few weeks earlier I'd spent 400 miles cycling through nothing but cornfields. There were times when I felt ill at odds surrounded by so many people, like a square peg trying to fit into a round hole. In those miles upon miles on the open road, I had changed. Cities felt more crowded than they used to. The noises were louder, everyone seemed to be going somewhere, and intent on getting there in a hurry.

As day broke on the second morning in the Windy City, Annabel-Zoe and I set about fulfilling our tourist duties. We dashed straight to Millennium Park, and to the highlight of Chicago's modern art – *The Bean*. I'd been pre-warned that this was a prime tourist spot, where out-of-towners amuse themselves by taking ludicrous shots of their grinning faces reflected in its shiny surface. I had naturally promised myself that I wouldn't engage in such juvenile behaviour. What a fool I was. One should never underestimate the power of a giant silver bean. I soon discovered that there is something irresistible about seeing the city mirrored at odd angles in an oversized haricot. We spent 30 minutes giggling and snorting like school children, executing the obligatory array of inventive poses before mixing up our Chicago diet by heading for a Chicago-style hot dog, a well-dressed frankfurter garnished with mustard, onions, pickle relish, a gherkin, tomatoes and a dash of celery salt. Basically, the hot dog is the least important part of a Chicago-style hot dog. It's all about the accessories.

Bean duties fulfilled and hot dogs consumed, I set about reading more about the Windy City and learned that like many great cities around the globe, Chicago has a river running through it. Only, Chicago's waterway has a dark secret – it actually used to run in the opposite direction. You what?! My thoughts entirely. When storms raged, the flood waters from the river used to push sewage into the lake, up to 'cribs', which collected the city's drinking water. In a bid to rid Lake Michigan of waterborne diseases (like cholera, for example), a few civil engineering bright sparks set about reversing the flow of the Chicago River in 1887. It hurt my brain, trying to understand how they managed to pull off such a feat of engineering, but here's how they did it: they built a 28-mile-long canal, which diverted the river water away from the lake and east, towards the Des Plaines River instead. Genius! The whole project was a major success. Well, it was a success for everyone apart from the residents in the now downstream cities, such as St Louis and Illinois, who received a flow of watery Chicago poop where there had been no poop before. Love thy neighbour? Nothing says love like the gift of raw sewage.

As if feats of engineering and lessons in sewage mastery weren't enough, Annabel-Zoe had decided that in order to fully immerse ourselves in the history of Chicago, we should take an architectural boat tour. Bobbling around on an open-topped boat in the middle of the city, the tour guide with the microphone (we named him 'Mike on the Mic') told us about the history of Chicago's impressive buildings. We learned that in 1871, a 'great fire' caused 6 square miles of destruction in Downtown. Bad news indeed, but like a grimy phoenix, and with the aid of famous architects from around the globe, a new Chicago rose from the flames. Architects flocked to the now blank city-canvas in a bid to leave their mark. They proceeded to fill the city with the most spectacular buildings, spanning a range of styles – the Gothic-style Tribune Tower, the art deco Merchandise Mart (my personal fave), the curvy, groovy Marina City (which looks like a series of records stacked on top of one another), the Wrigley Building (which is sadly not shaped like an oversized packet of chewing gum) and, by far the most famous, the 442-metre-high Sears Tower, once the tallest building in the world. There was something special about seeing these buildings from the water, an uninterrupted view of each of them as we glided gracefully by.

On the final night in town, I cashed in what was a birthday treat sent from my brothers in the UK – dinner at the Sky Deck in the Sears (now renamed, Willis) Tower. For some bizarre reason, no one else had booked dinner on the Sky Deck that night. So, at a tourist attraction that has 1.3 million visitors per year, Annabel-Zoe and I had the entire deck to ourselves. Talk about million-dollar dinner dining! We filled our faces with more Chicago-style pizza (because it had been at least 12 hours since I had last eaten any) and sipped on root beer. All the while, I looked out onto a grid of streetlights, headlights and tail lights, ambers, reds and white streaking and stretching into a never-ending dark night sky. I knew that tonight was my last night in the city and I had grown fond of Chicago. I felt like I'd really got under the skin of the place. I'd immersed myself in its history, culture and architecture – all things that were a welcome change from the monotony of the road and the recent flat landscapes of the Midwest. I knew I wouldn't have explored so much of it, or perhaps stopped so long, if I hadn't had Annabel-Zoe by my side, and for that I was grateful. Toasting our root beers and grappling with the last gooey pieces of mozzarella clinging to my chin, I felt refreshed. My mind was clear and my veins were full of deep-dish – I was ready for the road again.

FALL

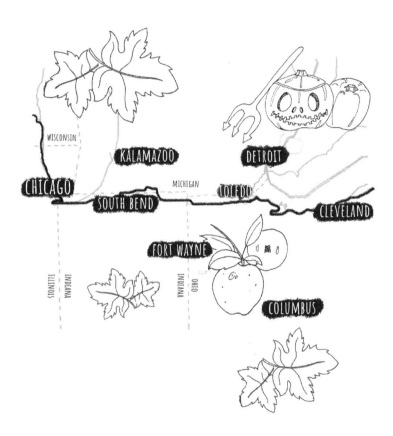

WISCONSIN

KALAMAZOO

DETROIT

CHICAGO

MICHIGAN

TOLEDO

SOUTH BEND

CLEVELAND

FORT WAYNE

ILLINOIS

INDIANA

INDIANA

OHIO

COLUMBUS

13

Falltum

Distance Cycled: 6,460 miles

States Completed: 19

It was daybreak in Illinois and the streets of Chicago were bathed in an early morning light. The skies glowed a soft shade of amber, as if someone had lit a fire just beyond the horizon. Now behind me were the skyscrapers, towers and spires that had kept me so entertained for the past few days. They cut striking black silhouettes against a golden sky, as stray rays of dawn light bounced between the buildings with mirrored glass on their upper floors.

I'd left Annabel-Zoe sleeping and managed to catch the city off-guard, just before it woke up. I've always found there to be a beauty to a city just as dawn breaks. There's something about the usually untouchable concrete heart of a metropolis, coated in layers of traffic, smog and noise, that seems exposed in the early morning. Vulnerable even. Like the moment you catch a busy mother resting her eyes as her newborn sleeps.

I followed a bike path along the shores of Lake Michigan, looking out on waters which had been whipped into a frenzy over the past week, and were now glass-like, as if they were reflecting the morning mood of the city. As I neared the southern end of the lake, I passed through the suburb of Jackson Park, and all of a sudden, I found that I was no longer alone – groups of cyclists began appearing from every direction, until I was swept up in a wave of wheels. Just as I was preparing to ask a fellow cyclist what was going on, a woman at the side of the road flagged me down. She had a notebook in her hand (just like in the movies) and a man with a large camera at her side. I pulled up next to her, and she pounced.

'How are you finding the new bike path today?' she asked, launching into her questions straight away.

'Err, this? It's great… I mean.' It was no good. I couldn't style it out. I fessed up. 'Is it new?!'

The woman looked confused. She cocked her head sideways; her fringe lifted momentarily by a passing gust of wind, revealing a furrowed top brow and a forehead crumpled like a sheet of paper about to be thrown into a waste bin.

'So, you didn't know that today is the day they opened this bike path?'

'Errr, no. I'm just leaving town and followed the lake…'

'Huh!' she said. 'Fabulous,' she continued, in a wonderful Chicagoan drawl.

'Was this not open yesterday?'

'No! Today is the first day this bike path has been open. City cyclists have been campaigning for it for years, which is why there are so many out here today.'

'Oh, great!' I replied, thinking that I was quite the lucky duck.

'So, you're not from Chicago?'

'Oh no. I'm from England.'

'Where are you headed?'

'Oh, umm… Michigan, then Ohio, then Pennsylvania, New York… I'm, um, riding through all fifty states.'

'Are you serious?' the reporter exclaimed, and I nodded. 'And you just happened to be here today?' I nodded again.

'Fabulous. Well, I'm from the *Chicago Tribune*. Can we take a quote from you for the paper?'

The next five minutes were filled with very excited chatter about how lovely it was to have a traffic-free cycle path to cycle on out of the city, how much I loved Chicago's architecture and the USA in general, and why I think more people should ride bicycles. I pedalled off feeling as high as a kite, fuelled by a love of cycling, and towards the town of Gary.

Gary was one of those places that intrigued me. My best friend at primary school had been called Gary. In fact, from the ages of 5 to 11, Gary and I were inseparable. Inseparable that was until I went to an all-girls secondary school and Gary went to the local mixed comprehensive. He popped up on my Facebook feed every now and then, and seemed to have been doing an awful lot of pumping iron in the gym since leaving the gates of Grand Avenue Primary. That, and spending a lot of time in Ibiza. Gary and I had grown apart.

But this Gary was a whole different ball game. I was fascinated to find that whenever I was asked to share details of my route, even when I was way out in Washington state, people would say, nine times out of ten, 'Oh, you're not planning on going through Gary, are you?' When my response was a firm yes, or rather a yes where I went up at the end like a question, the question poser would perform that windy face and sharp inhalation of breath. The sort of face one might pull when you see someone walk into a glass door. There was some grounding in their concern. In 1994, the *Chicago Tribune* ran a story which proclaimed that 'Gary takes over as the murder capital of the USA' as 'the city of 119,125 had a record 110 killings in 1993, translating into a murder rate of 91 per 100,000 residents'. Putting that next to the neighbouring city of Chicago, which had a murder rate that year of just 30.6 per 100,000, Chicago looked like a crime pussycat.

I rolled tentatively across the Illinois–Indiana state line, into state number 19 of the journey and into the outskirts of the infamous Gary. Because of its location right on the shores of Lake Michigan, there was no way 'around' the town. Well, not short of a gigantic detour south anyway, and besides, there was a magnetic pull which was drawing me to it. A fascination with a place that everyone in the US seemed to believe was so deadly, I couldn't help but want to find out for myself. At the corner of the street which marked the threshold into the town, I took a deep breath. I was caught between wanting to look at everything around me and keeping my eyes fixed firmly ahead.

I spent 20 minutes travelling through the town, trying to stay on the main roads where possible. I felt mildly uncomfortable, but it's always difficult in these situations to separate which fears are real and which are imagined. I certainly wasn't facing any real fears, only those in my head, but those types of fears often seemed bigger than the real ones and they were enough to fuel me with adrenaline. I cycled past gigantic industrial plants. Large blue metal buildings were punctuated by rusty towering machines next to steaming silver pipes, intertwined like an elaborate doodle someone might make during a particularly boring business meeting. Every now and then I'd catch a glimpse through a metal fence of a person somewhere in the midst of the smoke. Hard hat on head, headphones on, somewhere halfway up a precarious-looking tower and partly obscured by the incessant production of smoke. *How can they work in all the noise?* I wondered. In one sense the town was alive, alive with the noise and sights of a manufacturing industry that supported it, but in another sense, it felt entirely dead. As if it were the machines that were alive, overshadowing the presence of the humans who lived there.

Having managed not to melt under the weight of an overloaded imagination and to 'survive' Gary, I ground back into long days in the saddle. My strategy was to eat up as many miles as possible across the Midwest, making the most of flat land before I hit the mountains of New England. I chunked out days of 113 miles, 104 miles, 107 miles… and to my

delight I found that I could stay off the main highways by following farm tracks.

The farm tracks were laid out in a grid-like fashion, fenc-
ing in the surrounding cornfields. Most were called 120, 122,
121A, or similar, and they would switch between tarmac and
sand or gravel at a moment's notice, so choosing the 'best
route' became a lottery. It was always a gamble as to whether
I stayed on the path I'd chosen or went in search of the next
turning, hoping it might offer some smoother, faster riding. It
reminded me a lot of the fantasy 'choose your own adventure'
books I used to read as a kid, most of them by Ian Livingston.
These books had titles such as *The Warlock of Firetop Mountain*
and *The Forest of Doom*. On reading them, you were taken on
an adventure through the pages, but you had to choose between one course of action or another every few pages, which
may or may not have ended in your death. I'd always cheat
by keeping my finger in the page where I'd made the original
decision, just in case I met an awful end with an evil beast and
needed to return and change my decision. Alas, there was no
such option on these farm roads, but at least there were no
beasts waiting to gobble me up either.

I wound my way from one small suburb to the next and
had a great run of luck with WarmShowers hosts, before hop-
ping over the border into state number 20, Michigan. It was
a brief visit, and I vowed to come back one day to pay my
respects to the intriguingly named Wolverine state. Crossing
back into Indiana, I pedalled my way to the home of a woman

named Lou-Ann in the town of Angola, Indiana. Lou-Ann's profile on Warmshowers.org had made me smile as it described how she lived in a historic 100-year-old house, liked to hang her laundry out in the sunshine, and how her home was often full of music and theatre folk.

In between contacting Lou-Ann and arriving at her house, I had managed to lose her number and so hadn't been able to update her on my time of arrival. When I arrived at her house in the middle of the afternoon and knocked, I found that there was no one home. A neighbour called to me from across the street.

'Are you waiting on Lou-Ann?' I nodded. 'Oh, she's out at a party! Go ahead and let yourself in, I'm sure she'll be along.'

The neighbour came over, introduced himself as Lee, and helped me put my bike in the garage before showing me inside the house. Twenty minutes later I was sitting on the sofa in a living room of a woman whom I'd never met. I had gotten her number from Lee the neighbour and so I sent Lou-Ann a text.

'Hi Lou-Ann. Anna the British girl here. Lee let me in, I'm sitting on your couch. Hope that's okay! See you soon.' A reply came straight back. 'Am out gallivanting. Back soon!'. Gallivanting, now that was something that everyone should do a little more of.

Lou-Ann's delay in joining me gave me a chance to inspect her home. It was brimming with trinkets, theatre posters, instruments and photos and was, needless to say, a 'real' home. It had a personality, as opposed to simply being a physical space. There was a 'welcome wall' with quotes and signatures from previous guests – something that made me feel as if I were creating a little piece of history, just by crossing the threshold.

Lou-Ann returned an hour later and tumbled through the door. I think tumbled is the best description of it. She was a whirlwind of energy and enthusiasm; an auburn-haired Tasmanian Devil of thought and action; her mind seeming to shoot off in a new and inspired direction at a moment's notice. She was in her mid 60s, a mum of three and now a grandma too. Her bright shoulder-length red hair and white English-rose skin were accompanied by dark pool-like brown eyes that I could see were brimming with tales. I liked Lou-Ann immediately.

I soon gathered that Lou-Ann was not one to sit still. I think I was lucky to have caught her on a rare night in. She seemed to fill every available moment in her life with something – running local theatre groups, attending art classes, hosting storytelling workshops. As we chatted, I slowly pieced together the rich tapestry of her life. With each paragraph came a new activity, passion or contribution to the local community. She told me that she was a storyteller by trade, which, from what I could gather, involved touring the country and telling tales at local theatres and community festivals, or writing stories for local publications. She also spent summers on Ocracoke Island – off the coast of Virginia – telling ghost tales of the legendary Black Beard, whose ship sank nearby. She was also a literature professor at the local university, wrote and performed community plays, hosted seasonal and themed parties in her living room and contributed to a weekly column for Northern Indiana newspapers. To further warm your heart, Lou-Ann rode her shiny Dutch-style bike (a Mother's Day present) everywhere around town and was perplexed by those who didn't use two wheels instead of four.

'I did twelve errands on my bike today. It just makes good sense. I don't know what it is about being on a bike – that feeling you get. I can't quite describe it!' she said.

Over a take-out pizza and beer, Lou-Ann and I chatted and laughed the night away, and before we knew it, it was 10 p.m. I had sat in the same armchair since arriving at 4 p.m. and not even moved for a shower. As I made my way up the stairs to de-stink myself, Lou-Ann called to me.

'The wall! You must sign the wall!' To my right was the 'welcome wall' I had spotted when I'd first arrived. Like a surgeon about to perform a delicate procedure, I turned to Lou-Ann and stretched out my hand.

'Lou-Ann. Sharpie, please.' She nodded and handed me a pen. On the wall, I chose to leave one of my favourite Dr Seuss quotes:

'You have brains in your head.

You have feet in your shoes.

You can steer yourself any direction you choose.'

As I crawled into bed that night, I couldn't help but think about what direction my life had taken up until the start of this trip, and the direction Lou-Ann had chosen for her own. Her chosen profession, a storyteller, isn't one I'd come across before and certainly wasn't something you would see advertised in the local shop window. But stories are everything it means to be human. They make us think, feel, act. No matter how abrupt and transient our modern-day social media, text and email exchanges can become, there will surely always be space and a human need for a ruddy good story. It's food for the soul, and at this, Lou-Ann is a top-level chef. Perhaps I'd like to be a storyteller one day too, I thought.

It was 7 a.m. and still dark when I left Lou-Ann's the following morning, and I was well and truly on a mission. I had until 4 p.m. that day to make the town of Woodmere, Ohio, to visit a group of children at Woodmere Elementary School. As I set off, I wondered why I did this to myself, cut things so fine, put pressure on the days to make a certain amount of mileage in a certain amount of time, and then I was honest – I did it because I enjoyed the challenge. There was always the bigger challenge of making it through the 50 states, but that seemed too large a goal to focus on repeatedly. The realisation of it seemed too distant to bring any day-to-day satisfaction, and so I liked to set myself mini goals. Challenges within the larger challenge so to speak – and today was to be one of those.

I got off to a terrible start on account of the fact that it was still dark and the batteries were flat on my bike lights. I had to fumble my way off-route for a mile to find a gas station to buy new batteries, then attempt to fit them with fingers that were numb from the early morning frost, but soon I was on my way again. Sucking in the cold air, legs turning, mind spinning, heart beating. I calculated that I had to maintain an average speed of 12 mph to make it in time to Woodmere. I'll admit that speed doesn't sound very fast, but I'll remind you that I was lugging 30 kg worth of gear with me, and those panniers were spread out like sails.

Within 10 miles I had crossed the Indiana state line and entered into state number 21, Ohio. I did a speedy bike dismount at the 'Welcome to Ohio!' sign, leaping from Boudica to set up my camera and pose with the sign. I must have looked completely unhinged to any passing cars – rushing around, dropping my camera, hugging a sign, smiling and getting back on the bike all within the space of three minutes – but today was going to be tight and I couldn't be late to the school.

With just 35 miles left to go, I hit a beautifully paved bike path. I raced along it and passed two men on bikes going in the opposite direction.

'Hey! Hey! Where's the fire?!' they yelled. I felt guilty and impolite not stopping to say hello, so I pulled hard on my brakes and wheeled the bike back to them, panting.

'Sorry!' pant, pant, 'It's just I…' pant, pant, 'I've got a talk…' pant, pant, 'with some kids and I, I can't be late.'

'Which school?' asked one of the men.

'Woodmere Elementary.'

'Ah, we know the one! In that case, you need some energy!' said the taller of the two men. He reached into his pack and pulled out a bag of apples. Oh no, I thought, that's going to weigh me down even more, but I didn't have time to refuse, and besides – how could I? Instead, I accepted the apples graciously. 'That's so kind! Thank you.'

'You've gotta taste one. They're Ohio apples – the best!' said the other man. I shoved one apple in my mouth, like a pig about to be served up, and stuffed the others in my rear pannier bag. I took a bite and hopped back on the bike.

'Delicious!' I yelled, now starting to pedal away. 'Thank you!'

'Hey! What are you talking to the kids about?!' they called after me.

'I'm cycling the 50 states!' I yelled, already almost out of earshot.

'You're crazy!' he yelled back. 'Good luck!'

At 4.10 p.m., I skidded, red-faced and exhausted, into Woodmere Elementary School. There were 10 minutes to spare before beginning the talk and, having pedalled 104 miles without so much as a whiff of a break, I was pooped. There was time for a quick hello with the man who had organised the talk, and my host for the night, Gordon, before I shoved my USB stick of images into the school computer and dished out a 30-minute talk about the journey so far to a room of 50 kids from grades 4–6 and their parents. The teacher, Sally, had told me that these were kids who had been identified from the years as 'gifted', and she wanted to expose them to something that might make them believe they were capable of great things. I felt humbled that she believed I could do just that. Once the kids, and adults, had finished with their round of questioning, Sally came back to the front of the class.

'Now, we've got something we'd like to ask Anna, haven't we kids?'

'Yeeeeeaaaaaassss!' came the return chorus from the group.

'Toby… do you want to stand up and ask Anna?'

A little boy with bright blonde hair stood up in the second row. He was wearing a blue T-shirt with some kind of superhero on it, his little seven-year-old fingers fiddling with the hem of it as he spoke.

'We're… we're… having a party… upstairs.' Toby paused and took another deep breath. 'And we wanted you to come to the party too.' Toby sat back down and breathed a huge sigh of relief.

'Thank you, Toby' said Sally, turning to me. 'Anna, the children have laid out some cider and donuts for you. Would you like to join us?'

It was now 29 October, just two days shy of Halloween,

and early enough to be starting the celebrations if you asked me. Although I did have to clarify that what Sally was referring to as 'cider' was an American term for a sweet, warm version of apple juice, not cider in the British, alcoholic sense.

'I would love to come and have some cider and donuts,' I replied enthusiastically.

The class responded with a huge 'Yayyyyyy!'

There was the sound of scraping chairs, the slap, slap, slap of plimsoles running down the hall, and then what sounded like a herd of elephants as the kids made their way up the stairs and into the classroom on the floor above. I followed the excited rabble and spent the next 30 minutes signing autographs and talking to the kids about their adventurous dreams. I was presented with a Woodmere Elementary T-shirt before I left and promised to send them a picture of me wearing it when I made it to state number 50, Hawaii.

That night I hardly slept. My mind was buzzing with all the things the kids had said to me – all the things they wanted to be when they grew up. Artists, teachers, lawyers, policemen, scientists, writers, actors, singers. I wondered how many of them would stay true to doing the things that made them happy, and how many would get side-tracked – finding themselves aboard a life-train, moving so quickly and seemingly with so much purpose that they never quite found the time to ask where the train was headed. Most of all, I was struck by their boundless imagination, so wild and untamed. I resolved to stow away a little bit of that wildness in my panniers, for a rainy day.

Late autumn was in full swing as I pedalled eastward across Ohio and onto the southern shores of Lake Erie, and I found myself facing a fresh dilemma. I was caught between two naming conventions for the time of year. Autumn was the British term, but the American 'fall' described everything so much more accurately. I settled on a hybrid and decided to call it 'Falltum' (I'm diplomatic like that you see, someone make me Pres-minister already).

I had learned that passing through Indiana and Ohio during Falltum is a delight. It was as if the trees were having a party and everyone was invited. Well, except the evergreens. They evidently missed the memo and remained stubbornly clad in their verdurous robes as surrounding neighbours partook in a slow summer-end striptease. Of course, we have turning leaves in the UK during autumn, but nothing quite like the US. In the US, trees pop. They erupt. They explode in a multitude of colours, the likes of which I'd never seen before in shrub form. Fall in the north-east US is one thing about which you should definitely believe the hype.

By the time Halloween rolled around, I had rolled my way into the home of David and Monica Matia in the suburbs of Cleveland. I was only originally intending to stay one night, but when a wet and windy storm blew in, I was convinced to stay for two. Once again, I nestled into the bosom of family life, with fresh morning coffee and afternoons sitting on the windowsill, writing blogs and calling friends back home. David didn't even seem to mind when I accidentally locked his son, also called David, out of his own home for a few hours.

The extra day of rest meant that I was able to experience a real American Halloween. I am a huge fan of fancy dress and a firm believer that life in fancy dress is always more fun. I can back this up with maths:

Life = Fun.

Life + Fancy dress = Fun squared.

My penchant for ridiculous outfits could go some way to explain why I had run the length of the UK's Hadrian's Wall dressed as a Roman soldier and the length of the Jurassic Coast dressed as a dinosaur. And, of course, why I had rollerbladed 100 miles around Amsterdam, dressed in 80s clothing – let's not forget that one. So, I watched with glee as the Matias prepared for a full American Halloween. Even Roxy the chocolate Labrador got in on the action, though when I came down the stairs on Halloween evening to find her clad in a pink tutu and matching pink and purple bunny ears, I had some suspicions that she had had a little help in choosing her outfit. The Matias put together a huge bowl of sweets by the front door, and every 20 minutes the doorbell rang. Kids from the neighbourhood arrived by the bucketload dressed as devils, ghosts, Draculas, witches, fairies, pumpkins, Frankensteins and my personal favourite: a parsnip.

Once the stream of pumpkin-loving punters had quietened down (presumably because it was past many of their bedtimes), the Matias ordered in some pizzas and we sat around as a makeshift family, chomping on slices of stringy margarita and discussing the best outfit that had come to the door. I reflected on how lovely it was that the whole street had come to life that evening. Most of the kids who came to the door seemed to know the family in one way or other. And when I looked down the street I could see that the surrounding houses had their doors open and were dishing out treats too. I was gutted that I hadn't thought ahead and packed myself some Halloween get-up, or at least stopped to buy an outfit en route. I supposed that I could have borrowed Roxy's tutu if I'd asked nicely, but she seemed so happy in it and I hated to deprive any dog of her prima ballerina moment.

'So, is Halloween a big thing back home in the UK?' David asked, folding another slice of pizza neatly in two and taking a bite.

'It's a thing, but not a big thing. Some people get into it and some people don't… We actually get more excited about Bonfire Night,' I said.

'Bonfire night?!' David asked. It was then I realised that Bonfire Night was only a British tradition. I'd never really thought about that before. I went on to do my best to explain what the night entailed precisely, but during that process I realised I didn't know all the ins and outs of the gunpowder plot. I was, therefore, ill-equipped to relay those ins and outs to an international audience. By the time dinner was over and I went up to bed, all the Americans in the room seemed to believe that we British enjoy celebrating an attempt to blow up our monarch by throwing life-sized stuffed men on bonfires. I don't think Great British tourism will be offering me a job any time soon.

TORONTO
BUFFALO
SYRACUSE
ALBANY
NEW HAMPSHIRE
MASSACHUSETTS
BOSTON
CONNECTICUT
PROVIDENCE
RHODE ISLAND
NEW YORK
PENNSYLVANIA

WELCOME
TO
New Hampshire

NIAGARA FALLS

14

Betty 'the Hutch' Hutchinson

Distance Cycled: 6,892 miles
States Completed: 22

I had decided in advance that I wouldn't let myself get too attached to the states of Pennsylvania or New York, because these were the two states that I would be passing through twice doing my 50-state wiggle. I would enter into them for the first time as I travelled beneath the Great Lakes, and then again a month or so later as I pedalled along the East Coast. Having left the comfort of the Matia home, I continued onwards along the southern shores of Lake Erie, under clear skies and in crisp cold air. Boudica carried me into a 50-mile stretch of Pennsylvania, before crossing into upstate New York, which marked state number 24.

I'd been excited about visiting New York state for some time, and not just because it was home to New York City. I was still a few weeks from hitting those bright lights, but right now I was heading for another gold-star attraction, just beyond the skyscrapers and sprawl of the city of Buffalo: Niagara Falls.

This wasn't to be my first meeting with Lady Niagara. I had been lucky enough to visit the Falls as part of a Toronto school netball tour, at the tender age of 16. Experience tells me that not many American readers will be familiar with net-ball. It's like basketball, but you don't move. Yes, it's silly, but we (England that is) are really rather good at it. In fact, did you know that basketball originated as an adapted form of netball? Netball came first. Basketball second. So, let's have a little respect for netball, please. This time around, however, the journey to Niagara was to be different. For a start, I wasn't a teenager, dressed in skater clothing and desperately uncomfortable in my own skin. Nor was I listening to 90s punk band Blink 182. This time, I was making my Niagara assault as a full-grown, Lycra-clad adult via the US side of the Falls.

A visit from the American side of the Falls isn't especially scenic at first. The only way for me to describe it is as… industrial. For the past month, I had been working my way across what is affectionately known as America's Rust Belt. It was something I had learned about while reading Bill Bryson's book *One Summer*, which chronicles the events of the summer of 1927 in America, a year in which a whole load of monumental events happened (the invention of the TV, the first flight across the Atlantic by Charles Lindbergh and the great Mississippi flood – to name but a few). The book frequently refers to this strip of land across northern US as the backbone of the nineteenth-century engineering boom. Cities such as Detroit, Michigan and Gary were among those mentioned. It was on the Rust Belt that Henry Ford produced the first Model T. Yet, when the US economic depression hit in 1929, these cities suffered immeasurably.

I'd already decided not to judge Niagara on her rusty surroundings, so as I wheeled along the shore of the mighty Niagara River, I met the Falls with an open mind. I watched through the trees as the river rapids moved quicker and quicker, the flow growing ever more ferocious until the blue-green colour of the water was overtaken by swirling, exploding patches of white. The noise grew in intensity too, building and building, surging onwards in a deafening roar until at last reaching a cascade crescendo. And then, there she was, Lady Niagara, a rose amongst rusty thorns, millions of gallons of water tumbling into a deep plunge pool below. I thought of each water droplet as if it were a brave little parachute soldier, jumping out of a plane and free-falling for hundreds of metres before rejoining his fellow parachute water-droplet friends at the bottom.

Resting Boudica on a set of white railings next to the visitor centre, I took a walk out onto a viewing platform which juts out over the river below the Falls and offers the chance for a better view. It was well below zero that day, and despite having left my gloves tucked in my helmet on the bike, I stood there with numb hands and stared. For 20 minutes, I walked up and down, alone and in awe, on the concrete platform. From where I was standing, I could see the smaller portion of the Falls. It was throwing up mist as the water collided with boulders below, like a sack of flour dropped onto a concrete floor. A modest rainbow was dancing its way across the middle of the watery chute, fragments of red, green and blue being caught by the droplets. Looking out beyond the edge of the platform and across the border into Canada, I could see the more well-known section of Niagara, known as Horseshoe Falls – so named because of its shape. There were throngs of people lining the railings over there on the Canadian side, and I was thankful that it was quieter on the platform where I stood. I watched what looked like toy boats go about their journeys into and out of the base of Horseshoe Falls. I had been down there in those boats once, as a 16-year-old. I shut my eyes and tried to remember what it was like, but all I could remember was eating a sugar-coated waffle on the bank after the boat ride. Ah memories.

This was one of the few times on the journey when it felt like a shame to be experiencing the views alone. I didn't feel that I could accost a stranger and explode into excited chatter about how fabulous a sight of natural wonder it was, so I had to keep all those emotions to myself. All that joy, all that amazement. Surrounded by people sharing the sight together, I noted how their joy seemed to be doubled when shared. My thoughts shifted to how I almost didn't make the detour to see Niagara, because it added an extra day to my schedule. But no matter how many people I had met who told me that the US side of the Falls wasn't worth it, I found the place to be nothing short of spectacular.

At last, my body caved in to the cold and I dragged myself away from the platform and into the visitor centre for a cup of hot chocolate, before getting back on the bike. I continued my journey eastwards across upstate New York, skimming the tops of an area called the Finger Lakes – a place that gets its name because of 11 long lakes which splay out like (you guessed it) fingers. When I looked at the map, I actually thought they looked more like a bear claw had slashed the United States than a collection of fingers, but I suppose 'bear claw slash lakes' isn't quite as catchy. What the Finger Lakes lack in width they make up for in depth. They are some of the deepest lakes in the world, a number of them going well below sea level.

I stopped briefly at the northern end of six of the lakes to look out on their clear blue-green waters. Although the area around the lakes was flat, the land between them was anything but. My legs hurt more than usual over the days that followed. They had become accustomed to the flat landscapes of the Midwest, so the undulating hills of upstate New York were a shock to the system. I had to beat and slap them into life each morning and it seemed to take 50 miles before they started to propel me forwards, rather than me dragging them around. Still, it didn't bother me. The air up here seemed crisper and fresher than it had out west. There was an alpine feel to it. It smelled of evergreens and freshly cut grass and I liked that.

At the small town of Sprakers, I joined the banks of the Mohawk River and followed it eastwards through the fun-to-pronounce town of Schenectady (Schen-ect-tat-tie). I took a detour through the suburbs of what was a cute little town, weaving among cobbled residential streets, passing tall church spires and a 50s-style movie theatre. On one street, the shops were painted in bright, bold colours – reds, yellows, greens – that seemed to mirror the season of Falltum in full swing. Leaving Schenectady, I passed through Troy, and was sorely disappointed that there was no sign of Brad Pitt or a Trojan horse. I crossed the border into Vermont and entered into a little piece of home: New England.

Now it's confession time. Before leaving for the journey I had thought that New England was a state. My geography knowledge works on a need-to-know basis, you see, and I had never needed to know much about New England before. In fact, I had gone so far as to believe that this was perhaps a piece of land owned by England in the United States. I soon learned that New England is the name for an area of states – which covers the 'actual' states of New Hampshire, Vermont, Maine, Connecticut, Massachusetts and Rhode Island.

It was now early November in Vermont, and snowfall was becoming a more regular occurrence. I had one more mountain pass to take on before I could stick to the safer sea levels along the East Coast, and the thought of going up the mountain made me anxious. Pulling into a gas station in Bennington at the foot of Woodford Pass, I did my best to ignore the kind lady behind the counter who told me I was silly to be cycling up the mountain in winter. I also politely declined to listen to the man in the post-office queue who took it upon himself to point out that I didn't have winter cycling tyres. Instead, I resolved that I would just get on with it, and find out what it was like for myself.

Within 2 miles of beginning the nine-mile climb up to Woodford, I was alone, revelling in the silence and the solitude. The traffic was light; a few cars passed me that hour, but there was no one out there to tell me that I was a fool. Well, except myself, and I didn't fancy feeling foolish today. I slotted into a familiar rhythm, one that had guided me up the Sierra Nevada Mountains, across the Great Basin Desert and over the Rocky Mountains. One leg at a time, one pedal stroke more than before, thoughts turning and tumbling in sweet synchronicity with my legs.

When I came to from my meditative state, I was just a few hundred metres from the top of Woodford Pass. There was ice lining the edges of the road and patches of snow spilling from the verge onto the tarmac, claiming more and more of it each day, I presumed. But today was okay. Today I took it steady to the crest of the pass, and there I stopped to pull on more layers of clothing before beginning a solitary, cautious descent down the other side. Snow had now begun to fall, but only gently. I thought about how I was forever a student on this adventure. Today, that mountain taught me a lesson. As was the case with each and everything I had been nervous of, it turned out to be nothing much at all. In fact, it turned out to be a beautiful day on the bike.

I was soon through a narrow 40-mile-wide southern sliver of Vermont, and I found myself at a little house in the woods in Deerfield, New Hampshire. This house was quite literally the house that Jack built. I had managed to get hold of Jack

Hutchinson via Warmshowers.org – an organisation which was proving ever more useful as the days got shorter and the nights colder. Jack's profile described him as a retired teacher and engineer in his sixties, who enjoys a bit of bike racing and touring with his wife on a tandem.

Once across the threshold of the Hutchinson home, I was soon introduced to Jack's wife, Rebecca, and his mum, Betty. Betty was 93 years old, but young in every other sense of the word. Over a cup of tea around the kitchen table, I listened as Jack told me that every year Betty competes in the Manchester, New Hampshire, 5-k running race and tries to break the record for the 90–99 age group. It's a record that she's held for three years on the trot. Last year, she even smashed her own record by seven minutes. Every year, she runs the race surrounded by her 19 grandchildren and great grandchildren – all of who are, as you would expect, her greatest fans. During the race, they surround her like a pack of wolves for the entire 5 kilometres, passing men in their forties and fifties, as Grandma Betty ploughs on. As they pass, the grandchildren turn and point at the other runners and proudly announce, 'Dude! You just got beaten by my grandma!'

Every morning, Betty uses the mile between her house in the woods and the mailbox at the end of the driveway as a training run. During my two-day stopover at the house, I had the pleasure of joining her for a training session.

The daily ritual began at 7 a.m. I was already waiting by

the front door with Jack and Rebecca, as I watched Betty negotiate her way down the staircase. She made her way over to a wooden pew by the front door, where she had laid out two essential items of clothing. She paused and turned to her son Jack.

'It cold out?' she asked, still staring ahead at the door.

'It's pretty cold, ma,' said Jack in reply, and Betty nodded.

She picked up the first item of clothing – a yellow beanie – and pulled it down firmly onto her head so that I could see the word 'HUTCH' emblazoned in green letters across the brow. She shuffled sideways and picked up the second item of clothing, a yellow scarf, which she wrapped around her neck in two swift, sweeping movements. She then picked up a set of grey and blue hiking poles, which were resting next to the door. She looked at Jack again, but this time said nothing.

'You ready, ma?' he asked

'Ready,' Betty said, and I could have sworn I saw a faint hint of a smile creeping into the corners of her mouth.

Jack swung the front door open and I was taken aback by how brisk the air was. It must have been close to zero outside. It was a glorious morning, the sun had not long come up and the front lawn was a carpet of sparkling frost. The birds were far more awake than I was at that hour and danced to and fro on the pathway in front of the house. I soon gathered that Betty wasn't much of a talker, and so rather than rabbit on, I decided to enjoy the silence too. Betty settled into a rhythm, flicking her hiking poles backwards and forwards and propelling herself down the driveway at a pace that was part way between a run and a walk.

The brown dirt driveway wound away from the house, bobbing and weaving through the woods. We came to the first corner and Betty broke the silence for the first time. She looked sideways at me and said, 'I like to cut the corners,' before taking a line across the driveway that would make a racing-car driver proud. I was forced to leap out of the way and put in a burst of speed to keep up and move in her new, more direct trajectory. I fell back into step alongside her and noted that Betty was breathing hard. Poles swinging, legs shuffling, gaze fixed firmly ahead. We had been moving swiftly through the trees and were now onto a more undulating section of the driveway. At the crest of the first hill, Betty broke the silence again. She looked sideways at me and said, 'I like to speed up on the flats,' before upping her pace and quickening her step. I was finding it hard to keep up, without breaking into a full-blown run and began thinking about how Betty does this every morning. Just then the mailbox came into view. I'd seen it, and I could sense that Betty had seen it too. The sun was glinting off the corner of its blue metal edge. Betty looked sideways again, leant her body forwards, flicked her poles backwards and in a breathy voice said, 'I'm going for the finish!' And she was gone, into 5th Hutch gear and I was left for dust.

Spending time with Betty that morning was an eye opener.

I thought about how, over the years, she must have had her fair share of doctors telling her what she could and could not do, what she was and wasn't capable of. I'm sure that others in her community try to tell her on a daily basis that she should 'take it easy', and no doubt she would struggle with an inner voice that says she's 'too old'. But Betty hasn't listened. At 93, Betty is still aiming to be the best version of herself, and in pursuit of what makes her happy. Dear careers advisor, when I grow up, I want to be Betty 'the Hutch' Hutchinson.

***

After 7,000 miles of cycling and having followed a route that no satellite navigation system would ever advise, I crossed the Maine state line and reached the shores of the Atlantic Ocean. It'd been two months since I'd left the Pacific Ocean in San Francisco. I couldn't help but feel in a reflective mood as I stood on a rugged windswept beach in the shadow of a lighthouse and looked out from the north-eastern shores of the US, home towards the UK. In many ways, it had taken me an eternity to get here, 123 days to be precise, but I was also overcome by this odd feeling that the journey was going to be over all too soon. Making it to the Atlantic, and at last being able to turn to head south had been a goal for some time. Now that I was here, inhaling salty Atlantic air, surrounded by grey rocks, pebbles and seaweed, I almost didn't want to be here at all. I wanted to get in a time machine and go right back to the beginning of the journey and do things slower this time – to see more, but most of all to worry less about things that may not ever come to pass.

My journey into Maine only took me as far as the town of Kennebunkport, but I found it to be everything I had hoped it would be. Quaint buildings, small wooden-clad churches, brilliant sunshine, rocky shores, lighthouses, rugged untamed beaches, a fresh ocean breeze, lobster pots strewn across front lawns and the catch of the day being served up in a cafe on every corner. While in town, I stayed with a nice young man named Nathan, a friend of my great aunt who was studying boat building at the local university. I was blown away by the idea that you could do a whole degree in boat building, and thought what a wonderful thing that would be, to spend your days crafting and honing a vessel that could one day lead you on adventures into the open ocean. In many ways, I was envious of Nathan's degree choice. Much as I had enjoyed studying psychology at university, I wondered whether I might have been more suited to doing something where I used my hands as well as my mind. And that led me to thinking that perhaps this was something I could still do now – a direction I could take when I was home. On the shores of the Atlantic, I made a vow to myself. Inspired by Betty and Nathan, to believe that it was never too late to start trying to better yourself and your life, I vowed to spend less time behind a computer, and more time connecting, creating and building. It was a thought that filled me with hope about the future. A future of which I felt very much in control.

NEW YORK

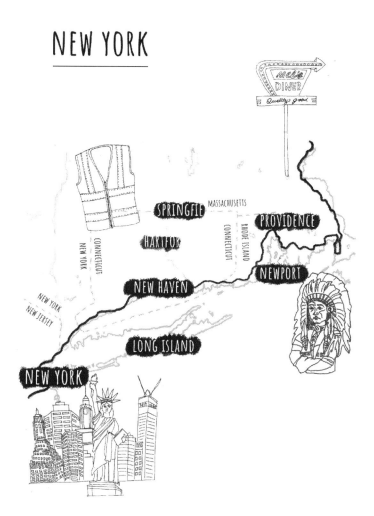

SPRINGFIE   MASSACHUSETTS

PROVIDENCE

HARTFOR

NEWPORT

NEW HAVEN

LONG ISLAND

NEW YORK

CONNECTICUT
NEW YORK

RHODE ISLAND
CONNECTICUT

NEW YORK
NEW JERSEY

DINER
Quality good

15

Oh, Brother!

Distance Cycled: 7,743 miles

States Completed: 27

'This could be a complete disaster. Or it could be fun. Either way – let's be 'avin it.'

These were the wise words from my younger sibling, Jonty, sent via text as he boarded a plane to meet me in Boston, Massachusetts. Our holidays together hadn't always gone to plan, and I had led Jonty down many a tangled path. Like the time I took him with some friends on a trip to Wales and a 16-year-old Jonty had rather too much to drink. So much so that I ended up cleaning up the baked beans he later scatter-gun-vomited on the toilet wall. Then there was the time that I convinced Jonty to join me and my friend Becky in Athens, to watch the 2004 Olympics. We ended up staying in a shell of a building with no running water and walking for five hours in the scorching Grecian heat to a ferry port after missing the only bus to it. And yet, all of these things hadn't put Jonty off. He had agreed to fly to state number 28, Massachusetts, to ride the 360 miles from Boston into New York City – where his then girlfriend (now wife) Kate would be waiting for him to begin a romantic holiday together.

I have always felt an overwhelming sense of protectiveness over my 'little brother'. It was a feeling that had begun at a young age, and so I suspect it is innate. Jonty looked the spit of the Milky Bar Kid as a young boy. Bright blonde hair, large glasses and cheeks so peachy you couldn't help but poke them (as I did on many occasions). Aged seven, I overheard a nine-year-old boy calling Jonty 'specky four eyes' on account of his large glasses. Primary school kids can be mean, and so when I overhead this bully picking on Jonty, I walked up to him and I slapped him. I don't condone violence in any form, I am not a violent person, but mess with my little brother, and I will get buck wild on your ass. The fact that I was seven at the time and the bully was nine apparently didn't matter. Justice got served up whatever the age of my brother's attacker.

As there are only 14 months between us, we share many things. And that naturally began with the sharing of baths when we were nippers. I am still haunted by a vivid memory of the time we shared a bath and Jonty deposited a brown coloured gift in the water, aged three. As the years wore on, we stopped sharing baths and Jonty stopped gifting me brown parcels, but we shared many other things: friends, parties, holidays, rowing kits.

I met Jonty at a subway station on the outskirts of Boston, in a town called Braintree. After almost five months away from home, it was strange to see a figure so familiar in unfamiliar surroundings. He looked out of place there, his tall frame and wide shoulders clad in a green jacket and jeans, accompanied by a broad grin and long gangly McNuff arms, poised for an embrace.

'Hello sis!' he beamed. 'Fancy seeing you here!'

'Hello little broski,' I replied, now halfway into an unbreakable sibling hug.

I was excited if a little nervous to have Jonty join me for the week. Excited because I got to spend a week with someone who has known me since the year dot and nervous that I now had someone to look after besides myself. (Although being 27 years old, 6 ft 3 and having big man-muscles, Jonty was more than capable of looking after himself.)

We had six days to ride the 360 miles from Boston to New York City together. We'd also scheduled to take one day of rest in the middle, to spend some time with a great aunt of ours in New Haven, Connecticut. Well, I think she's my great aunt – she is my dad's cousin's wife's mum. What does that make her? Anyway, that left five days to cover the 360 miles, meaning an average of 72 miles per day, which, in light of the long days covered across the Midwest, was rather civilised. There was certainly no need to subject Jonty to 100-mile days; he was on a holiday after all. I wanted us to have time to stop, explore and eat.

Of equal importance as making it safely to NYC was the bucket list of items Jonty had said he'd like to experience during his time back in the States. We'd been a couple of times together as kids and back then it all was about the food.

Especially when most of it is larger than your infant head. When we were kids, America meant big – big cars, big people and big food.

The route I'd chosen wasn't the most direct route between Boston and NYC, because I'd decided that we couldn't possibly pass Cape Cod without giving it a little visit. Cape Cod is a little hook-shaped piece of land which extends from the eastern shores of the US in Massachusetts. It's famous for sailing, vineyards and beaches. We wouldn't have time to see much of it – and being late November, it was the wrong time of year anyway – but I certainly fancied having a good nose around, if only for a day or two, so I'd arranged for us to stay with some hosts in the town of Falmouth, at the southern end of Cape Cod.

Making sure we didn't always stay in motels was important for me this week. As well as feeling a sense of responsibility for Jonty's safety, which I dutifully fulfilled on day one by presenting him with a high-vis vest, I felt a sense of responsibility to make sure he had a good time. I wanted him to experience a week of adventure, a snapshot of a week of my life on the road. I wanted him to experience the kindness of staying in strangers' homes, I wanted to show him off to these strangers. In short, I just wanted everything to be perfect.

It was a cold, crisp morning when we set off from Braintree and began to wind our way out of the tangled web of the city suburbs, inching closer to our first night's stopover on Cape Cod.

It began to drizzle lightly and, eventually, the houses thinned out, the number of route options dwindled and we found ourselves riding peacefully along beige-coloured dusty farm tracks, past cranberry bog after cranberry bog. We stuck as close to the coastline as we could, never straying too far from the salty air of Massachusetts Bay and swooping seagulls overhead. We gave a little cheer as we passed through Kingston – a town with the same name as the one in which we were both born in the UK – and settled into the rhythm of riding as a two.

One of the things high up on Jonty's US bucket list was to eat at a dirty roadhouse-style diner. The kind of place that serves pancakes and waffles, washed down with an endless stream of water-weak coffee. In the movies, these places are always run by slightly bitter, albeit amusing, waitresses who have a wit sharper than any knife held by the overweight, miserable chef in the diner's kitchen. Places like that had been plentiful out west, but I was doubtful that we'd find anything like them on the East Coast. Here the chain coffee houses had taken over and independent dirty diners were few and far between. Still, I hoped to make up for it in other ways.

It was late morning on the first day of the double McNuff journey to NYC. I was blowing away the cobwebs after a few days of rest in Boston, and Jonty was flushing out a seven-hour flight and the accompanying jet lag from his system. We turned a bend and were greeted by the usual sight of another long straight, beige-coloured road. I looked over my shoulder at Jonty, as I had started to do to check he was still there and hadn't veered violently off-course into one of the many cranberry bogs. Just then I spotted something shiny out of the corner of my eye. Set back from the road, 50 metres from where we were, was a big silver Airstream-style camper van, with a neon sign that unmistakably read 'Diner'.

'Jontyyyyy! Dinnnneeeerrrr!' I pulled on my brakes and turned the bike around. Jonty stopped too and looked in the direction I was pointing.

'There's a diner!' I repeated.

'Really?!' He looked suspicious as this wasn't really the place for a diner to be. Traffic had been light, after all, and I wondered how they got the business, especially as they were set back from the road.

'I swear it. Well, it looks like a diner! Come on!'

We rolled into the shabby-looking car park and propped up our bikes next to two small trucks. We took off our high-vis vests (for fear of the locals mocking us) and slid our helmets over the bars of our bikes, before shoving open the flimsy plastic-framed door to the diner. Punters in truckers' hats turned to look at us as we entered, and a waitress in her mid 50s with ash-blonde hair and a pink shirt smiled at us from behind the counter.

The inside of the Airstream was fresh out of a movie set. Stainless steel panels, with horizontal lines carved into them, ran around the front of a long counter that had a line of red-topped, round stools perched on hour-glass-shaped stainless-steel trunks – making them look like mushrooms with flattened tops – positioned in front of it. Behind the counter, I could see coffee pots on the go, one full, another still dripping. There was a window into a kitchen to the left of the counter, which was steamed up with condensation. Beyond the counter, the rest of the Airstream was taken up with booths, sporting tattered beige upholstery. It looked to be leatherette, but I couldn't quite be sure. Right at the end of the diner was one long table with normal freestanding chairs.

'Morning darlins,' said an auburn-haired waitress. 'Go ahead and take a seat. I'll be right with you.'

I turned to Jonty and grinned. Jonty grinned right on back.

'This is AWESOME!' I mouthed, before we moved off, past the counter and to the table at the end of the room.

Ten minutes later, Jonty and I were two cups deep into our refillable water-weak coffee and waiting on our food. Jonty had ordered the biggest thing on the menu: a plate of crispy bacon, two eggs, potato fries, two buttermilk pancakes, grits (a grainy, more liquid form of porridge) and biscuits (or scones to us in the UK). I went on the modest side and just ordered buttermilk pancakes, two eggs and some crispy bacon. I was beaming with pride, feeling so chuffed that we'd managed to magic together a dirty diner experience for Jonty.

The diner experience turned out to be the highlight of the

day, and things got a little soggy as it started to tip with rain in the afternoon. There are no two ways about it, cycling in the rain is never fun. Much less fun when you've taken a detour to Cape Cod to experience the scenery. It was early evening by the time we made it to the town of Falmouth. We knocked on the door of Jim and his family's house (yet another Warm-Showers host) and once we'd had our warm shower we got to talking about clams, lobsters and cranberry farms, before the conversation moved on to talking about Wampanoag.

'Wampa-what?' I said to Jim.

'Wampanoags,' he replied. 'They're a Native American tribe. Well, they used to be spread all across Massachusetts, but they've been all but wiped out now.'

I was fascinated to learn that the spoken language of the Mashpee Wampanoag tribe died out 100 years ago, but one woman, with the aid of a linguistics degree from MIT, has been working since 1993 to revive it from written documents. Her name is Jesse Little Doe Baird, and she began her mission because of dreams in which she was visited by her ancestors speaking the language. She's been successful, and although it's now her second language, it's the mother tongue of her 11-year-old daughter Mae – who is the first native Wampanoag speaker for over a century. Other members of the community, descendants of the tribe, are now learning to speak the language and plans are underway to open a Wampanoag immersion school on Cape Cod.

The following morning, we waved Jim and his family farewell and prepared to head back to the mainland, towards state number 29 and Rhode Island. As we saddled up and got ready to go, I was thinking about how perfect this journey had been so far, and how I had managed to bag Jonty yet another authentic adventure experience by staying with Jim on Cape Cod. Then Jonty turned to me.

'Ansie,' he said, using the nickname he's had for me since I was young. 'Can I go off first?'

'Yeah, of course you can. Is the pace okay?'

'Yeah, it's fine. It's just that my back brake doesn't work, so I've only got one set of brakes and I'm worried I won't stop and crash into the back of you.'

'What?! You've only got one set of brakes?! Why didn't you tell me?!'

'Yeah. I thought it'd be alright, I was coping, but all the rain yesterday has worn the front ones down too, so they're not much good at stopping either.'

'Jont! How have you flown across the Atlantic for a week of cycling with only one set of brakes on your bike?!'

'Oh no, I mean, I do have two. The back one will work, it just then stays jammed on. So it's like an emergency brake.' He grinned.

Brothers!

In the two days that followed our visit to Cape Cod, Jonty was storming along. He pounded out the mileage, showing no signs of struggling at all, a fact that perplexed me and caused me to question whether I was quite as fit as I had thought. After a brief stopover with another kind host in Providence, Rhode Island, the natural course of the adventure began to flow.

We stopped in a cafe to meet a friend's girlfriend's mum. The mum owned the cafe, and so we were treated to a free breakfast. A local reporter heard that we were in town, so she turned up at the cafe to interview this crazed adventurer who was cycling the 50 states. She greeted Jonty and me, and then sat down opposite Jonty, which struck me as odd, but I supposed she could sit wherever she liked. She then began her round of questioning.

'So, Jonty, is it?'

Jonty nodded, and looked confused.

'This is quite some feat you've taken on.'

'Err, is it?' he replied.

'How many states have you ridden through so far?'

Jonty chewed on a piece of pancake, and looked even more confused, then he smiled. 'Errr, I think you mean my sister. She's the one doing the fifty-state ride. I'm just here for a week.'

'Oh, I'm sorry… it's just. Well, I mean, I thought that…'

I said nothing and just smiled at her. I couldn't help but find it amusing that she'd just assumed that big burly Jonty was the one on the grand adventure.

'Well, I mean, it's unusual for women to do these kinds of things, isn't it?' the reporter continued.

'Is it?' I said, looking back at her but saying nothing else. Honestly, I felt a bit let down. I wanted to stand up and shout: 'SISTER OF THE WORLD, FELLOW SHE-RAH – CAN YOU HEAR YOURSELF?! HELP ME OUT HERE. HELP YOUR DAUGHTERS OUT HERE!!'

She looked visibly flustered and I didn't want to make her feel any worse, so I explained that one of the reasons for this adventure was actually thanks to my brother. In fact, thanks to both my brothers. It was because of them that I grew up simply 'doing what the boys did'. But one day I hoped that there would no longer be a difference between what the boys and the girls did, especially when it came to taking on adventures. That seemed to calm the reporter down a little and so we went on and had a nice 20-minute chat after that. I rode off feeling that Boudica and I, as two women of the world, had even more of a reason to complete this 50-state challenge than ever before.

As Jonty and I continued to weave our way south towards New York, it continued to rain. Then the wind started to join in too, making the going even tougher, but still Jonty kept chugging on. More than that, he insisted on shielding me from the wind and the rain by riding at the front of our two-man peloton all day every day. He said that it was so I could save my energy for the rest of the journey, but I knew he was just being chivalrous. It was very sweet, and so I obliged and took the easy position on the first few days of riding together.

Just when I was beginning to wonder whether Jonty was super-human, or whether I was just going very slowly, the wheels fell off the brother-wagon. After 220 miles of wet and windy riding, as we rolled into the town of New London, it became clear he was a broken man. His cheeks were flushed red, he went very quiet and he could barely keep his eyes open by late afternoon. It was like looking at a toddler that had run around for too long and desperately needed a nap. After a hearty and healthy dinner of Domino's Pizza, followed by Taco Bell (where we were very disappointed to discover that the burritos had shrunk since we were kids), Jonty was flat-out asleep by 7 p.m. Naturally, I did the sisterly thing of taking an unflattering picture and sending it to the whole family, plus his girlfriend, Kate.

For the next few days, Jonty let me take my turn at the front, and we continued as a merry little duo down the coast. Riding with a member of the opposite sex for a few days proved rather educational. Too many times I'd set off and find myself alone 100 metres down the road. I'd look back and spot Jonty with his hands down his pants, rearranging 'the furniture'. Apparently, it's all too easy to mount your bike in an excited leap and land on one of your testicles. Who knew?

Singing levels hit an all-time high one day, as we decided that everything should be expressed via the medium of song. Were you to buy the *East Coast Hits* album from that week, you'd enjoy classic tracks such as 'I need a pee', 'Where is Lockwood Avenue?' and 'Can I turn right, at this red light?' (radio edit). We also created a game which involved spotting Dunkin' Donut shops. The East Coast is littered with them, and the rules of the game were simple. Whoever spotted the Dunkin' Donut shop first had to scream 'DUNKIN'!', and the other person bought the coffees at the next stop. Over the rest of the week, I watched Jonty bounce back from his exhausted state in New London and really get into the groove of things. He seemed upbeat, relaxed and to embrace the unknown a little more than he had when leaving Boston.

As planned, we took a rest day with our great aunt Ann in Hamden, Connecticut – state number 30. Fuelled by a day of rest and having been very well looked after by our extended family, we left Hamden bound for New York City.

I had made the executive decision that we would ride into New York City by continuing to follow the East Coast. This meant navigating the sprawling New York suburbs of Bridgeport, Stamford, New Rochelle and, lastly, the Bronx. There was the option of catching a ferry from Bridgeport to Long Island and going via Queens, but sticking to the coast seemed the more 'logical route'. Plus, given that my opinion of the Bronx was based solely on Hollywood movies and J-Lo songs, I wanted to see what it was really like. So Jonty and I rolled up our sleeves and waded headlong into the Bronx urban jungle.

We made an early start from Hamden and hoped to cover the 70 miles to Hell's Kitchen in New York City by mid-afternoon. It was only 70 miles after all. Of course, as usual, my plan was optimistic and, after the first few hours of riding, it became apparent that this was going to take us much longer than we'd hoped. The first few hours weren't too much trouble, though the riding was far from glamorous as we jostled for position on roads packed curb to curb with traffic. The smog was suffocating, in stark contrast to the mountain air of Colorado, Wyoming and Montana – oh, how I longed for a lungful of that endless horizon air now.

Seven miles out from the Bronx, in the town of New Rochelle, we got 'stuck' in a traffic jam. Quite an impressive feat when on a bike, I thought. Our pannier bags made us too wide to sneak between the lines of traffic, and as there were two lanes of it in both directions, we found ourselves in a car sandwich. The pavements were packed with walkers, so using them was a no-go, and we simply had to wait in line with the cars. We nudged, patiently, nervously, forward. Jonty was doing his best to maintain a chipper smile, which I could see fell from his face every time I wasn't looking.

Approaching the outskirts of the Bronx, I could hold it together no longer, quite literally. We had just finished hogging the road over a highway flyover, being beeped and honked by a large truck with several cars on the back of it, when I finally cracked.

'Jonty! Jonty!' I screamed above the cacophony of outer-city sounds. 'I need a pee! Like, now!'

I had been clenching my pelvic floor muscles since we left Hamden, not wanting to stop for a wee on account of being nervous of the ever-shrinking time window to make it into the city before dark. The riding that day demanded constant concentration. I had been doing my best to remember directions, at the same time as being on high alert for turning vehicles, any cars coming too close or turning left across our path. Pile on top of that the weighty responsibility I felt for keeping Jonty safe, and the double dollop of guilt I felt for making him cycle such a ridiculous route, and my mind was almost as exhausted as my pelvic floor muscles.

Jonty nodded at my request and we pulled off into the nearest petrol station, just on the northern end of the Bronx neighbourhood. Pee successfully ejected from my body, and Jonty having also done a 'splash 'n' dash' himself, I made a vow then and there that no amount of riding was worth wetting myself over. I needed to get my priorities in order and I made a new rule: pee before panic. I had done too much panicking that day, and not enough peeing. Feeling more comfortable now, I turned my attention to the map and the final 12 miles onto Manhattan Island.

I knew from previous visits to New York that the city was laid out in a rather helpful grid formation. I wanted to make sure I didn't stop as we went through the roughest area of our journey, because stupid tourists stopped, and asking for directions could be looking for trouble. So I had decided that I would remember the route from this point, and once we made it to 100th Street, I could navigate us from there using the grid system. I repeated the directions out loud like a mantra.

'Straight. Left. Right. Straight over. Through the park. Left.' I then took a deep breath and looked around.

The only way to describe the Northern Bronx is as an assault of the senses. It's as if a scene from *The Fast and the Furious* (1–6) collided with the UK's bustling Tooting High Street, in the midst of an M25 traffic jam. The place made me feel a little uneasy and I couldn't help but feel that we were being stared at. In fact, I knew that we were being stared at. After all, we were two tall white middle-class Brits, one on a giant pink bike, both wearing high-vis vests. Who am I kidding, we stood out like sore thumbs.

The skin on my arms began to tingle as I repeated the directions under my breath one last time. 'Straight. Left. Right. Straight over. Through the park. Left.'

'Anna… Anna,' Jonty interrupted me, and I stopped and looked up at him.

'Yep?'

'Can we get going… please?' I could see he was nervous too. Little brothers were like dogs; they could smell the fear.

I took a deep breath and off we went. Weaving and winding, ducking and diving, lefting and righting, using every sense possible (including my sixth one) to avoid being run off the road. I didn't take it personally. The swearing, honking and bumper-dodging weren't reserved solely for us after all – although I'd wager that we had more car doors opened in our faces than most.

We stopped briefly at a set of traffic lights and I looked back at Jonty, who flashed me a nervous smile. It was starting to get dark now. I was doing my best to keep my gaze dead ahead at lights and not look sideways at the men in low-slung jeans, gathered around cars parked on the pavement. The shop fronts were mostly graffitied. A lot of them seemed to be selling car parts and were adorned with tyres and exhaust pipes. Just then I spotted a man get off the hood of one of the cars and start making his way towards us. He looked left and right before stepping into the road and making his way through the stopped traffic to the front of our bikes.

'You two,' he said looking directly at me. 'You be careful out here.'

He didn't seem to be threatening us, more offering a genuine warning. It was a good job I had just been to the bathroom, because if there was anything that will make you wet yourself with fear, it is likely to be a man in the Bronx warning you to be careful.

The lights changed and with a renewed injection of

adrenaline, we were off again! 'Straight. Left. Right. Straight over. Through the park. Left.' At last, we hit Third Avenue and took a straight shot for the Third Avenue Bridge. Pedalling over the bridge and onto Manhattan Island, I breathed a huge sigh of relief. By the time we made 125th Street, my heart rate had just about returned to normal levels. And it was only then that I realised I was absolutely famished. In all the excitement and the incessant need to keep moving forwards for fear of getting ourselves into trouble, we had barely eaten since breakfast. We pulled into a parking bay on Lexington Avenue to briefly inhale the honey sandwiches that Ann had packed us off with that morning. It had taken us 3.5 hours to ride the last 20 miles but we were in New York City at last, and although it was long after dark, the city was alive with colour.

Yellow taxis whooshed and weaved in front of us, having little regard for our path. My eyes darted from side to side, trying to take it all in. There were glimpses of buildings through a sea of people clad in gloves, hats and winter jackets. There was my cold breath on the night air, as I watched the droplets suspended for a moment in front of my face and then disappearing, carried by the biting wind. There was Jonty's smiling face. His red cheeks. And all around him sparkled. Red lights, white lights, green lights. Blue lights suspended in trees. Christmas trees. Christmas markets. Holly and ivy.

I caught sight of the Chrysler Building, and then the Empire State, their spires reaching into the clouds and being engulfed by them. Sirens, horns, high heels clip-clopping on concrete pavements, bursts of laughter from the open doors of sports bars, waves of chatter. Vendors on street corners selling hot dogs, pretzels, slices of pizza. Wafts of freshly cooked popcorn and honey-roasted nuts flooded my nostrils. The heat from the car engines warmed my legs as I passed. My heart pounded. And then at last, the corner of 47th Street and 9th Avenue – home for now, at least.

We pulled on our brakes one last time in Hell's Kitchen and pushed on the buzzer of Annabel-Zoe's Manhattan apartment block. After 11 hours of riding and a dramatic traffic-dodging finale to end the week, Jonty was safely delivered to his awaiting girlfriend, Kate, and so ended my duty as a big sister for the time being.

As we waited for the girls to make their way downstairs to let us into the apartment block, I turned to Jonty and gave him a hug.

'We made it!'

'Yayyy!' he replied.

'Thanks for coming, broski. You did so well. I'm sorry that last bit got so ugly.'

'No way. Thank you, sis. It was a complete disaster, everything I could have hoped for.'

And he gave me one last hug as the apartment door swung open.

Thanksgiving

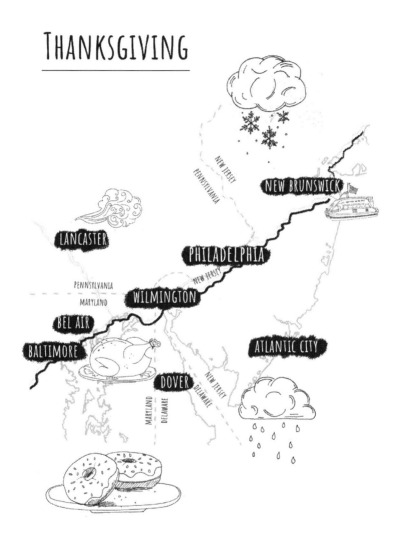

16

'Mum, the turkey smells like farts'

Distance Cycled: 8,133 miles

States Completed: 30

I spent the following five days in New York City. Resting, exploring and indulging in my favourite pastime of sitting in coffee-shop windows and watching the world go by. One morning, I couldn't sleep, so I snuck out of Annabel-Zoe's apartment in Hell's Kitchen at 5 a.m. to sit in a coffee shop in Times Square. From there, I watched the city come to life – yawning and stretching, footsteps on the pavement, a sea of commuters with take-out coffees in hands, heads nestled deep into the collars of thick winter coats. For each person that passed the window, I built a fictitious world in my mind. Their names, where they were headed, their occupations, their families, their troubles, their loves, their losses, their joy and their grief. I wondered about everything that made them who they were at that moment when they passed the window. *Are they happy?* I wondered. *Do they know what they are supposed to be doing with their life?* Most were purposeful in their gait, moving swiftly along the street, as if being compelled by a force greater than their own. But there was a melancholy in some of their faces, a preoccupation in their eyes, which hinted that they might not be so sure where they were going or why, after all. I watched the passers-by until each was out of sight, before beginning again on the next one.

In between people-watching in the city, I spent some quality family time with Jonty, Kate and Annabel-Zoe. We ate Mexican, Italian, cronuts, donuts, seafood and seaweed. Naturally that was all washed down with wine, beer, martinis and margaritas. We went ice skating in Central Park, took a walk down 5th Avenue, waved at the Statue of Liberty from the bottom of Wall Street and took in a show on Broadway. I also visited the students at New York Harbor School, where I was fascinated to learn that it's the only school in America where water studies form the core of the curriculum. That is, the kids learn how to build and operate boats, spawn and harvest oysters, design submarines, conduct environmental marine research and dive underwater. Everything that might set the younger generation up for a life supporting the New York Harbor and Hudson River. The school sits on Governors Island and, quite aptly, the only way to get there is by ferry. I loved my time at the school, which was so different from the norm and seemed to be showing the kids so many unique options for careers later in life. Best of all, I was even given a stuffed seal by the kids as a thank you – I named him Hudson.

On the fourth day in New York City, I hugged Jonty and Kate goodbye as they got into a shuttle bus bound for JFK airport. I went back to Annabel-Zoe's apartment, flicked on the TV, and began to pack for my own departure the following morning. To my horror, the weather channel reported that new winter storm Boreas was rolling on up the East Coast and was due to hit just as I prepared to leave the city. My heart sank.

Since the incident in Iowa where I set out to ride 120 miles and ended up verging on hyperthermia and in a motel after 50 of those miles, I'd resolved to be more sensible with any decision to ride in strong winds and heavy rain. The only problem was I had allowed just two days to make good on a promise to spend Thanksgiving with a friend in Baltimore. Looking back now, such promises seemed arbitrary – surely my friend would have understood if I had got held up in a storm? But she had recently moved to Baltimore from the UK and I knew she was struggling to settle in, so I wanted to pay her a visit when I had said I would. Being a let-down was not an option, storm or no storm. Baltimore was a 220-mile ride from NYC, and 110 miles was a long way to cycle each day in the face of storm Boreas.

The following morning, the temperature was sitting just above zero – warm enough to give riding a crack at least and so, at 5.30 a.m., I snuck out of Annabel-Zoe's Manhattan apartment and was on my way. I had no choice except to go for it and make it as far towards Baltimore as I could.

Wheeling through the still dark, subdued, city streets, I enjoyed the slight nip in the air and the sensation of being in motion once again. Just as I had in Chicago, I revelled in the quiet of the city at that time of the morning. At the chance to be alone with the skyscrapers, pavements and rivers of tarmac as they flowed endlessly out of sight. At the bottom of Wall Street, I dismounted from Boudica and wheeled her onto Pier 11.

Looking back on the experience of riding into New York City, I knew that I didn't fancy riding out of the city too, and so had opted to get the ferry over to the next state, New Jersey, and continue my journey down the East Coast in that way. Sitting on the ferry dock, sipping a coffee I'd acquired from a shack at the entrance, it felt odd to be on my own again. The five days spent in New York with Jonty and the girls had never felt like reality. Not the reality I was living at the moment, anyway. They were too comfortable, too far-removed from the day-to-day of the adventure to consider them to be a part of it. For the five days spent in the city, it'd felt like the trip had been placed on pause. I always knew it would restart, but taking another glug of coffee, alone on Pier 11, I wasn't sure that I was entirely ready for it to, not just yet anyway.

The ferries on the pier seemed to come and go at an alarming rate. In true British style, I had expected that someone would dutifully inform me that my ferry was about to depart. I soon realised, after missing two ferries for Bedford, New Jersey, that you must have cat-like reactions so as not to miss the swift docking, loading and departure of the ferry.

Forty-five minutes later, the ferry docked in the sleepy and deserted town of Newport. I decided I needed to warm up a little before carrying on, so I stayed in the ferry terminal for 20 minutes. Munching on a muffin purchased from the small shop inside the ferry terminal, I let the warmth of a large coffee be pumped through my veins. I took my first pedal strokes into state number 31, New Jersey, and to my delight, discovered a bike path. I was sure to take the time to congratulate myself on the decision to take the ferry route. It had allowed me to be catapulted directly from the middle of a busy hectic city to the relative calm of suburbia. I was now feeling warm again, from both the coffee and the self-congratulation. That storm I had been so concerned about as I'd left the apartment that morning seemed nowhere to be seen. I concluded that perhaps it was all hype, after all, and went on to bash out my first 55 miles in New Jersey by midday.

Alas, as I left my lunch stop the skies darkened overhead. The heavens opened and it began to pour. And my, how it poured. Big freezing globules of rain dropped like shells from the sky, splashing onto my rain jacket and creating rivers that ran down my sleeves and into my gloves. The wind soon drove the icy rain sideways, so that it clawed at my already reddened cheeks. I had a small cycling cap on, which kept the worst of it from my eyes and allowed me to still just about see – I took this as a major positive.

For the next three hours, the rain continued to pour and I gave a little whimper as I felt the first stages of it creep through my thick winter jacket. I crossed a state line once again and was back in Pennsylvania. Contrary to the start of the day's ride in New Jersey, the riding became ugly as I fought for space among streams of traffic on the outskirts of Chester, riding through broken glass and often slamming poor Boudica's front wheels down unseen potholes. Having ridden 90 miles, I was still 30 miles shy of the target for the day but decided to take refuge in a motel and hoped to make up the lost miles the following day.

On the second day of my battle with storm Boreas, I woke at 7.30 a.m. to find that it was pouring with rain again. I searched for a modicum of joy in the idea of going cycling, but, still tired and downtrodden from the previous day's ride, I struggled.

'There's no point in starting out in this,' I said to myself.

I resolved that I would leave it 30 minutes or so, but with my unbelievable ability to faff, 30 minutes naturally turned into an hour and a half, and when I finally wheeled my way up the road from the motel, it was raining just as heavily as it had been when I woke up. I cursed myself for not leaving earlier.

The route from Chester put the U, the G, the L and the Y into ugly. Although the Y was mostly a question I was asking myself. The terrible weather was doing little to dispel my now terrible mood. My mind was as saturated as my jacket with negative thoughts, and those thoughts continued to rain down too. In the hours that followed I began to convince myself that the whole trip was a waste of time. That no one really cared what I was doing and that I was foolish to be out here, riding in this sodding storm, traffic dodging, and for what?!

The web of outer-city streets led me on many twists and turns. Navigating began to require constant attention and trying to repeatedly use my now soggy phone to load up maps, as I cowered under tunnels and bridges in respite from the rain and the wind, was getting old very quickly.

'This is CRAP!' I shouted as I stood under one tunnel, my words reverberating off the dark brick arches and bouncing around and landing back onto my ears. It was crap. I was cold, tired and in no way enjoying the day. The tunnel confessional seemed to do something to shift the dial, however, if only a little. As always, in admitting that a situation was almost 100% crap, I had released a little bit of steam from the crap-filled pressure valve.

Fifteen miles further on, now clear of the worst of the city at least, I wrestled my thoughts into the semblance of a better mood. I told myself that the weather might ease up and clung to that idea. Instead, the wind picked up and it hailed. I went into a weird saddle-based trance, removing myself from the situation entirely and pretending I wasn't really there on the road.

I couldn't tell you exactly what went through my head that day, only that I tried to remain chipper at all times. This meant lying to myself and to others on many occasions. To questions of 'Aren't you cold?' and 'Isn't it miserable to be so wet?' I retorted 'Oh no, I'm fine, it's not so bad, I love the feel of the driving rain against my frozen skin.' If all else failed, I told myself I only had an hour left on the bike. Then carried on for six. I cried a little as I cycled – nothing special, no dramatics, just a small sob every three minutes or so. I'd mumble something to myself through the tears, usually 'This is shit' or 'Sod off, just sod off, why can't you just sod off and stop raining. You sodding rain.'

My tears were borne of a frustration. This was the kind of day I shouldn't be riding; I should be able to make a sensible call and just stay indoors and sit it out. But with the winter weather closing in fast and the incessant need to make miles, sitting tight wasn't an option. I felt an overwhelming sense of hopelessness. Like nobody cared. It didn't help that I'd managed to lose my high-vis vest on the ferry over from NYC. Ever since I'd been given one by Cindy in Colorado, I'd never wanted to be without it. In this weather, on these busy roads, I felt like a sitting duck as traffic passed within inches of the bike.

By lunchtime I'd begun to obsess about my high-vis vest, or lack thereof. So, after crossing into a narrow sliver of land that marked the state of Delaware, I pulled into a K-Mart and treated myself to a fluorescent orange hunter's vest. I wasn't really in the mood to celebrate state-bagging today, but I took the purchase of the vest as a gift to myself and a memento of the smallest of all of the US states. Normally these vests would be used to avoid being shot in the forest on a hunt; I would be using it to avoid being run over in the urban jungle. I paired the vest with a back-up high-vis belt I had sitting at the bottom of my pannier, which left me looking like a cross between Captain Bucky O'Hare and Flash Gordon. I looked ridiculous in my bright orange Delaware-chic ensemble, seated atop my pink bike, but I'd be darned if anyone was going to miss seeing me on the road now.

During my high-vis purchase, I had stopped to check the map. I'd hoped to carry directly on down Route 40 into Baltimore, in the state of Maryland. But on closer inspection, I saw that the green-marked bicycle route went up to the bridge over the Susquehanna River, stopped, and continued the other side. What did that mean?! There had to be a good reason for it. There were usually pedestrian walkways on bridges that I could normally wheel my bike over, but it didn't look like there was even a walkway on this one. I cursed myself for not noticing this crucial piece of information earlier, because I could have made a direct beeline for what looked like a more cycle-friendly bridge higher up the river. As it stood, going up to that bridge now and back down would add an extra 30 miles to today's 120-mile ride.

It was already 2 p.m., and fast becoming apparent that I either had to find a way to get across that bridge, or that I'd be stopping short of Baltimore tonight, missing Thanksgiving with my friend and breaking a promise I'd tried so hard to keep. I decided that the latter was a terrible option. I hadn't ridden through a day and a half of torrential rain, only to not make it in time.

I racked my brain for ideas and decided to go for it – I'd rock up at the bridge and see what transpired. Upon arriving at the crossroads in front of the bridge, I immediately spotted the reason there were no bikes allowed. Not only was the way across narrow, with just enough space to allow two lanes of fast moving traffic through, but the sides of the bridge were sheer concrete slabs. Sheer girl-on-a-bicycle-squishing slabs. Not in a million years would I have attempted to make my way across that! I'd seen some death-trap bridges in my time, but this one took the Baltimore biscuit.

Sitting at the crossroads just before the bridge, I became increasingly aware that people were staring at me. I tried to ignore them, instead choosing to look wistfully ahead, towards the bridge, as if I had some kind of plan, when the reality was I had no plan at all. *Why are there no directions for long-distance cycle tourists who have made promises to their friends for Thanksgiving?!* I thought. Just then a woman in the car next to me wound down her window. 'You're not going across are you?!' she asked, a look of horror on her face.

'Oh no.' I smiled. 'I'm trying to find a way to get a ride over,' I replied.

'Good – it's not safe to be on your bike around here. There's a station down there, maybe they can help?' she said, gesturing to a set of white single-storey buildings up ahead to the left. I felt humbled by her concern and a little embarrassed. I stood out like a sore thumb. It would have been like spotting a cyclist in the UK's Dartford tunnel. What a prize plum.

Just as I approached the white set of buildings, it started to snow and I smiled. I couldn't help it. This was getting ridiculous, and in fact, the sheer insanity of the situation had now cheered me right up. It was then I realised that the white buildings were in fact a police station, and that cheered me up even more. It is a well-known fact that police are lovely. Yes, yes, American police officers are the loveliest of them all. They save people's lives and things. I had seen it in the movies. So when I entered into the lobby of the station and the other people milling around asked me, 'Jeez, guurl, ain't you cold out there in that storm?!' I replied, 'It's not so bad you know.' And I meant it.

Naturally, the police officers thought I was certifiably insane. They couldn't seem to get over the fact that I was cycling in America, let alone the fact that I was cycling in a storm and, worse still, I was determined to find a way to get a ride across the bridge. I was sort of hoping one of the nice officers would come to my aid and offer to sling my bike in the back of one of their police cars and give me a ride across, but alas, they didn't seem to be offering. Fair enough – the good American public weren't paying their taxes for me to use the police like a taxi service. Just then, the man in the queue behind me piped up.

'You wanting to get across that bridge?'

I swung round to see a man in his late 50s, with grey balding hair and large specs.

'Yes, I'm hoping to… only it doesn't seem so friendly for bikes.'

'Jeez. You've got some nuts, coming down here in the storm, but I'll give you a ride over.'

'You will?!'

'Sure,' said the man, who now seemed to find my predicament amusing.

I threw my bike in the back of Earl's truck and, in the three-minute ride across the bridge, we covered everything about him, his life and his family. Having not spoken to anyone properly since leaving New York, and upon deciding that Earl really was a rather lovely man, I bathed in the warmth of his company. Safe in the knowledge that people seemed to be willing to lend a helping hand no matter where I was in the country, I waved Earl off, saddled back up on Boudica and crossed into the state of Maryland. That left me 33 states down, with just 17 to go. Looking down Route 40 towards Baltimore, I narrowed my eyes.

'Game on, Baltimore' I said aloud. Operation Thanksgiving was go.

At 7.30 p.m., I made it to my friend Lizzie's flat in downtown. I wanted to collapse on the pavement outside, to yell up at the window and wail at her about the few days of horrific riding through Boreas that I'd taken to ensure I made it to her in time. I wanted to rant and rave about how cold I was, how hungry I was, how all I wanted to do right that very second was curl up in a ball and fall asleep. Instead, I swallowed all of these things down, took a deep breath and knocked calmly on the door. A moment later it flung open.

'You made it!!' Lizzie shouted, flinging her arms into the air. 'How was the ride?'

'Oh, you know, okay. A bit cold. Here, I bought you some doughnuts,' I said handing her a box of Krispy Kremes I'd stopped to buy at a gas station a mile earlier. 'Could I have a shower please?'

The following day was Thanksgiving and I made up for the tough few days of riding into to Baltimore by doing very little. In fact, I had been so focused in my efforts to do nothing that much of the day had disappeared, and it was now late afternoon.

'What *is* that smell?!' Lizzie cried from the kitchen.

I hauled myself off the sofa and poked my head around the corner to find Lizzie with her head in the fridge, nose to nose with a dead bird. I stuck my head into the fridge and inhaled deeply too, gagging as a rotten stench flooded my nostrils and hit the back of my throat. That was surely not good.

Five minutes of repeated turkey sniffing ensued (surely this is now a contender for an Olympic sport in years to come), and after much discussion about the possible logical next steps we could take, Lizzie decided to call her mum, who was at home in Henley-on-Thames in the UK.

'Mum,' she said, and there was a long pause. 'The turkey smells like farts.'

'What kind of fart, darling?' came the swift reply from her mum, and I wondered at this point how many kinds of fart there were. I could think of at least three, and relevant subcategories to boot.

'Well. Sort of an eggy fart,' Lizzie continued. 'Like a mixture of egg and death.'

'Ah, a sulphur dioxide fart,' Lizzie's mum replied.

Dammit! I forgot that kind of fart! I thought.

'That doesn't sound good. Is there any discolouration on the bird?' her mum pressed on with her line of turkey questioning. 'Errr… Hang on…,' Lizzie said, holding the phone away from her face as we all took a pause for Olympic sport number two: turkey staring. She poked the turkey a little with her finger before concluding. 'It's yellow, Mum.'

And so, with a jaundiced, farting turkey, our hopes of a perfect first-ever Thanksgiving dinner went up in a puff of yellow sulphuric smoke. Thank goodness for the late-night store over the road and crispy chicken strips. I'm pretty sure the pilgrims would have gone in for chicken strips anyway, had they been offered them first by the Native Americans. The terrible food didn't dampen the mood and, with each chicken strip I ingested, and a few extra slices of pumpkin pie, I could feel my spirits lift.

As with all good friends, it seemed like I had seen Lizzie only yesterday. There was something about the company of an old friend that put my recent woes into stark perspective. No storm lasts forever, after all, and with every change in weather, town and scenery, I knew that I would keep moving forwards – even though it felt as if I was doing it slowly at times. With a belly full of pumpkin pie, I checked the forecast for the next few days and saw that it was set to be cold, but dry, at least. Boreas the Ugly had passed me by, or rather I had passed through it, and I was more than excited about my next stop – Washington DC.

PENNSYLVANIA

MARYLAND

WEST
VIRGINIA

VIRGINIA

WASHINGTON D.C

CHARLOTTESVILLE

RICHMOND

MT ROGERS

VIRGINIA

NORTH CAROLINA

RALEIGH

WILMINGTON

COLUMBIA

MYRTLE BEACH

CHARLESTON

WASHINGTON D.C

17

Dreaming of Dixie

Distance Cycled: 8,329 miles
States Completed: 33

It had been a while since I'd experienced the stomach jump that comes from seeing a famous landmark for the first time. Rounding the bend on the bike path into Washington DC, the unmistakable dome of the Capitol Building came into view. It was perfectly silhouetted against a clear blue sky, so I squealed. Then giggled. Then mouthed, 'That. Is. So. Cool,' and stared at it so long I almost rode my bike into a fence.

I had never really thought much about what Washington DC might be like until it became a part of the 50-state journey, but, nevertheless, I was won over. The bike lanes in and around town were some of the most impressive I'd come across since Seattle, as was the attitude of the drivers to cyclists using them – a key indicator of how well supported cycling really is in a city. I couldn't get over the fact that many of the lanes were in the middle of the road – keeping cyclists out of harm's way while the traffic went about its business around the edges.

I stayed with friend of a friend, Martha, and her husband, on the outskirts of the city and decided to take a day off to soak it up. The number of things to see and do within a compact area was overwhelming. I'm not what you might call a culture vulture; I prefer being outdoors getting muddy to being inside reading things on walls or looking at pictures, but I just had the feeling that I should spend a little time immersing myself in the history lessons on offer in DC. So I stayed up late to plan a jam-packed schedule for the following day.

I woke up the next morning at 7 a.m. and leapt out of bed. I got dressed, threw some breakfast in the general direction of my face and hopped on the metro, bound for downtown Washington DC. One by one, I worked my way through art galleries, covering French, Chinese, Greek, American and Russian work with indoor and outdoor collections spanning everything from the Byzantine era in A.D 330 to the twenty-first century. I spent an hour in the National Museum of the American Indian, followed by the Museum of Natural History, and rounded everything off with a trip to the National Museum of American History. There, I learnt about the Battle of Baltimore, which was where the Americans fought a historic battle against the Brits in 1812, after (as far as I could gather) the Brits got all up in the US' business and waded in to meddle with their international trading. That exhibition was my favourite of them all because they had on display the original 200-year-old American flag. A flag which had been painstakingly handmade over seven weeks and raised up above that battlefield for the first time all those years ago. It was seeing the 'broad stripes and bright stars' fluttering against the sky that day that inspired lyrical dude Francis Scott Key to write the American national anthem that's so widely recognised today. Throughout the journey, I'd always found Americans to be patriotic and extremely proud of their homeland, so to see *the* American flag in the flesh made me feel a little bit proud as a temporary citizen of the country too.

Museums conquered, with a coffee in hand, I moved on to the monuments, whose greatest triumphs are to lend a sense of depth and soul to a city which is so young in comparison to other more established ones around the globe. I marvelled at the needle-like structure of the Washington Monument, fighting every urge to wade out into the lake like Jenny in *Forrest Gump*.

Last, but not least, I went to see Mr Lincoln. It wasn't until I spent time at the Lincoln Memorial that I truly understood how he altered the course of the history of the USA so dramatically. I decided then and there, looking up at him from the front of his giant cast feet, that he was not only tenacious, but also way ahead of his time. His irrepressible belief that every man was created equal became a driving force in the eventual abolition of US slavery. Any man who sets such a morally righteous ball in motion, whilst maintaining immaculate facial hair, gets my respect.

When I slipped into bed that night, after a home-cooked dinner of soup, fresh bread and roast chicken with Martha and her family, I felt I had a better understanding of why America is the way it is. Coming into the city having experienced over 8,000 miles of the country myself and accompanying that with a day immersed in tales of American history, I couldn't help but fall a little bit deeper in love with the USA; a country fragmented and united by its history all at once.

The following day, Martha escorted me from her home to the outskirts of DC. After 20 miles we parted ways and I pedalled off down the Chesapeake and Ohio canal path, which I followed for a blissfully solitary 75 miles. As dusk began to lay a blanket of scarlet over the canal, I wheeled over the Potomac River and crossed into state number 34, West Virginia.

'Well, helllooooo, West Virginia!' I yelled at the top of my voice. 'Nice to meet you!'

I was delighted to be here, in the *real* south. Land of *Duck Dynasty*, moonshiners, bootleggers, country roads and the Shenandoah River.

A month earlier, I'd received a message from Drea and Joe, whom I'd stayed with in Portland, which read: 'Hey Anna! I noticed from your route that you will go near Shepherdstown, WV. Some of our best cycling buddies live there and would be more than happy to host you, I'm sure. Just let me know if you're interested and I'll put you in touch!'

Those cycling buddies were Laurie and Marty, plus their two adorable kids, five-year-old Dimas and seven-year-old Ella. As always, I spent the first few minutes after crossing the threshold into a new home feeling a little nervous. I wanted to be polite, to be kind, to do all the things I'd been brought up to do when meeting strangers. But I needn't have worried – within 30 minutes I was fully immersed in family life, playing (and losing) a Star Wars lightsabre battle with Dimas, while Ella clambered on my back.

'No, no Anna, *you* need to die now,' said Dimas, as he stood back from what had apparently been a fatal blow with his lightsabre.

'Do I? But I'm Darth Vader, I have an invincible lightsabre, which I blocked your sabre with,' I replied.

'No, I just took your sabre away – it's over there on the floor, see?' pleaded Dimas, now looking visibly upset.

'Ah. Yes, I see!' I said, before commencing an elaborate Oscar-worthy death scene.

Fifteen seconds later, I was resurrected by Ella shouting, 'Be my pony! Be my pony!' closely followed by, 'I'm a tiger! – raaaaaarrrrrr!'

When the time came for Marty to put the kids to bed that night, I was exhausted. I had cycled 80 miles and re-enacted seven elaborate death scenes in many imaginary universes. I slunk onto the sofa next to Laurie and joined her in indulging in what she dubbed her guilty pleasure: *The Real Housewives of Atlanta*. Beers in hand, we chatted back and forth about life and all its wonderings, stopping any serious conversation every now and then to discuss whether Atlanta housewife Kenya's butt was real or fake.

I felt so at home in Laurie's house, surrounded by kind people with lovely kids, who watched trashy TV to relax just like I do from time to time. At home, normality frustrated me. I did everything I could *not* to be normal, sedate, still. But when away from it, when life was an ever-changing carousel of emotions, people and places, it was these moments of normality that kept the motion sickness of the road at bay.

The following morning, I was up and at 'em early doors. I stuffed down a breakfast of porridge oats and raisins, bid my farewells to Dimas and Elsa, giving Dimas my lightsabre for 'safekeeping' and waved goodbye to yet another family I may or may not see again. I wheeled back over the Potomac River, through the town of Sharpsburg, and to the battlefield of Antietam.

Now, I'm no history buff. In fact, you could likely attribute everything historical I learnt at school to a little wooden ruler with the names of past British monarchs printed on it. I had always found history… dull. I never really cared for 'facts' for a start, which were apparently a cornerstone of the subject. Litres of Mr Saunders' (long-suffering purveyor of secondary school education) red ink were wasted on correcting my fictitious and elaborate essay-like accounts of what Henry VIII *would* have said had he been a witty, light-hearted dude instead of a gluttonous, wife-slaying tyrant. But when Laurie and Marty had told me the previous night that the site of America's bloodiest civil war battle was just a few miles away from their home, something very odd happened – I was intrigued.

After a brief tour of the on-site museum and a short chat with the local ranger – who was a little bemused by both my mode of transport and my level of cheeriness so early in the morning – I went outside to look out on the battlefield. Perhaps it was because it was a foggy morning, and the rolling fields at Antietam were blanketed in a heavy haze, which parted every now and then to reveal a distant cannon or monument to the dead. It could have been that I had arrived at a place where over 3,000 souls took their last breath, and a further 18,000 were wounded – all in a single day. Whatever the cause, Antietam had a real 'feel' to it. A murky effervescence, bubbling just above non-existent and just below the tangible. I wouldn't have been entirely surprised if a ghostly figure had wandered from the field to shake my hand. I wasn't creeped out; I was just moved. Antietam is an eerie place, especially for someone with an overactive imagination.

Before long, I bid the ranger farewell and was on my way again, heading across the next state line into state number 35, Virginia. Virginia had one of the prettiest state signs I'd seen so far. A red cardinal perched on a brown branch, which led into two yellow and green flowers in full bloom. 'Virginia Welcomes You' it read, and I welcomed it too.

***

A few days before crossing the Mason–Dixon line, a historic boundary that marks the North–South divide, I had made the decision to change my route through the South. The original, pre-departure plan had been to skirt inland, covering Virginia, the Carolinas and Florida in as few miles as physically possible. In that way, I would also be able to take in one of the most scenic roads in the world: the Skyline Highway, a 105-mile highway that follows a ridge line in the Blue Ridge Mountains and the entire length of Shenandoah National Park.

Sadly, the weather had other ideas. It was now early December and with the recent storms and snow, I had been warned that the Skyline Highway was closed for the season. If I couldn't have mountains, I decided that I would have the next best thing – the ocean. So I went rogue and, like a muscular moth to a flame, I decided to add on a 'few' extra miles.

I took a straight shot south through Virginia and moved swiftly from town to town and city to city, staying with friends of friends and WarmShowers hosts in the cities of Fredericksburg and Richmond, before crossing the state line into state number 36, North Carolina.

On my first night in North Carolina, I stayed in the home of a chiropractor called Adam near the city of Raleigh, in which (much to my disappointment) everyone is not riding around on 80s vintage bikes. I celebrated the first day of Hanukkah with him and his two kids and explored his home, which was one fit for *MTV Cribs*, complete with a bathroom fully themed in the green, blue and orange colours of the Florida Gators basketball team – his university town's best team. As my never-ending search for what it is I was supposed to be doing with my life continued, I left Adam's house convinced that I was going to be a chiropractor. Not only because he seemed to earn a good living, but also because he was helping people. I liked both of those elements of the job, and Adam even went so far as to sit with me and look up some courses at American universities. The idea lasted for approximately three days, until I read I would have to do a week's worth of work experience in a chiropractor's practice to even get on a course. It was then I understood that if work experience wasn't for me, and that if I just wanted to get on with the business of helping people and cracking them back into place, then a seven-year chiropractor's course probably wasn't the right career path.

In the city of Goldsboro, I stayed with a young chap named Sam, who had hiked the Appalachian trail the previous year. On the morning I left town, we decided to go for breakfast together. It was early, before 8 a.m., and we were the only two people in the restaurant, except for an elderly man sitting in the corner. I had naturally ordered my usual pancake platter and went big on the maple syrup and crispy bacon too. Sam had held back at first, but for fear of getting 'food envy' (this is a real thing), he caved and ordered a similar-sized feast. When we got up to pay at the end of the meal, the waitress said, 'Oh, no worries – you're all set. That man over there got you all paid up.'

Sam and I looked at one another and then at the man, only he had gone. We left the waitress a tip, and dashed outside, on the hunt for our pancake prince. We looked all around, but the prince was nowhere to be found. He had just secretly bought us a pancake breakfast and... disappeared.

As my first week in the South wore on, I realised that I had been so distracted by the hosts, and so engulfed by their kindness, that I had missed seeing the landscape around me changing ever so subtly, day by day, bit by bit. The temperature rose by a fraction every day, and the warmth was a welcome change from the snow, wind and rain of the northern states. I was mostly riding on sandy farm tracks, past fields filled with strange-looking plants. Spindly chest-height shrubs with thin brown branches, more like twigs with little bobbles of white on the ends of them. From afar the whole field looked like 1,000 miniature doves had landed on the branches of miniature dead trees. *What in the world were they?* I wondered. I was thinking about what kind of vegetable might be growing beneath the surface in winter, when I came across one field where the plants were lined close to the fence, and the penny dropped. 'Cotton!' I called out, pulling on Boudica's brakes and screeching to a halt. They were cotton plants.

I had never really thought about how cotton grew before and I had certainly never seen a cotton plant. How have I worn it day-in, day-out over the years yet have such little understanding of where it actually comes from? It made me think about how many other materials there were in the world, and how I had never really considered where or how they grew. It made me feel uneasy about being so disconnected from the start of the chain. I consumed, but I didn't think. In the next field, I spotted something even cooler than just the plants: a giant ball of harvested cotton. It was all squidged up and wrapped in yellow plastic so that it resembled an enormous Liquorice Allsort. I chuckled to myself and wondered if a giant Bertie Bassett might be lying in wait just around the corner too. There was something wonderfully cartoonish about this Liquorice Allsort cotton ball. It looked entirely out of place in that field, like something from a Salvador Dalí painting.

It wasn't only the landscapes that were beginning to change. In North Carolina, I felt a shift in the level of interest that Boudica and I received too. People seemed more intrigued than ever about our journey, and I soon learned that if you want some attention in the US, anywhere south of Virginia, here's what you must do: 1) Be a woman, 2) Ride a pink bike, and 3) Have a British accent.

I had grown used to getting funny looks over the past six months, but the southern states were taking staring to a whole new level. I seemed to attract far more of an audience than usual at my snack stops at convenience stores and gas stations. My first enquiry had come from a man dressed head to toe in camouflage gear, wearing a beige baseball cap, set at a jaunty angle on his head. As he got closer, I could see that he was chewing on tobacco and seemed to think nothing of spitting it on the floor just in front of me before he spoke. Perhaps this was the polite thing to do when one is chewing tobacco? To spit before speaking. A sign of respect, so to speak.

In another gas station, I entered and passed a group of four men chatting in the small space between the food aisles and the counter. They seemed like work colleagues and I noted some sort of attempt at a uniform, although it was subtle enough to be misconstrued as fashion. They were all clad in denim jackets, faded baseball caps, thick steel-toed boots and a mix of khaki trousers and jeans. When I walked in, they all stopped talking and turned to look me up and down, before smiling at me – and I smiled back. As I approached the till to pay for my goodies, the men began chatting to me and I told them about my trip. They couldn't quite believe that I had ridden over 8,500 miles to this point, and through 36 states. There was a lot of 'Dammmn, gurll!' and 'Well, would you listen to that!'

We had a nice chat, about where I was headed, who I was and where I was from before the guys took it upon themselves to discuss the best route I should take south. Ordinarily, this would have bothered me – being told what to do 'n' all, and especially if I felt like it was because I was a woman – but on this occasion I didn't feel like that at all. They seemed unusually concerned for my safety and had just got a bit carried away among themselves. As I prepared to leave the gas station and get on my merry way, the conversation between John, Pete, Mike and Dougie started to get a little heated:

Pete: She be takin' the fitty-faw, I tells you. (Which I translated as Route 54.)

Dougie: Oh, no, no, no – the fitty-faw got construction on it, she best be on the thirty-one. That'll get her there safe...

Mike: Are you crazy?! There ain't no shoulder on the thirty-one, them trucks'll sneak up on her real fast. She be takin' the fitty-faw to the south junction then onto the twenty-three.

Pete: See, I tolds you – the fitty-faw, it's gotta be the fitty-faw.

Dougie: You didn't told me nothin', Pete, I drive that road all the time...

John: The thirty-one gots a big ole hill in it though boys, she don't wanna be goin' up no hill. How about the farm road, just off the twenty? Ain't no trucks on that there road.

Mike: The twenty?! John, are you outta your mind?!

The debate among 'the boys' got so heated and went on for so long that I tried to interrupt a few times, but to no avail. Instead, I just decided it best to sneak out the door while they were still yammering away and get back on the bike. I couldn't help but smile as I pedalled off; the genuine care for my safety was heart-warming. I was still smiling about 'the boys' and their insistence on keeping me safe when I crossed the state line into South Carolina and hit the shores of the Atlantic Ocean once more, at the town of North Myrtle Beach.

If you talk to Americans about Myrtle Beach, you'll become familiar with its reputation as 'Dirty Myrtle' or the 'Redneck Riviera'. Riding in, I could see the roots of such a reputation. The main highway is a migraine sufferer's worst nightmare. As far as the eye can see are bargain stores, chain restaurants and fast-food joints, all announcing the delights on offer with big flashing lights. But I soon discovered that Myrtle was one beach book I couldn't judge by its lightbulb-lit cover. Away from the busy highway, just one street over, I uncovered the reason that the area had become so popular in the first place: a beautiful windswept golden beach, surrounded by tufts of wild grass and punctuated with boardwalks and modest dunes. I was early for my arrival at my host's house in town, so I locked Boudica to a nearby lamppost and took a walk along the shore. With it being winter, the beach was as good as deserted and just when I thought things couldn't get any more blissfully solitary, a heavy fog rolled in, transforming my stroll from the marginally tranquil to the downright serene. I walked for another half an hour along the beach, disturbing large flocks of seagulls as I went and, every now and then, stopping to do a cartwheel. Why? Because I could. (I mean, I was impressed I still could at 28.)

When I was 19, fresh out of school and eyes ablaze with the wonder of the world, I decided to move to Australia for a while. There I became BFF-OUIGH (best friends forever – or until I go home) with a girl named Amy. Although, at the time of writing, Amy has represented Australia in the sport of rowing at two Olympics, she is originally from (drum roll, please) North Myrtle Beach, South Carolina. So, as soon as I hatched the new route, I thought of Amy and decided that I simply had to visit her home town. So, ten years after I had met their daughter in a country 9,000 miles away, I appeared on the doorstep of Amy's parents' house in North Myrtle Beach, and was welcomed by Price and Barbara like a long-lost child.

During my two-day stopover in town, Price told me that North Myrtle hadn't always been such a tourist trap and that, in the 70s, it was just a small town with less than a third of the population it has today. He and his sister Cookie took me out to show me the 'real' Myrtle – one full of quiet suburbs and community-centred block parties in the evening – where everyone knew everyone except, of course, the strange girl from Britain. Naturally, as part of my immersive Myrtle experience, I was treated to a proper Southern-style feast at the local all-you-can-eat buffet.

Cookie was a quick-witted woman who reminded me of a cross between Pink and Meryl Streep. She had short-cut, no nonsense white hair, cheek bones you could hang your washing off, a pixie-like smile and green-blue eyes with a twinkle of mischief running through them. The conversation flowed easily between the three of us as I worked my way through a plate full of the local fare – including collard greens (kale-cabbage stuff), biscuits (scones), gravy (a bit like bread sauce, only thicker), fried chicken (chicken, fried) – and washed it all down with sweet tea (cold tea with ten tablespoons of sugar in it).

Not being satisfied with the sugar fix from the tea, I agreed to a dessert of peach cobbler – mostly because it was 'tradition' and therefore had to be done.

Riding out (or rather rolling out) of town two days later, I saw the whole area through new eyes. I was grateful for my time spent in Price and Barbara's home because they had helped me find a deeper appreciation for Myrtle's history and beauty. Had I just ridden on through, I am sure my report of the town would have been entirely different – a fact that made me wonder how many towns I had already passed through and made a snap judgement about, only to miss something much more endearing beneath a brash veneer.

Leaving North Myrtle Beach, I continued to track along the shores of the Atlantic Ocean, through Murrells Inlet, Pawleys Island and Georgetown and into the historic city of Charleston. It was over those next few days that I started to notice a lot of new plants popping up at the sides of the roads. There were no longer just cotton fields I was seeing, but a whole host of other things. I failed to learn the official name for all the trees I saw in the swamps and forests of South Carolina, but the Beardy oak (*Muchos Hairyiculus*), the Mr Tickle tree (*Armus Gargantuan*) and the Spikey Hand Fan-Fern (*Highus Fivus*) were among those that repeated most frequently.

The change in shrubbery could be attributed to the fact that the climate in the south of the state had started to get a little sticky. Even though it was now nearing mid-December, the further south I rode, the more I seemed to become encased in a treacle-like heat. The heat was often accompanied by outbursts of rain, but the heat was there all the same. One particular day, it was only 25°C, but humidity was up at 85% and I'd neglected to take enough water with me for the morning, which was spent making my way along small sandy farm tracks. By the time late afternoon rolled around, I was beyond parched.

The air grated my throat as I swallowed it down and although I had been sweating profusely for the past hour, my body seemed to have given up on that – try as it might, the pores could produce sweat no longer in the treacle-like air surrounding them. My jersey clung to my back and shoulders without even the faintest sliver of space for any air to flow between my skin and the sodden Lycra. I came to a fork in the road and just before filtering onto the road, I looked back to my right. Like a mirage in the desert, there it was – a gas station. Glory be! I let out a little yelp, knowing the amber-sweet nectar of a bottle of orange soda followed by one of chocolate milk (and possibly some water after that) were now within a moment's reach.

I parked Boudica up outside and shoved open the door of the gas station. As I walked in, a customer standing at the counter seemed especially amused at my entrance. He kept looking from me to Boudica, and then back at me, but said nothing. He was a slim-built black man wearing a ragged denim jacket and a bright red cap. He smiled at me and I smiled back, before slinking off into the aisle to begin making my gas-gourmet selection for the day.

I began scanning the vast array of Michelin-starred delights on offer. The choice was a tough one: a soggy-looking white bread ham sandwich, a muffin that had been left out just that bit too long or a jar of gherkins. Sense prevailed and I went for the ham sandwich, grabbing the muffin as an after-thought, just in case it had some of my five-a-day within the blueberries. Of course, I would need something to wash down the meal, so I selected a 2013 vintage bottle of chocolate milk and some water. I passed the man again on my way from the till to sit down at one of the booths by the window, and as I began stuffing pieces of the ham-like substance into my pie hole, he appeared next to me.

'Say, miss – can I join you?' he said, gesturing to the empty seat in the booth opposite me.

'Of course,' I replied, swallowing down hard on the dry ham sandwich, which seemed to have decided to cling to the sides of my oesophagus like a chimney sweep.

'I'm Eddie,' he said, removing his cap and sliding into the booth.

'Nice to meet you, Eddie,' I said, extending my hand across the table for a handshake. Usually I was one for hugging, but I was a little tired and being all wedged under the table 'n' all, I went for the shake. Eddie, however, had other ideas. He took my hand, turned it over as if I were a princess and he prince charming, and he kissed the back of it. It wasn't seedy, it wasn't weird; a strange man had just kissed my hand in a gas station and yet it felt harmless. There was a gentle nature to Eddie, his movements were slow but purposeful and I got the impression right away that he wouldn't harm a fly.

With the hat now off of his head, I could get a good look at Eddie's face. Despite looking to be in his late 50s, he still had a good head of hair, which sat close to his head in tight black curls. Wisps of grey around his temples hinted at his age and I noted the odd stray chest hair escaping from his thin navy-blue T-shirt – its sagging neckline mirroring the drooping bags underneath his large cobalt-blue eyes – eyes which were puppy-like and looked as though he was on the verge of tears. If there was one thing Eddie clearly took care of, it was his teeth – they were pearly white, and he flashed them in a smile at me once more.

'Now what in the world are you doing all the way out here?' he said.

I told him the story. That I had now made it through 37 of the 50 states and would be carrying on for a while yet. I spoke for a few minutes, with Eddie pitching in every now and then with a 'Mmmm hummm, and then what?' and when I was done, Eddie fell silent.

'Well. In't that just something?' he said, sitting back in his chair and scratching his head. 'I can't even get me the kahunas to make it across that there state line, and here you are, li'l

Miss England, going wee wee wee all over those states like a piggy who ain't never going home for tea.'

He drew a wiggly line in the air with his hand to mimic what I assumed was meant to be my route for the journey and smiled again, although this time he was smiling to himself and shaking his head. There was another brief silence before he said, 'Say Anna, take my number, won't you?'

'Okay, Eddie, I'll take it. What would I use your number for though?' I asked.

'Well, you know, I just wanna check in on how you're doin' down the road. Nothing strange, like. Just tell me how you're gettin' along. What it's like out there. How the peoples of the States are treatin' you. You know?'

I didn't see any harm in taking his number. If it made Eddie happy, then it made me happy too.

'Sure thing, Eddie, I'll let you know how I'm getting along. What is it?'

'What's what?'

'Your number, Eddie, your number?'

'Oh! Yeah. It's hmmm… hang on there. Now jus' gimme a minute.'

Eddie pulled out a phone from his trouser pocket, one that looked like the first Nokia ever released onto the market. He put the phone purposefully on the table before reaching into the breast pocket of his denim jacket and producing a pair of folded-up reading glasses. He untangled the glasses piece by piece, one fold at a time before placing them delicately across the bridge of his nose. That task done, he turned his attention back to the phone and flipped it over to reveal a piece of paper Sellotaped to the battery on the back.

'I got it taped here, see? So I don't forget it.' He smiled, seemingly proud of himself. Eddie read me the number off the back of his phone and leapt excitedly from his chair when my 'test message' to him from across the table arrived on his phone.

'Well, gurl,' he said decisively, gently placing both palms onto the table and using them to lift him from his chair. 'I gots to be goin' now. I gots places to be and peoples to see. I hope you make it. I know you can.'

And with that, Eddie leaned forwards, put one hand around the back of my head and tipped it towards him, kissing me on the forehead.

'God bless you, my child,' he said as he moved back away and to a standing position. 'God bless you,' he said again as he swung open the door and walked across the forecourt.

As I watched Eddie walk off down the road, I wondered where he was going, where he lived, what his life was like... and what reports I might send him from the road ahead.

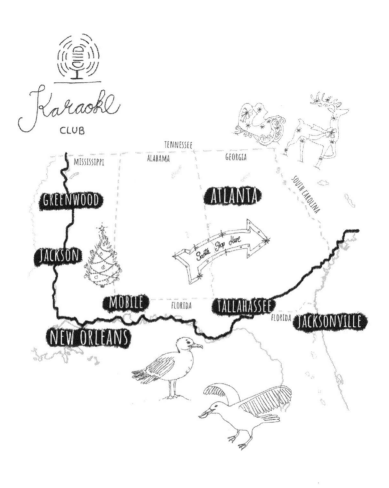

Karaoke
CLUB

TENNESSEE

MISSISSIPPI   ALABAMA   GEORGIA

SOUTH CAROLINA

GREENWOOD

ATLANTA

JACKSON

Santa Stop Here

MOBILE   FLORIDA   TALLAHASSEE

FLORIDA   JACKSONVILLE

NEW ORLEANS

THE DEEP SOUTH

18

Honk. Honk. Honk

Distance Cycled: 9,243 miles
States Completed: 37

The south-east US was turning out to be a wonderful place to meet storybook-esque characters, but not necessarily such a great place to ride a bike. I was grateful that I'd been hosted so much since leaving Washington DC. When I counted the hosts up, I realised it had been seven families over 10 nights. These strangers-cum-friends had become comfortable, safe bookends to what were long days of uncomfortable, anxious riding along busy roads with very little shoulder space to ride on. I was doing my best to control my nerves as I went and to make sensible choices to seek out quieter routes where possible. Near Charleston in South Carolina, for example, I had taken an 80-mile detour through Francis Marion National Forest to try to give myself at least a little respite from the busy main Highway 17, but the detours were taking their toll on my schedule. On account of all my dallying around earlier in the journey, and my extra miles to go and visit Amy's folks in South Carolina, I now had to take the most direct route possible through state number 38, Georgia.

I had loosely organised roads in the States into three

categories. They were either narrow roads with no shoulders but equally no traffic like those in Nevada, Wyoming or North Dakota. Or they were huge highways with large amounts of traffic but giant 3-metre-wide shoulders, like in South Dakota. Then there were the city streets, with dozens of options and back roads aplenty where you would always be surrounded by slow-moving but heavy traffic.

Here in the South, however, I was breaking new truck-filled, narrow-highway-category ground. The past two weeks had been fraught with struggles to find any space to ride safely. Through southern Georgia especially, there always seemed to be just one road going in the direction I was headed, and I was sharing it with every other Tom, Dick and Harry. The Dicks honked at me louder than the Toms and the Harrys – but all day, every day, people seemed to be honkin'. Honk. Honk. Honk. Sigh. Needless to say that much honkin' can really start to get a girl down.

On top of the busy roads, it was now 12 December. Everywhere was covered in tinsel or blasting out Yuletide songs and starting to feel Christmassy. Everywhere, that was, except inside my heart, which was mostly just feeling sad about having made the decision to be away from home for Christmas. What was Christmas about if it wasn't about your family, after all? No one had forced me to come out here and be away from them. I had done this to myself and I began to feel deflated. I ground back into long 100-mile days, but I took little joy from being on the bike. I tried distraction techniques, blasting music from my phone, which helped for a while. And on some days, I turned off the music and let my thoughts roam free. On those days, dark thoughts would rise from my mind like a swirling mass of emerald-tinged smoke above a witch's cauldron.

With only a month to go until the trip was due to end, I thought a lot about my impending return home, and an inevitable return to office work. *Did I want to go back to work?* I wondered. There was a voice that told me I had to. There were practicalities to think about, after all; my bank balance was well below zero for one. But I was beginning to wonder whether money was the only reason I would be going back, and in that case… what was this thing called money about? What did it bring me if it wasn't the freedom I craved?

I began to grow concerned that I would struggle to enjoy the final month on the road and that if things carried on like this, all ugly highways and fast trucks, then misery was surely a foregone conclusion. I then decided that there must surely be something on the road that lay ahead that would be interesting. I went into a research frenzy, looking up places of historical and cultural interest to look forward to seeing. That helped a little too. That week became a strange cocktail of emotions. I was sad to be away from home, not enjoying the riding, and all the while knowing that when I was home I would long to be back out here again, even if the riding was ugly and lonesome.

To add a cherry to the already overloaded ugly cake, it had been raining a lot over the past week – although the rain didn't bother me as much as it did further north. It was a welcome change from the sticky heat, at least. Georgia was experiencing a series of monsoon-like storms which mostly felt like cycling in a warm bath – that, or as if I had wet myself. My now sodden foam padding in my cycling shorts had collected much of the rain water, which ran off my jacket and down my legs. The rain made me even less visible to the fast-moving trucks, leaving me feeling more like a sitting duck than ever. Through the sogginess, the sense of unease and the slow creep of homesickness that was beginning to appear, I was doing my best to remain chipper, but by the time I crossed the border into Florida, I was mentally exhausted.

***

It was my first day in Florida. I'd only been cycling for 5 miles and already I was in tears. This wasn't the first time I'd sobbed from the saddle, but today felt different, and worryingly so. I should have been celebrating the 39th state, gorging on freshly picked oranges, hanging with Mickey Mouse at Disney, riding alligators into the swamp sunset and all those other things Florida is famous for. Instead, I could barely summon up the energy to get off the bike and take a selfie with the 'Sunshine State' sign. I was now in one of the lowest states of the whole journey – in every sense. Every minute on the bike felt like an hour. I couldn't concentrate, I had no focus, no motivation and I was turning the pedals with such a pathetic effort that I was hardly moving. I was tired, just so very tired – of everything. It felt like someone had tied 100 little lead weights on my body, and they were just hanging there, dragging me down. And there were several hung around my heart too – I missed my family terribly.

My mood hadn't been helped by a stop at a gas station that morning, where the attendant had made the not unusual enquiry about what I was doing and where I was headed. It had taken me a while to remember where I had come from and where I was going that day – something I was beginning to get used to. The days, names, places and faces were all beginning to merge into one. After some prompting from the attendant of the possible places I could be headed, I remembered that I was riding to the city of Tallahassee.

'Oh, my, that's an awful long ride,' said the attendant, her blushed southern-belle cheeks glowing.

'Mmm hmmm,' I said wearily, just wanting to pay for my goods and get out of the gas station and be on my own again. That, or be given permission to curl up on the floor of the gas station and sleep for 1,000 years. I would have taken either option at that point.

'You know it's eighty miles to Tallahassee, don't you?'

'Yes, thanks. I do,' I said, doing my best to muster a smile that might challenge hers, but getting nowhere near it.

'I'm not sure you'll make that. Not today,' she said, still

smiling. Ordinarily these comments would run off me like water off a duck's back. But my feathers were saturated, clogged with the oil of months on the road.

Worse than the weariness was the fact that I was marginally concerned that I was officially going mental. I kept having bizarre dreams about my brake blocks. Ordinary women may dream of men on white horses, of becoming famous, swimming with dolphins, sipping margaritas on a deck... I, on the other hand, was dreaming about my brake blocks. The specialist hydraulic rim blocks were starting to wear down faster than usual due to all of the recent rain. I had ordered a replacement set which were waiting for me in Alabama, but that was still a week from now and I wasn't sure if my current set would last that long. It was your classic first-world problem and it was crippling me.

As I went to bed each night, I could feel the sensation of my hands squeezing my brake levers and them taking a while to stop. I kept dreaming that I didn't stop at all and flew off the road into ditches, into the back of trucks or off cliff edges. Any inhumane way to die at the hands of failed brakes – you name it, I was lucid dreaming about it. It was a sensation that kept me from falling asleep at night and then made me feel sick when I woke up. It was completely irrational; I can only imagine that in some form I'd projected all of my worries about the final few weeks of the journey onto my brake blocks. Eat your heart out, Freud.

That day, I felt uncomfortably alone. Like a child lost in a crowd at a theme park. There was no one here for me to talk to, and I knew that if I had mustered the will to call someone back home then I would struggle to explain precisely what it was I was so upset about that very day. I knew no way to cope other than to aim to snap out of it.

I decided that if this was going to be the lowest point in the whole trip, and it certainly felt that way, then I was going to make some good of it. I pulled over to the side of the road, left Boudica on her stand at the roadside and waded into the forest a little and got out my camera. I turned the lens to face me and began to talk to it.

I cried a little more and got angry when I recounted how I was fed up of the weather, the roads and people telling me I couldn't achieve what I'd set out to do. Then there was the brake-block chat. I admitted I was obsessed.

'I'm obsessed with my bloody brake blocks! It's ridiculous. Completely ridiculous! I don't know what I think's going to happen. It's not like I'm going to die if they wear down!' Immediately – even though I knew I might never share that video with anyone following the journey online – it felt like a weight had been lifted. I'd had a release. I'd stopped trying to cheer myself up and instead indulged in the glorious ugly truth – I was miserable and today was a crap day. As if by magic, I felt better.

The road conditions past Tallahassee started to improve.

Ribbons of freshly laid tarmac flowed in front of me and smaller, well-surfaced backcountry roads took me away from the traffic-heavy main highway beneath a low-hanging tree canopy. I had a feeling that in Florida, things were going to get better.

By the time I arrived on the southern coast of the US at the Gulf of Mexico, Florida was continuing to do its best to drag me out of my slump, and for that I was grateful. It was still humid, but the muggy air was accompanied by a cool on-shore breeze. My arrival on the Gulf Coast coincided with the parting of the heavy curtain of thunderous grey which had suffocated me for the past week, revealing bright, crisp, cloudless blue skies. It was as if the South had been testing me, treating me to a baptism of fire to check just how badly I wanted to complete this journey, and at last the master in charge, the sorcerer of the South, had said, 'Enough! She's had enough. The poor girl's had a sob and is dreaming about her brake blocks. Let's give her a li'l sunshine, shall we?'

I watched my shadow ride alongside me, cast by the late afternoon sun onto the concrete sides of the bridge into Panama City, and at last I found the Florida I had read and heard so much about. Oversized yachts bobbed on a deep blue ocean, gathered in plush marinas, their pearly white fibre-glass hulls and wooden decking twinkling in the bright winter sun. Smaller rubber dinghies whizzed to and fro between the yachts like worker bees in a hive. Parasailers cut across the rays of the sun every now and then, suspended high and free above the warm Caribbean water, fringed by white sand. The whole scene looked like something from a high-end property catalogue. *What was it like to live here?* I wondered. *Did the people of Florida's panhandle know just how dreamy their world was?*

After pedalling from Panama City to Pensacola, I opted to take Route 30A, a road that runs right next to the shoreline and would lead me to the appropriately named seaside town of Seacrest. I'd been told by recent hosts in Florida that this road was swollen with traffic in the summertime. 'Bumper to bumper!' they said. But as it was 'winter' (ahem, 21°C and sunny), the small, immaculately maintained towns and silky smooth sandbars along Route 30A were all but deserted.

Seacrest itself looked like a town fresh out of *The Truman Show*. It was immaculate, almost suspiciously so. Bright green patches of grass were neatly cut in squares, dotted between silky smooth tarmac roads with not a pothole or cracked road marking in sight. The town itself had a European feel – quaint cream-coloured coffee shops and bars with open fronts, outdoor seating and bike racks outside. And then there were the Christmas trees: triangular, full-branched evergreens decorated with perfectly spherical, evenly distributed red baubles, and red and gold wrapped presents at their base. I thought about how long such a structure would last in many parts of London before someone peed on it, vomited over it, or stumbled into it while drunk. I grew suspicious that Seacrest was breathing in, holding it all together so that it might appear picture-perfect as I passed through it and the second I was out of sight, it would relax – allowing its bulging, unsightly belly to flop out and cause the button on its favourite pair of jeans to burst. Yet, for now, I was grateful that Seacrest could keep it all together to save me from starting to fall apart.

I was early for my arrival at my host's house in town, so I decided to take a ride down to the beach and chill out there for a bit. Riding onto the beach was a great idea in theory. The reality was that the way down to the beach was via a set of 50 wooden steps. I locked Boudica to a lamppost at the top and started to go down to enjoy the beach myself, but something told me that wasn't fair. I'd had a tough week and wanted a little beach time, but Boudica deserved it too. I caressed her chipped pink paintwork and well-worn leather saddle and muttered, 'Get your bikini on, Boudie, we're going to the beach.' I then proceeded to carry 30 kg of bike and bags down the 50 wooden steps to the whitest beach I had ever had the pleasure to set foot on.

With Boudica propped next to me, I lay on my back and let the warmth from a day of sunshine transferred from the sand to my cycling jersey. I watched seagulls swoop and play above me. I made sand angels. I then got intrigued as to just how close I could get the seagulls to come and so laid a ring of jelly sweets around my body and lay back down. Sure enough the seagulls swooped down next to me. At first, I yelped – their wings seemed huge just centimetres from my face – and then I relaxed. I shut my eyes (hoping the seagulls wouldn't decide to express their gratitude for the sugary feast by pooping on me), exhaled a long breath and let go. Five more weeks, another 900 miles and I'd be lying on my back on a beach in Hawaii, I thought. Just five more weeks.

In the week that followed my visit to Seacrest, I picked my way along the National Seashore Park, and mostly rode with my mouth wide open. It was just so pure, untouched and pristine. Not pristine in the way that manicured Seacrest had been – this was naturally pristine, with emeralds and blues of the ocean lapping against shores of snow-white sand. I wasn't alone on the seashore: dotted along it were fishermen, casting single rods from small bright-red boats. I crossed the Florida state border and into Alabama, before spending a night on a tiny spit of land called Dauphin Island. I treated myself to a night of solitude in a modest motel there, and from my bedroom on the ground floor I could hear the waves breaking on the beach, just beyond the dunes. I was the only one in the motel that night and yet, just as I'd been told in Florida, apparently the motel was jam-packed with people in the summer months. Lucky, lucky me.

That night, when I could see that the sun had started to slink from view, I wrapped up warm, pulled on my beanie and scampered out to the beach. It had been an overcast day and the clouds had now thinned out, creating a patchwork of blues, whites and greys across the sky. I sat on the sand and watched and waited as the sun continued to drop below the horizon. At last, it reached a point where the sun's rays could sneak through the clouds. They cast a yellow glow over the watery sheen on the beach, creating a mirror on the sand that reflected the patchwork colours of the sky. I would have never thought in a million years that one of the finest sunsets I would experience on this journey would be in Alabama, but it was fast becoming true.

***

I had arranged to meet Annabel-Zoe in Memphis, Tennessee, in less than a week's time, so I made short work of nipping through Alabama, through Mississippi and on to spend a night in state number 42, Louisiana. I was only in Louisiana for 120 miles, taking in the south-eastern corner of it, a fact that broke my heart. Originally, I had intended to head into New Orleans and take a few days off the bike to soak up the legendary French Creole, colonial vibes in the city. But time was ticking on, and on top of that I had grown tired of riding into big cities on a bike. When I researched the route into New Orleans, it looked unfriendly to say the least. Big main roads, bridges and no clear, quiet path for a touring cyclist, let alone one on an ever-shrinking schedule. I had to be honest with myself that it would not be a pleasant ride, and as much as I desperately wanted to visit the city, I resolved that I would just have to come back another time. Instead of a culture-rich visit to New Orleans I simply spent one night in a crummy Louisiana motel, and pedalled out of the state and back into Mississippi the following day. Glorious.

Mississippi was one state that always had the upper hand. I could never remember how to spell it and would mostly end up with several variations along the lines of Missippippi (which sounds like someone had missed episodes of *Pippi Longstocking* on TV), Missi-pissi (which sounds like what often happens when a man aims for the toilet) or Mippissippi (which sounds like someone who misses *Pippy Longstocking* and misses the toilet when they pee). Sadly, not one of these spellings was correct. Thankfully, my hosts on the first night in the state taught me a rhyme to remember how to spell it (please repeat the following in a Deep Southern accent).

'Emmm, aye, crooked letter, crooked letter, ayeeee. Crooked letter, crooked letter, aye, humpback, humpback... aye!' (Which translated to M-I-S-S-I-S-S-I-P-P-I.) They made me repeat it in unison with them until I had the spelling down to a tee.

I wound my way through the depths of Mississippi with my eyes wide open. I'd heard a mixture of things about the state, many of which I found to be true. For example, I saw extreme wealth and extreme poverty sitting side by side. I'd pass a huge mansion with a mile drive and acres of land 10 minutes before entering a small town with nothing more than small brick shacks and scruffily dressed kids playing in the broken tarmacked streets. However, Mississippi was also a state where I never knew what to expect, and with every turn of a corner, it would change.

By 20 December, I had made it midway through Mississippi and was feeling much more okay with the idea of spending Christmas away from my family. Something about the beauty and warmth of Florida, Alabama and Mississippi had plastered over the cracks that had started to form in my mental state, and I was feeling much more upbeat. In the wake of so much beauty in the week that had passed, I'd also realised that I had made a foolish assumption about the weeks that lay ahead, and that was that I had 'seen it all'. I had already been proven wrong and I was very keen for that to continue to be the case.

***

On the morning I woke up in McComb, Mississippi, I decided it was high time that I 'Christmassed up' my bike. I had made a trip to the dollar store the previous day to stock up on all the Christmas decor essentials and waded headlong into the challenge. By 10 a.m. that morning, the motel room looked like the floor of a primary-school classroom. Strands of tinsel were scattered across the floor, the remains of an antler headband were in the corner (I'd glued the antlers to my helmet) and discarded Sellotape and duct tape were strewn across the bed. I stepped back to admire the finished product. Not too shabby, I thought, not shabby at all.

'You look beautiful, Boudica,' I said aloud. Like a true Christmas engineer, I'd taken care to avoid tinsel rubbing on any brake cables. I had even considered a way to hook up fairy lights to a battery pack but decided that was possibly excessive. Besides, it was probably going to rain again, and I didn't fancy electrocution all because of some fairy lights.

In the city of Jackson, I spent a night with the Sykes, who – after introducing me to their miniature pony called Starlight that lived in the garden – told me that they would like to take me out to the local karaoke bar. Karaoke. Urgh. I imagined a small box room, condensation on the windows, faded sofas, a large screen and several embarrassed and/or inebriated souls sitting around the edges, 'reluctantly' taking the microphone before either going all out with Bon Jovi's 'Living on a Prayer' or spending the entire song ending every line of the verse with 'Sorry' or 'Oh, I dunno this part!'

As it turns out, karaoke in mid-state Mississippi is an altogether different affair. This is because people in Mississippi actually *enjoy* singing and, what's more, they are not afraid to let the audience know it. Within the karaoke pub, instead of men in their early 20s chanting at one another to drink large quantities of alcohol from a companion's sweaty shoe, they slap each other on the back, whoop and cheer as their mate gets on stage and serenades the audience, stone-cold sober. The quality was also astounding. Singer after singer came to the stage and belted out a performance that wouldn't have been out of place in a TV talent show. These people clearly loved music. It was in their soul and their blood. Before I knew it, I was joining in too, swaying, arm in arm with the Sykes to the southern anthem of

'I've got friends in low places…' My favourite act of that night was a man named Pete. Over the two hours I was in the pub, he took to the stage three times and each visit was accompanied by a more elaborate and risqué dance performance. Without fail, there would always be a comedy-genius opening line to his performance.

'Hi there, my name's Pete. All you ladies out there, I hope you've taken your birth control pills. Because I'm about to make you pregnant, with the power of my rock…' These were his words on his first visit. The second time he took to the stage, he announced, 'I want to apologise to all the guys out there for the immaculate erection. And to all you ladies for the immaculate conception…'

Before the night was out, the Sykes' son-in-law had stepped on stage and blasted out Bon Jovi's 'Bed of Roses'. I'd cheered and clapped and whistled, feeling totally immersed and entirely out of place all at once.

The following morning was 23 December. The Sykes offered me to stay and spend Christmas with them and Starlight the pony. Part of me desperately wanted to accept the offer, but I'd made the decision before hitting Mississippi that spending Christmas Day with a family other than my own might just make me sadder about my decision to spend it away from them. And besides, on a practical note, it was another two full days until Christmas. Although I didn't have an awful lot of miles to make in those days, I really did need to get a wriggle on. My flight to Hawaii was leaving from Dallas in less than three weeks and I still had seven states to pedal through to make Texas. So, with a slight rumble in my stomach, I loaded up Boudica again, hugged the Sykes goodbye and pedalled off, bound for Memphis, Tennessee.

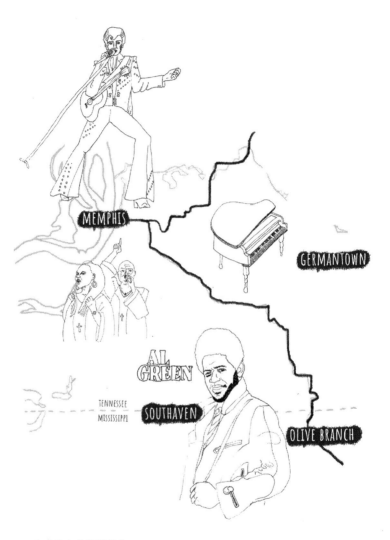

MEMPHIS

GERMANTOWN

AL
GREEN

TENNESSEE
MISSISSIPPI

SOUTHAVEN

OLIVE BRANCH

MEMPHIS

19

The Land of the Delta Blues

Distance Cycled: 10,721 miles

States Completed: 42

When I came up with the idea to pedal my way through the States, there was one gold star I had stuck on the map in the south of the US that was deemed by the goddesses and gods of the musical universe as immovable. The star was situated over the blue-collar town of Memphis, Tennessee. I wholeheartedly believed that Memphis was going to be a magical place. I'd been looking forward to arriving in town since leaving New York. I had a feeling it would be a city with a different vibe from those I'd encountered on the East Coast – a little rougher around the edges, more real, more soulful. Above all though, Memphis was about the music, baby – exactly the kind of music that I loved.

Being from white middle-class Kingston upon Thames, I was naturally raised on a mixture of country, reggae, soft rock, blues and soul. Shania Twain was my sunshine. Motown was my lifeblood. The Eagles were my oxygen. Growing up, I knew more Al Green lyrics than any 11-year-old ever should and never tired of Otis Redding being played on repeat. I once went to a Christmas party where the theme was to dress as 'what I want to be when I grow up' – I went as Tina Turner.

I wouldn't classify myself as a musical person, though I do love a good sing-song in the shower, and we can't discount the fact that I made it to grade three on the violin back in my primary school days. But I do love *real* music – with a beat that would send any restless foot into a fidget frenzy and with lyrics that make the hairs on your neck stand on end. For the real music lover, Memphis is just a must.

In the days leading up to my arrival in the city of soul and rock 'n' roll, I'd read a lot about the place. I'd learned that Memphis is set deep in what's known as the Delta – an area of alluvial land, characterised by frequent flooding of the Mississippi and famous for its fertile soil, abundance of cotton farms and, most importantly of all, blues music. Back in the 1920s, the folk in the cotton fields would sing to distract themselves from their suffering. Heavily influenced by church gospel music, their melodies spoke of the hardships they faced in daily life. It's these hardships that defined the music of the era. Their lyrics arose from a necessity, an irrepressible urge to sing in a bid to ease the pain and toil of long days out in the fields. When I think about that kind of music compared to many more modern songs – peppered with sex, violence and the glamorisation of a material life – I can't help but feel that there is something that is much purer about the blues songs of the 20s.

***

It was a cold, bright, cloudless day when I rolled through the city limits and towards a sculpture of a giant record set on the side of the road, alongside the words, 'Welcome to Memphis!' The centre of the record was pink, its surrounding black circle held in place by a jaunty, yellow base. Looking at that welcome sign, set against the blue sky and nestled amid bright green bushes, I began to suspect that Memphis would be a colourful place. They could have chosen to cast that state out of bronze or copper, but instead it seemed deliberately retro, a sign that said welcome to our city, and welcome to the past.

Rolling into the centre of the city, I was immediately struck by how much quieter it was than I'd expected it to be. After all the traffic-heavy city battles on the East Coast, I'd mentally prepared for a hectic ride in, and instead I found it to be civilised. There were several bridges surrounding the city, offering safe passage over the Mississippi River. Dotted around the centre were large buildings with some well-executed architecture. These buildings were too short to be classed as skyscrapers, but they were tall enough to feel imposing. There was even a pyramid-like glass structure that reminded me of the Louvre in Paris. Despite the large and impressive buildings, Memphis still had a part-finished, almost sleepy feel to it. It looked as if someone had been playing Monopoly and begun to put all the pieces in place for a metropolis, but was called away from the game part way through construction.

I made my way to the downtown apartment I'd rented for the next few days – where I would be meeting Annabel-Zoe, as she flew in from New York to join me on a cultural tour of yet another American city. I hadn't been able to celebrate Christmas with my immediate family and, due to the expense of flying home to the UK, nor had Annabel-Zoe. Our families usually spend Christmas day together, so we'd both decided that we would celebrate it, just the two of us, on 27 December instead.

I soon learned that Memphis is not a sprawling place, and with good reason. It is the Danny DeVito of cities: small, high-quality and jam-packed with entertainment. Seeing as we were looking for some entertainment, there was one place where it was rumoured we were guaranteed to find some hustle to add to our bustle – the iconic Beale Street. I'd read that back in its '20s heyday, Beale Street was a normal high street by day, and a musical mecca by night. Locals went to see their doctor there, do their shopping, meet their neighbours for a gossip and get a haircut. At night, they would return to the street, but this time for the music and the food. And the rum. But mainly for the music.

Annabel-Zoe and I wasted no time in getting cleaned up and out the door to the heart of the action. We soon learned that a visit to Beale in the dark hours is a sensory feast. Just a few paces into our walk and my ears began to tingle as the soulful sounds of the South escaped through every cracked window pane to wrap themselves around me like a blanket of blues. I looked sideways at Annabel-Zoe and saw the neon sign of the B. B. King's Blues Club reflected in her eyes. My stomach began to rumble with the beat of the surrounding bassline, as wafts of freshly cooked barbecue ribs broke free from the nearby eateries and flooded my nostrils. Annabel-Zoe grinned at me and I grinned right back. I took a deep breath and we both stood stock-still. It was pure dynamite.

I could have stood in the middle of Beale Street all night, watching the comings and goings and soaking up the atmosphere, but we decided to experience the magic from the Rum Boogie Cafe. Surrounded by 1,000 signed guitars of the legends who'd played there, including Billy Gibbons, Bon Jovi and Sting, I drank rum from a plastic cup, ate a giant rack of ribs dripping with BBQ sauce and listened to live covers of Johnny Cash and Garth Brooks being played with gusto from the nearby stage. Leaving Rum Boogie, we boogied our rum-filled tums down the road to catch a tribute show at the Jerry-Lee Lewis' Cafe & Honky Tonk. Complete with slicked back hair and accompanied by a glamorous assistant with her boobies hanging out, fake Jerry-Lee did things to those ivories I'm sure were illegal. Hands and limbs and fingers moving frantically in every direction like a floor full of spiders. When fake Jerry played 'Great Balls of Fire' and set the piano ablaze, no one panicked or reached for the fire extinguishers, they just whooped and cheered, egging him on.

Fully recovered and only mildly smoke-infused from our night on 'the Beale', we continued the tourist rampage by visiting Sun Studio – where an 18-year-old kid called Elvis recorded his first demo track. It was also at Sun Studio, back in the day, that the predominantly black blues music of the Delta collided with the predominantly white country music of Nashville. The result? Rock and roll, baby – and the kids went nuts for it. Having had our fill of soul and rock 'n' roll at the studio, we skipped off to Graceland – a place that I fully expected to be a tourist trap. After a three-hour tour, lots of snooping, and a fair amount of listening and reading, I can officially confirm that it wasn't nearly as bad as I'd feared it to be. Of course, there were a few rhinestone renegades, and it is without a doubt up there with the more 'touristy' experiences I've had (standing in line for an hour to get on a bus which takes you across the road is ridiculous, for a start), but after learning about Elvis' humanitarian side, I actually found the whole experience to be rather humbling.

On our final day in Memphis, and after a trip to taste what was apparently the best fried chicken in all of America (it wasn't), we headed to the edges of the city for a Sunday service at the Full Gospel Tabernacle Church in South Memphis. It might seem a little odd that a non-religious soul like myself would head to church on a Sunday, but I was here out of curiosity and to experience a service that was rumoured to be akin to any musical on Broadway. We arrived a little early so we snuck in the back door and onto a pew to catch the end of Sunday school. I felt rather awkward, like I'd just invited myself to dinner at someone's house and I was now sitting at the table with a spoon in my hand, heading for the mashed potatoes. But after re-reading on Wikipedia (during Sunday school:

shocker!) that the church was definitely open to 'drop-ins', my anxiety dissipated.

As the next half an hour wore on, more people began to arrive. Characterised by their casual attire and sheepish facial expressions, it was clear many weren't part of the usual church congregation. I sat and watched as band members filtered from the wings behind the altar. The service started with a man sitting down at the piano and singing. A well-dressed black lady to my left then joined in, slowly rising from her pew – both arms aloft, as if ready to receive the music into her heart – and making her way forwards to harmonise with the piano man. The church choir then began to file in, adding layer upon layer to an already divine gospel chorus. By the time the service 'officially' began at 11.30 a.m., the church was filled to the rafters – not only with people, half local, half tourist, but with the sumptuous sound of gospel music.

There was a brief announcement and some local notices were read by a short elderly woman with grey hair, partly obscured by a large purple hat, before the choir and the band started up again. As they did, Motown-legend-cum-preacher Al 'Let's Stay Together' Green glided out of the archway. He was sporting a cream and navy robe with patent black Converse sneakers and had accessorised his whole outfit with a beaming full-teethed grin. There was not one tooth I could not see in Al Green's mouth. I watched as he moved purposefully among the choir and ministers, shaking their hands and smiling.

I sat quietly, listening, watching and smiling, full of joy and feeling emotional to be a part of such an uplifting experience. Al settled into a rhythm through the service – he'd speak a little, preach a little, converse a little, then break into song – swiftly accompanied by the band and choir who seemed to know what to do without so much as a nod. The two-hour programme was like a gospel version of *The Sound of Music*.

It really didn't seem to matter a jot at the Tabernacle if you were religious – it wasn't about religion, said one member of the congregation. It was about sheer joy. A celebration of life. Gratitude expressed via the medium of gospel music and positivity via the medium of prayer. I'm sure if doctors prescribed a morning at the Tabernacle instead of therapy or drugs, the world would benefit immeasurably.

Something about Rev Green's music put me back on a high. As the sun set on my final day in Memphis, I was now more in love with blues and soul music than I had ever been. My high was further elevated by the purple and pink hues which lit up the sky: a brightly coloured bow around what had been a rich and wonderful few days in the city. As one local said to me, 'Memphis is just a blue-collar town, always has been, always will be. Some people like it, some people don't. But it sure got soul.' I couldn't argue with that.

Looking out on that sunset from the apartment balcony, with Boudica still sleeping in the hall, I thought about the final section of the journey that lay ahead. There were now just 10 days left until my flight out of Dallas, Texas, to the final state of Hawaii. All I had to do from here in Memphis was nip north to say hello to Kentucky (state 44), then wiggle westwards along the borders of Missouri (45) and Arkansas (46), before taking a little detour north to touch the corner of Kansas (47). Then I would have to turn south and make a final bid through Oklahoma (48) to Texas, state number 49. My soul was well fed, my body strong and my mind stronger still. Whatever those final 10 days had in store for me, Elvis, Jerry-Lee, Johnny Cash, Tina Turner and Al Green had made sure I was ready for them.

DALLAS

KANSAS
OKLAHOMA

SPRINGFIELD

MISSOURI

OKLAHOMA CITY

ARKANSAS
OKLAHOMA

LITTLE ROCK

MEMPHIS

OKLAHOMA
TEXAS

BISCUITS & GRAVY

ARKANSAS
MISSISSIPPI

DENTON

DALLAS

ARKANSAS
LOUISIANA

GREENWOOD

20

The Dash for Dallas

Distance Cycled: 10,721 miles

States Completed: 43

The first few flakes of winter storm Hercules fell just as I saddled up and rode out of Memphis. They were barely even wisps, so I thought no more of it and continued to wind my way northwards through Tennessee. Moving along small country roads, I loosely followed the path of the Mississippi River. I took a small detour into the town of Nutbush, Tennessee, and loaded up the Tina Turner classic 'Nutbush City Limits' on my iPhone. In a bid to pay full tribute to my long-time idol, I sang at the top of my lungs, shaking my butt and dancing as much as is possible from the seat of a bicycle. When the dancing was done, it was time to cross the border into state number 44, Kentucky. Originally, I'd intended to ride a fair way north into Kentucky, but the temperature had begun to drop, the snow flurries came more frequently and something told me that I needed to keep moving through the remaining states as briskly as I could.

The Mississippi River ran between Kentucky and the next state of Missouri, and it was a long way north to the next road bridge at the town of Cairo. I was growing concerned that I might end up with a long cold day in the saddle and finish up riding in the dark, but when I pulled into a gas station to warm up my toes (and the rest of my body for that matter), a group of locals told me that I could catch a ferry across the river from the small town of Hickman, Kentucky.

There wasn't much to the town of Hickman, just a few white houses and industrial yards, which seemed all but deserted as I pedalled through that afternoon. Wheeling over a railway line, I turned down a dusty track, before stopping at the banks of the Mississippi. It was huge! It looked nothing like the Mississippi I had crossed in Wisconsin. A swirling mass of brown foaming water, big logs and clumps of collected debris moved past at an alarming speed. I could just about see the other side, lined with tall green trees, although they were coated in a dull haze, so the colours seemed subdued. There was no sign of the ferry on the river, and I wasn't entirely sure what I should be looking out for. I had a feeling that this wouldn't be a Caribbean cruise kind of affair and there would be no all-you-can-eat buffet on board. Then I spotted a sign that read, 'Press bell and WAIT HERE FOR FERRY.' I followed the instructions, pressed a little black button in a yellow box and waited. I felt somewhat frustrated that I had nothing to tell me exactly how long I would be waiting, and I also wondered whether a boat would bother to come all the way over here just for one lone cyclist. It was all very un-British. No one had handed me a ticket and told me to wait in line. I was not placed on hold and forced to listen to 'Greensleeves'. I had nothing to confirm that a ferry would turn up at all, but there was no choice but to wait and see.

Waiting for the ferry, I thought about a guy I'd been chatting to via email over the past few months called Kevin Brady. I'd come across Kev online and had enjoyed following his own mad-cap adventures, which were, at the time, leading him by canoe down the Mississippi River. We'd tried to meet up when I last crossed the Mississippi in Wisconsin but had missed one another, which wasn't surprising given that we were both on slightly erratic, weather-governed, adventure schedules. I had, however, met a number of people who had seen Kev, heard about him, or nipped down to the riverbank to cheer him on. Most of his social media posts featured some mention of the weather and that didn't surprise me. He was navigating the Mississippi in the depths of winter and camping along its banks too. I'd been keeping tabs on Kev's progress and knew that he had made it into Memphis just as I'd left town. I looked out on the violent, icy river, littered with eddies and driftwood, and thought about Kev. How in the world was he out there on this? Everything I could see in front of me spelled 'death trap'.

Eventually, a white and orange boat appeared on the horizon. It was a basic ferry with space to fit two cars at the most, but there was ample space for me and Boudica. A man with a thick brown beard, wearing navy waterproofs, nodded and waved me onto the ferry. He went about the business of loading me on very matter-of-factly, without uttering any words at all. As soon as we pulled away from the shore, the man turned to me and said, 'Are you British?!'

'I sure am!' I smiled, proud that he had noticed the little flag dangling from Boudica's bottom.

'Thought so. You Brits are crazy! We had a guy come through here a few days ago. British boy, canoeing the whole Mississippi… in winter!'

'That's my friend Kev!' I said.

'What?! You know that guy?'

'Yep! He's actually just made it to Memphis.'

'Memphis?! I was sure he was gonna die out there, it's been real cold the past week. Nice to know he's made it. I told him he's crazy. You're crazy too, missy. You're all crazy, you Brits. What in the world do they put in the water over there?!'

'Ah, it must be because we're raised on a diet of tea, stout and Digestive biscuits. Sends us a little kooky, you know? Plus, we're a tiny island. We've got to get out somehow!' I replied.

Pedalling away from the ferry, I began to feel proud to be a crazy Brit. Being crazy was awesome. Being normal, average, that was like vanilla ice cream to me. And I didn't much like vanilla ice cream. Especially without the sprinkles, or some raspberry ripple running through it. You've got to have a little raspberry ripple in you, at least.

***

On my first morning in state number 45, Missouri, I woke up to a howling wind and a light dusting of snow on the ground. I checked the weather forecast and saw that the temperature had now dropped to -10°C, with a wind chill of -15°C. The cherry on top of the icy cake was a 23-mph headwind. I let out a big sigh. I had a feeling that the director at the Department of Destiny had decided that I'd got a little too big for my cowgirl boots. He had clearly sensed my belief that the final 10 days from here to Dallas would be a mere formality, and so he had plunged his hands deep into the weather well and begun drawing out things to throw in my pedal-path. 'Flood? Hmm, no, we've done that one. How about a blizzard? Come on now, that's so last year…' Then he must have happened across a little bottle marked 'Polar Vortex' and muttered 'I wonder…'

After reading as much as possible about the impressively named Polar Vortex – the newspapers reported it was sweeping across the south of the US – I came up with what I thought was a Grade A plan. I would move slowly from small town to small town, making as much headway as I could until the storm passed. But something was stopping me from leaving the motel to get on the road. I couldn't seem to get Operation Creep underway, as I was caught between wondering if I was a fool to go out in such temperatures or whether I'd gone soft because I was even considering not to. My guts had gone glacial. My lady-balls were below zero. My can of (wo)man-up was frozen. I needed back-up. I dropped a message to the person I deemed to always know the answer.

'Mum? Are you around for a chat?' I waited for a few minutes and continued looking out the window at the howling wind.

'Hi pet! I'm here. Are you okay? It looks cold over there.'

I flipped open my tablet and hit call immediately.

'Hello petal,' came a familiar voice, and I felt better already. I chatted out the options for the next few days with Mum, who is by nature a detail-oriented woman. She's also an experienced outdoors woman, having taken on 24-hour mountain marathons and raced in a Hawaiian-style outrigger canoe across the Pacific Ocean with hammerhead sharks chasing her, once upon a time (that's a whole 'nother story). Needless to say, I trusted Mum's judgement.

'Okay, Anna. I agree that you've got to keep moving out there. The weather is due to get worse from what I can see. You'll find a way, there's always a way.' Mothers – you've gotta love 'em.

I shut down the video call. In a bid to give my tyres as much grip as possible on the icy roads, I let some air out of them. Then I embarked on three days of wind-battered, icicle-encrusted, hill-tastic riding. When the wind chill hit -17°C, my legs stung as if they were being stabbed by itty bitty knives, despite wearing two layers of leggings. An icicle beard formed on my chin, frozen droplets took up residence on my eyebrows, my eyelashes began to stick together and my water bottles turned to solid blocks of ice. When I lost feeling in my toes, I pulled into the next gas station I could find and let them come back to life before setting off again. I was rather impressed that I only slipped off my bike once in those three days, on sheet ice in a gas-station forecourt – an act which in reality hurt my pride more than it did my body. I will maintain that I was distracted by the impending inhalation of a gas-station doughnut.

I made good, slow, steady progress westwards, dancing back and forth along the Missouri–Arkansas border, ticking off state number 46 and all the while edging closer to my flight from Dallas.

The scenery was a welcome distraction as I picked my way over the many lumps of the Ozark Mountains. The soft rolling peaks of the green Ozarks stood out in a stark contrast to a cloudless blue sky. The roads were quiet, presumably on account of the cold, and so I often found myself alone in the mountains – lungs burning, nose dribbling and with a huge grin plastered on my face. Oddly enough, through the stinging and the pain, I was loving the challenge of it all. The uncertainty of the journey spurred me on, daily. After almost 200 days on the road, cycling 100 miles was no longer a challenge. For those few days out in the cold, I was filled with uncertainty and it pulsed through my veins like a drug. I was careful to listen to the soft whispers of Captain Sensible, however, who reminded me (at intervals) that no matter how good I felt, it was still ruddy cold.

I was convinced that I would manage to thwart the weather, that I would be lucky enough to have battled through the worst of it. Alas, I made it two-thirds of the way across the Ozarks before things slid off the scale of silliness. When I awoke at the home of Larry and Lajunta Plumfield in the tiny town of Oak Grove, Arkansas, there was a foot of snow on the ground and not a scrap of tarmac in sight. Larry had met me at a gas station on the main highway the afternoon of the previous day and ridden with me to his home. It was cold enough, but there wasn't a whiff of snow, so we had expected to ride out together again the following day. Now looking out of the window from his living room, it was clear that both of us were going nowhere. Worse than the snow, the sub-zero temperatures had caused a layer of solid ice to form on the roads. Riding Boudica out of Oak Grove was not an option.

Larry and Lajunta's home wasn't a bad place to be stuck, of course – far from it. It was wonderfully warm, wood was always on the fire, the fridge was full and I never had to ask for anything. Larry grinned at me often from behind his large Dennis Taylor-style glasses, saying repeatedly that he counted his lucky stars when I'd accepted his offer to come and stay, and I felt the same. Lajunta's heart matched the warmth of the fire, her shoulder length grey-white hair complementing bright blue eyes that sparkled when she talked about her 9 grandchildren. I wasn't sure if it was the cold air or the heat of the fire, but Larry and Lajunta both had the loveliest rosy cheeks, and they bubbled with life. Outwardly, I was calm as

I chatted to Lajunta and Larry, but inside I was riddled with anxiety. I was so close to finishing the journey and completing what I'd set out to do. When Larry spoke to me, I could feel that I was frequently distracted, desperately trying to think of ways to get back on the road.

Over a traditional southern-style breakfast of biscuits, grits, beans and gravy, Lajunta talked of her love for her country and for all of America.

'You love every single state?' I asked.

'Every single state,' she replied, smiling. 'You know, Anna, on Independence Day, when I see that flag go up the pole and watch those stars flutter in the wind – I can't help but well up. I am so proud to be here, so grateful.'

If there was one thing I had learned about Americans over the past six months, it is that they love their country. Their sense of patriotism is like nothing I had encountered before. Don't get me wrong, I love being British. I love the Queen, our scones, country walks and our small villages – I love everything about our tiny island. Well, except the football hooligans and binge-drinking culture, that I would leave out, but I love everything else. I even love that we take seats on public transport as far away from one another as possible – we're a small island, after all, and space is at a premium. But I am not sure that my love for Great Britain could do anything to rival the way Lajunta spoke about America.

According to the weather reports, the Polar Vortex would

only last five more days, but with a visa expiring, a flight booked from Dallas to Hawaii and my parents already bound to meet me there, sitting tight just wasn't an option. I began to contemplate others.

Option one was to cycle directly south-west from Oak Grove once the snow cleared, passing through Oklahoma and Texas. That would save me a few days of riding, but would mean missing out Kansas, and I would finish the journey having only cycled in 49 states. *Did that extra state matter?* I wondered. It seemed a shame, and I concluded that it really did. It wasn't about Kansas per se, it was about finishing what I had set out to do. At that point, Kansas was a total pain in the arse. I had toyed with trying to ride through it months earlier as I headed east across the States, but then decided against it. And now there it was, 100 miles north-west of where I sat, locked right in the middle of the country, colluding against me, a thorn in my side.

Chewing on a biscuit soaked in gravy, I fell silent at the table and realised that I could no longer have it all. It simply wasn't possible to make my flight in Dallas without finding a way to make up some lost time. So, after a long chat with Larry, I did something that made me die inside – I agreed to take four-wheeled assistance.

'I can't see another way, Anna,' said Larry, as he did the dishes.

'I know,' I said, pushing a bit of biscuit around on

my plate.

I was gutted. Absolutely gutted. But perhaps if I could just get a little further on, I could cycle from there. Still, even driving in these conditions wasn't especially sensible. Even so, Larry, armed with nerves of steel (and studded tyres) drove me 60 miles through snowy back roads, round steep curves and over mountain passes. Each time we hit a steep incline, Larry turned to me and said, 'Well, if we make it up this one, Anna, I think we'll be okay.'

My heart crept higher into my mouth and my feet pressed a little further into the footwell. At one point, I wondered if they might break clean through the floor and we'd wind up in a Flintstones-mobile. At Springdale, Arkansas, Larry's work was done. Like precious cargo, Boudica and I were handed over to our new host, Jay, who drove me the final few miles to his family home in Gentry.

Jay was a strong-looking man. A square jaw, wide chest, firm handshake and silver-grey hair. He was a lawyer by day and I could tell he was the kind of man who made things happen. Unfortunately, he couldn't make the weather clear up and the following morning in Gentry the mercury dropped to -22°C, with a wind chill of -28°C. When I discovered that it was warmer at that point in Alaska than it was in Arkansas, I began to feel foolish, embarrassed even. Who rides their bike through southern America in the winter?! But I'd done research before leaving. I'd checked the average temperatures for the times I'd be going through each state, and not found anything to suggest I might hit this kind of cold. But, of course, like the flood and the blizzard, I was assured by Jay and his wife Shirley that this kind of weather wasn't 'normal'.

As one of my favourite quotes from G. K. Chesterton goes, 'An adventure is only an inconvenience rightly considered', and I am always amazed how what are seemingly hold-ups become a blessing in disguise. Jay and Shirley could see that I was doing my best to remain chipper through the vortex hold-up, so they invited over their eight-strong Gentry cycling gang for an evening of storytelling. Think of it as if the cast of *Friends* rode bicycles. That was the energy around the dinner table that night.

I was touched to discover that the gang had been following my blog and I enjoyed answering question after question between mouthfuls of Mexican nosh. In turn, the Gentry bike gang shared tales of their own – of dog chases, near crashes, actual crashes, post-ride feasts and random acts of kindness they'd experienced on their journeys together across the US. To be part of such a close-knit group of friends for the evening made me forget all about the dash for Dallas. I retired to the land of nod that night with cheeks weary from smiling and a belly that ached from laughing (that, and OD'ing on the guacamole).

I stayed a further three days with Jay and Shirley, each morning hoping against hope that the cold would subside and

I'd get a clear shot at making a bid for Kansas. Jay had said a number of times that he could find me rides north towards the state line – where I would be clear of the snow and could get back on the bike, but I refused. Each morning, I woke up and looked out the window and, each morning, I whimpered a little more as the dream of riding the final miles slipped from my grasp.

Shirley was, of course, a master of distraction and dangled many shiny and exciting things in my path to take my mind off the snow-stuck situation. I got treated to a massage, went for lunches with her friends, played board games with 'the girls' and had dinner with both sets of grandparents. I even went on a million micro-adventures from the comfort and warmth of Jay's couch, as he took me through photos of previous family bicycle, hiking and four-wheeled trips. Jay clearly loved adventures, and when he reached for a book from his shelf, I was already grinning.

'You should read this!' he said, holding *Thunder and Sunshine* by Al Humphreys in his hand.

'I have and I loved it!

Jay set about thumbing through the rest of his adventure shelf, which included a host of other books I recognised.

'Sarah Outen?' Jay asked.

'Read it.'

'Mark Beaumont?'

'Read it.'

'Sean Conway?'

'Read it. Say, Jay! Maybe I'll write a book about this trip one day, eh? And you can have that on your shelf?'

Jay turned to me and looked stern. 'Only if you put me in it,' he said.

'Oh, I don't know about that,' I smiled.

On the fourth morning, over a breakfast of grapefruit and pancakes, I looked out the kitchen window again and checked the weather. Still a wind chill of -27°C. Still snow covering the ground. Still here. I let out a long sigh and turned to Jay.

'Jay? You know you said you might be able to get me a ride towards Kansas and clear of the snow.'

'Yes?' he replied, looking up from his paper.

'Well, I think I'd like to take you up on that.'

'You sure?' he asked, furrowing his brow.

'I'm sure.' I nodded.

'Okay, kid,' he said, getting up and coming over to put his hands on my shoulders. 'Let's get you out of here.'

I felt deeply saddened that I wasn't going to be able to ride every mile from here to Dallas. I felt like a child who had just painted something at school in bright acrylic colours, only to accidently tip a glass of water over it right at the last brush stroke. The adventure was still there, the energy that I had ploughed into trying to make it the best that it could be, but it now felt tarnished somewhat, washed away, a blurred mess. But I also knew that I had made my choice. There will always be elements of life out of your control, after all. I had learned that a lot over this past half a year in the States, and in those moments, you have two choices – live with it and accept it, or change it. I couldn't change the fact that there was a polar vortex going on outside, but I did get to choose how and where I travelled from here. Once the choice was made, I accepted responsibility for it. It was my choice and I would get used to it eventually.

Once the decision was made, it was like I had lit the fuse on a firework. Jay had been poised, ready to strike and he swung into action. He called Shirley's dad, who arranged to get me clear of the ice and more cold weather with a ride to Kansas with his friends Arlene and Don, who happened to be going that way the following morning. Gentry bike gang member Tod called his mum, who agreed to put me up for my first night in Oklahoma, and his sister, Robin, offered to take me out for dinner. Jay then called his bike friend Dan. Dan called his brother who worked at a bookshop near Dallas. The brother called the bookshop manager, Erin, who said I could stay with her before my flight to Hawaii. (Are you still with me? Good…). Dan then called another friend who said he would source me a bike box in Dallas, drop it off at Erin's house, then come back at 3 a.m. to take me to the airport. Who gives strangers a ride to the airport at 3 a.m.?! Kind people, that's who. And that wasn't even the half of it. I had friends of friends across Kansas, Oklahoma and Texas on standby, to host me and ride with me, should my yet-to-be determined route take me to their area. I watched all of this unfold in awe. It. Was. Awesome.

Over the next 18 hours, I decided to let go of any angst about not being able to ride those miles. I had made a decision, it was done; there was no sense in dwelling on it any longer. State number 47 Kansas was calling and I was, at last, a-comin'!

***

I hopped out of Arlene and Don's truck and dragged Boudica out of the back. On the journey to the northern tip of Arkansas, I had watched out of the window as the snow had slowly disappeared and beautiful black rivers of tarmac had become visible once again. Never had I been so pleased to see tarmac! I waved my knights in shining armour goodbye, loaded my bags onto Boudica and pedalled off. Fifteen minutes later, I saw the sight I had longed to see for days. 'There you are, you little blighter!' I said out loud, as the Kansas state sign appeared on the (as promised) flat, featureless horizon. As I had done for the previous 46 states, I set up my camera on a timer, and posed with the sign. I squeezed and hugged the sign as hard as I could, pressing its cold metal legs into the side of my face. Had it not been so cold that my tongue might get stuck, I might have even considered licking it, I was that excited. I cycled for 10 minutes into the state before stopping at a junction and looking westwards. *I wonder what Kansas is really like?* I thought, sad that I wouldn't be finding out this time around. I turned south and pedalled across the border into state number 48, Oklahoma.

For the next few days, I felt unstoppable, munching through the miles, bound for Texas. Even when a heavy fog rolled into Oklahoma and I was forced from the highways onto the side farms roads, I kept on trucking away. And when those farm roads turned to clay, and I had to run with my bike for a few miles, I kept on truckin'. All the while, I kept thinking things had to get to the plain-sailing stage soon. Sure enough, with T-minus three days until my flight to Hawaii, I was riding towards Dallas, zooming past cactus plants lining the road and pedalling under sunshine and blue skies, with the wind on my back.

***

I woke up in Texas, opened my eyes and stared at the ceiling. I blinked a few times and shut them again. This is it, I thought. The last day of cycling on the US mainland. I opened them again and turned my head to the left so I could see the time: 7.30 a.m. I felt weird. Very weird. I'd slept terribly. Partly because I didn't want to allow myself to fall asleep, because then it would be over, and partly because I was excited about the final day of pedalling. Six weeks ago, I had been ready to go home. This morning, I was staring out of the window at a Texan landscape and overcome with a mixture of sadness and pride.

I'll leave in an hour, I thought, and spent a further three doing what I do best: faffing. The majority of the mud from the Oklahoma clay fest had now dried and was easy enough to dislodge from Boudica's nooks and crannies. I pulled out my camera and made a video for posterity:

'So, it's the morning of my last ride… and I'm feeling really weird. Just so weird. It's twenty past ten… I really should have left by now, but I just can't bring myself to leave. The sun's shining, it's a beautiful day, I've packed up… but I kind of don't want it to be over. And I'm really sad. I'm actually getting really really sad now. So I think I probably just need to get on with it, rather than just sit here and be sad…

I'm happy and sad all at once. Is that possible?

I just got a text to say that my parents have just landed in Hawaii… which is incredible. The fiftieth state. I can't quite believe I'm going to Hawaii. I didn't believe it when I started and I still don't believe it now…'

At 10.30 a.m., I finally rolled out of the town of Bowie and began heading south toward Dallas. The ride was a joy. I pedalled in sunshine with a gentle breeze on my back moving me forwards towards a vast horizon. Oh, how I would miss that horizon. I couldn't have asked for a more perfect final day. I tried my best to enjoy every moment – to exist only in the now – and I managed it for most of the day.

I once watched a lecture on the art of listening and how it can help you to be more present. The lecture advised that the best way to fine-tune your listening skills is to attempt to separate out the sounds that make up the orchestra around you. So I concentrated on the hum of my wheels over the tarmac. The sporadic clicking from the back cassette. The sigh of the rim as I squeezed on my brakes. The rhythm of my breath. The noise my inner thigh made as the material from my shorts made contact with the seat. I soaked it all up. Every little decibel. New sounds were revealing themselves with every minute that went by.

I had decided earlier on that day to come off the busy Highway 287 and take minor roads, largely because the irrational side of my brain was convinced I was going to be hit by a truck. I could see the newspaper headlines now: 'British girl never makes the 50th state!' 'She was so close.' '50-state dream destroyed by 287.' Imagination is a wonderful thing, isn't it?

Fifteen miles away from where I was due to stop for the night, I pulled into a small roadside diner. Over a questionably fresh chicken baguette and a bottle of chocolate milk, I began chatting to a couple of grandparents and their grandson. As had hundreds that had come before them, they asked me what I was doing here, and so I told them.

'I'm errmm… riding the fifty states. I mean, well, I'm on state forty-nine now. Texas is state forty-nine. Just Hawaii to go.'

'You've bicycled through forty-nine states?! C'mon now. Are you serious?' came the southern drawl from the table next to me.

'Yes.' I smiled, thinking back to those first few weeks when I'd tell people what I was doing and feel embarrassed I was only on state number two. Although, even now I felt a little uncomfortable. I should be boastful, right? I should beat my chest and say, 'Yes I have!!! Hear me now, I am a cycling GOD-DESSS!!' But I shrunk back into my seat like a small child. I felt detached. To the outside world, it might have seemed like I'd achieved more than I had at the start, but I felt very much like the same me as before.

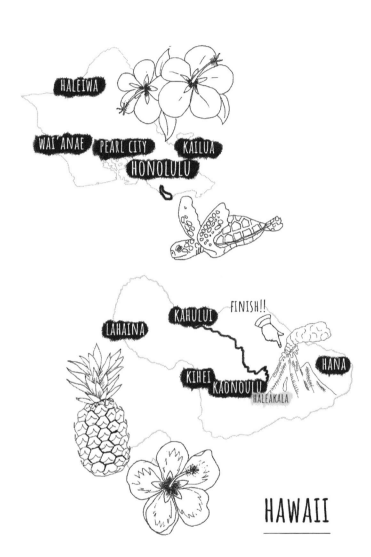

HALEIWA

WAI'ANAE   PEARL CITY   KAILUA

HONOLULU

KAHULUI   FINISH!!

LAHAINA

KIHEI   KAONOULU

HALEAKALA

HANA

HAWAII

21

Hawaii, the 50th State

Distance Cycled: 11,668 miles

States Completed: 49

Sitting in my airplane seat at Dallas Fort Worth Airport, it dawned on me that we'd been stationary at the gate for quite some time. The pilot, Peter, came on the tannoy. His soothing words were to the effect of: 'A part of the plane isn't working. In fact, we're concerned it's missing entirely. We just need to make sure everything's okay before taking you up to thirty thousand feet and letting you plunge to your death.' I couldn't help but marvel at such a flawless execution of customer care – Peter clearly missed the training memo about ignorance being bliss.

A commotion erupted among the passengers. There was a wave of passive-aggressive tutting, sighing and murmuring. One middle-aged man behind me got especially aggravated. He had a face that looked like he'd sucked on one too many lemons in life and began reeling off his schedule for the following 24 hours, much to the delight of the surrounding passengers.

I managed to hop-skip myself onto another flight and eight hours later I touched down in Honolulu, on the island of

Oahu. The big glass doors of the arrivals lounge slid back and standing there, holding hands and smiling, were my parents. I bounded towards them, my smile almost escaping from my face it was spread so wide as I plunged into their arms. Until this point, the thought of seeing them had been overwhelming. There really is nothing better than a loving hug from your mum and a bear hug from your dad, or better still a parent hug sandwich. Well, pass the mayo, because I was now the filling in that sandwich.

It was then that something within me released. I let go. I exhaled a long deep outward breath that I had been dying to make for the past six months. I could relax. I didn't have to hold it all together anymore. These two could help me hold it together for the final state.

In one way or another, both my parents had been with me for the entire journey. For all her worry, Mum had proved an invaluable base-camp support liaison, especially in the final month when the Polar Vortex took hold. I treasured that hug because I knew it would put Mum's mind at rest. I was here, safe and sound, and she needn't worry about me anymore.

After several more hugs, we moved off to the over-sized-baggage area to await the final member of the Hono-lulu party – Boudica. Only, Boudica never arrived. As I wait-ed for her beautifully decorated pink gaffer-taped cardboard box to appear, it dawned on me – she'd gone AWOL. In the broken-plane-change-of-flight debacle, Boudica had been left behind. She was like Kevin in *Home Alone*, left to fend for herself. (So much for my detailed marker-pen instructions that I had scrawled on the box to 'treat her like a lady'.)

Following the confirmation by the help desk that they had no idea where Boudica was, Mum proceeded to go into level-one panic mode (this is the highest level of mothership panic).

'What do you mean she's not here? How can she not be here?!'

I, on the other hand, felt rather calm, and that surprised me. Unlike how I had felt in Arkansas, it didn't seem to matter much anymore. I would be disappointed if Boudica never showed up, but in the grand scheme of it all, after over 11,000 miles of riding high atop that beautiful pink beast, if she didn't make it, then I accepted that that would just be the order of things. If she never made it to the 50th state, I was okay with that. I'd go and ride around on another one. And I'd just tell people that I'd had the most incredible adventure on a beautiful pink bike in 49 states. I left the airport with my folks in tow and we headed to our hotel at Waikiki Beach.

On the first day I cycled into the Nevada Desert with JP, he had mentioned a place in Hawaii called Mount Haleakalā. Excited by what he told me about the road up to the top of the mountain, I'd done some research and found it to be the longest paved road ascent in the world. The road to Mount Haleakalā (which is actually a volcano) runs from sea level to

3,048 metres of elevation, in one go. I had floated the idea to Master of Hawaii Logistics, Sue McNuff (aka Mum), and she agreed that a side trip to the island of Maui to cycle up Mount Haleakalā was a great way to end the trip. Mum's not a big fan of cycling on 'skinny wheels', as she puts it, so she would be our support wagon for the day, and my dad and I would pedal from sea level to the top.

With Boudica still AWOL, we hopped on a plane to the island of Maui and hired two beautiful carbon racing bikes from a bike shop not far from the foot of the mountain. On the test ride before our ascent day, Dad and I went for a little pootle through the downtown area. With no weight on the bike to keep me centred, I could barely ride the thing. I felt like a grizzly bear trying to ride a toy motorcycle, steering it with toothpicks. The bike twitched and jumped beneath me and I struggled to keep its delicate frame in a straight line. I didn't even name my temporary steed, for fear that Boudica would find out and feel like I had cheated on her.

Although excited about riding up a volcano with my dad, I was somewhat apprehensive. On one hand – and as *all* dads are – my dad is superhuman. An Olympic bronze medallist with a resting heart rate of 29, his body is built for endurance. That said, on this ride, we would be going up to high altitudes and I knew that was something to take seriously. Plus, there comes a point in your late 20s when your parents begin to gradually come down from the pedestal you have placed them upon as long as you've known them. They are no longer invincible individuals. They are human. They seem more fragile than they once were and so, much like the Chicago River, the flow of worry begins to reverse and move in the opposite direction. I was worried about my dad.

'Dad, did you manage to do some training back home for this?' I asked casually, as we went out on our test ride.

'Some… a little… it'll be fine,' was his succinct reply. This was good enough for me, as I had no choice but to trust that he would be sensible, but Mum was a little more concerned.

'Take it easy, Ian. The last thing your daughter needs is you kicking the bucket halfway up that volcano! That would really ruin her trip!' she said.

We set off from the shore of the Pacific Ocean at 9 a.m. Mum had done some prep work on our nutrition for the day, and I had watched as she smeared cream cheese on multiple tortilla wraps. With no knives on hand in the hotel room, she had taken a 'No cutlery? No problem' approach and dutifully completed the task with her fingers alone – all of us giggling away as she went, in full agreement that a bare-handed application of cream cheese could only add to the nutritional value of the wraps. The plan was for us to make the 40-mile journey up to 3,048 metres, stopping at intervals to inhale these delicately pre-cheese-smeared wraps.

Following the winding road and its many switchbacks upwards, upwards, upwards, I felt like Jack of Jack-and-the-Beanstalk fame. We pushed closer and closer to the clouds, until we were at last in them, and then above them, looking down. I kept a good handle on my breathing: I hadn't been up at altitude in a few months and, beyond 2,000 metres high, I started to get short of breath.

After 28 years of life, I was struck by how often our conversations with our parents are merely a transaction. Very rarely do we take the time to find out more about them and who they were before kids crashed their life-party. And so, as we turned one corner, it dawned on me that I had never actually asked my dad about the details of him being part of the British rowing crew that won a bronze medal at the Moscow 1980 Olympics. Of course, over the years, I had gathered scraps of information here and there, but I had no idea how he had felt about it all, what he'd been thinking that day when he crossed the line at the Olympics – none of it. With hours to pass together that day, I decided that it was as good a time as any to ask. So, for the following hour, Dad talked and I listened.

As it turned out, his Olympics had gotten off to a rocky start. Having won bronze medals in his coxless four at the 1978 and 1979 World Championships, Dad explained that the crew had an 'absolute shocker' in the first heat at the Games in 1980.

'What happened?' I asked.

'I don't know. Something was just off. Maybe we were nervous, maybe we were feeling overwhelmed, but we just never settled into a rhythm.'

I figured that was understandable, given that Dad and most of the crew were just 23 years old at the time. He continued.

'So we didn't get through to the final from that heat, and we had to go to the repêchage race to try to get a spot.'

I knew from my own rowing career that going to a 'rep' wasn't ideal. It meant that you had to do an extra race and potentially tire yourself out more than those who had made it straight through to the final.

'I remember as we went down to put the boat in the water for that next rep race, I was feeling superstitious – thinking that if the boat slid into the water a certain way, that meant we'd have a good row.'

'And did the boat go on the water right?!' I asked.

'It did! It slid onto the lake with a satisfying "schhhluuup" and we rowed the best we ever had. We came in clear from the field and went through to the Olympic final.'

It made me smile that my dad would be superstitious about how the boat was placed on the water before a race. I knew him to be a realist, often objective and seeing things as very clean cut. It was why he had become such a successful business consultant in later life. But to hear that when the stakes were high, he'd allowed a little superstition in – that made me smile.

'So… you're in the final. What happened there? How did it all go down?' I asked, now wondering how much Dad would be able to remember of a six-minute race that happened almost 40 years ago.

'Well, in the final there was us, the Swiss, the Russians, the Czechs and the East Germans. We knew that the Russians and the East Germans would likely be out of our league, and by halfway gone in the race they were out the front – but we were still in the mix with the other crews, and I knew that the bronze was up for grabs.'

I was now riding right alongside my dad and he was staring up the road – eyes fixed firmly ahead. My skin was starting to tingle, my heart was beating faster – I could see he was back there, back in that boat in Moscow in the middle of the race and, although we were halfway up a volcano in Hawaii, I was right there with him too. He carried on.

'There was a call to push on at the halfway marker and I absolutely floored myself, I gave it everything I had. I completely emptied the tank and in the third five hundred metres of the two-kilometre race we became the fastest moving boat in that race. We even started pulling back on the Russians and East Germans. But with five hundred metres to go, I had nothing left. I was gone, completely spent – I was still moving up and down, but I couldn't tell you what was going through my mind. I was just willing the finish line to come. The rest of the crew definitely dragged me through in that final five hundred metres and at last we crossed the line in third place and took the bronze medal.'

I sat up on my bike and exhaled, raising one arm into the air in celebration. 'Woooo! And how did it feel?!'

'Mostly relief. I was too tired to show it, but I was elated,' he replied, then he started to smile as he said, 'The medal ceremony was right after the race... I was feeling pretty ropey and so I chucked up my scrambled eggs all over the red ceremony carpet.'

'Ewww! Dad!' I said, laughing at how he had just shattered the picture-perfect image I had in my mind of him receiving his Olympic medal. Dad just looked sideways at me and grinned. I let the story sink in for the next few minutes as we pedalled in silence, but I knew I had one more question to ask.

'Dad?'

'Yes, petal?'

'If you could tell yourself anything now, talk to your 23-year-old self at that Olympics – what would you say?'

He thought for a moment and the turning of his pedals slowed. 'I would set my sights even higher. I would have more confidence in myself. Back then, the goal was just to get a medal, but looking back there was no reason why we shouldn't have been aiming for a gold medal. We just took it as a given that the East Germans and the Russians were beyond our reach. Of course, we might not have got there, we might have still ended up with a bronze, but I would definitely go back and tell myself to think even bigger than I dared and go for that. Because you never know what you might come away with.'

At that moment in time, I was filled with so much love for my dad. To have him as a parent, combined with an Olympian mum too, was pretty special. Seeing how they constantly pushed themselves, dug deep, went in search of being the best they could be – they really were the best heroes a girl could ever ask for.

In the hours that followed, we chatted on and off about a variety of things – the surroundings, general musings on life, music, sport, my brothers, a shared love of a decent coffee and a *petit pain au chocolat* – things that were important and unimportant all at once. Sometimes we rode together, at other times we rode apart, lost in our own worlds – just a dad and his daughter taking on a volcano.

After six hours of steady climbing, stopping every now and then to take in the view or wolf down a cheese wrap provided by Mum out the back of the van, Dad and I approached the 'finish line', an indiscriminate point in the car park which we both agreed marked the end of our journey into the clouds together. The last 200 metres kicked up to a 14% gradient, which normally wouldn't be too taxing, but at 3,000 metres and with heavy legs, we were both left gasping and silent. We collapsed over the handlebars of our bikes, panting, caught halfway between smiling and grimacing, and reached out to one another for a hug. Mum came bounding through the car park shortly afterwards, whooping and waving a piece of paper in the air. Since we weren't actually at the summit, which was in fact 20 metres ahead on a footpath up at the visitors' centre, Mum had gone on and got us a certificate each to mark the occasion. I dismounted my temporary steed and balanced the bike next to the car, before taking a few unsteady footsteps to look out over the edge.

I breathed in deeply and let out a long sigh. It was the first time I'd been up to the top of a volcano and I was immediately struck by the uninterrupted view from 3,000 metres up. It was spectacular. There were no neighbouring peaks – all I could see around me was Maui, the whole of it. From one end to the other and all the way across. I gazed back down the mountain, letting my eyes drift over the brown cindery desert slopes, dotted with shrubs and wild flowers. I marvelled at how the landscape looked so different at the foot of the volcano – so lush and so very green. I looked further out to the reef below – a swirling mass of whites, blues and aquamarines – and onto the offshore Molokini crater, which was shaped like a neat little crescent moon. Level with my eye line, against a backdrop of blue, were endless delicate wisps of cloud suspended as if someone had hurriedly dismantled an oversized candy floss and just… left it there.

I swallowed down a small lump in my throat and breathed a huge sigh of relief. There was a calmness about Maui that day which seemed so much at odds with all the struggle and strife it had taken me to get there. All of the logistical hurdles, the weather hold-ups, the obsession with my dwindling brake blocks, my worry at making the flight from Dallas – they all melted away until all that remained was me and the mountain. That day, in the 50th state, it had been as simple as turning the pedals until I reached the top.

***

Back on Oahu at Waikiki Beach, I had been starting to feel saddened by the fact that Boudica still hadn't turned up. Then, on the final day, right before we were due to fly home, I came back from a morning run and, lo and behold, there she was in our hotel room, still stowed neatly in her box, pink gaffer tape perfectly intact, acting as if nothing had happened.

'You little minx, Boudica,' I said, softly. 'I thought I might never see you again.'

I cut open the box and put my beloved pink bike together for one final time. I noted the missing part of her stand that I'd lost in a ditch after the floods in Colorado and the chip from her paintwork after I had hit the deck on ice in that gas station in Arkansas. There were small pieces of tinsel still attached to her frame from having 'Christmassed up' my bike in Mississippi. I looked down at my speedo: 11,668 miles.

As Boudica and I rode away from Waikiki Beach and towards Diamond Head Crater, I realised I hadn't even put her pannier racks on. There were no mudguards, no bags. There was a weightlessness to Boudica, and I felt weightless too. I knew she was only a hunk of metal and rubber, but that bike had been my constant through the never-ending twists and turns of the past seven months. She was an anchor in an often stormy sea and it would have felt weird to have left the 50th state having not taken her for one last spin. She deserved that too.

When I reached the foot of Diamond Head, I propped Boudica up next to a palm tree and stopped to look out over the Pacific Ocean. I thought back to the beginning of the journey. To the girl who had squeezed herself into cycling Lycra for the first time at Vancouver Airport and felt so uncomfortable, in every sense. I barely recognised her. She seemed nervous, naive, fearful, even. She seemed laden with expectations and obligations that were not her own.

I thought back through the States – to a sea of faces, of soft beds, of wild-camping spots, of mountain tops, of valley floors, vibrant colours, big cities, and towns with three houses. I replayed each precious memory like an old black and white movie in my mind. I recalled watching grizzly bears forage in the shadow of Mount McKinley. Stargazing at 2 a.m. in the Sierra Nevada Mountains at a sky so full that I feared it might just cave in under the weight of its own sparkle. I thought back on pedalling across the plains of Wyoming, with a herd of wild mustangs running alongside me, and of riding alone at dawn through the desert, with no sound beyond the whirr of my wheels. There seemed to be so many memories and I wondered how I would possibly manage to keep them all safe. So I decided in that moment that I would move them from my head to my heart, because I knew they would last a lifetime there.

That day, I was deeply in love with life. I was deeply in love with the USA. Every single state, even the seemingly uneventful ones or those I'd only pedalled through for a few meagre miles, had all gifted me something in their own special way. At the centre of everything, I felt a deep sense of pride and a quiet confidence that I knew no one could ever take from me. I had done it. I was here. Of course, I had no idea where I would go from here, but that didn't seem to matter – because I was exactly where I wanted to be at that moment in time. Just before I swung my leg over Boudica to ride back to the hotel, something clicked into place. I was overwhelmed with calm. I felt free, I felt relieved, but best of all – I felt like me.

Epilogue

Life is about choices. Day in, day out, the hours skip by. Those hours are defined by the things we choose to accept as part and parcel of life, and those that we choose to shove aside. The reality is that most of the everyday revolves around micro-choices. Decisions made within a framework for the life that we have, mostly unknowingly, already created.

It's a framework shaped by our upbringing, our parents, our peers, where we were born, what we watch, what we read, what our teachers thought of us at school, possibly even whether we're the kind of person who likes Marmite or not. For those of us who are fortunate enough to exist in a framework where we needn't worry about the basics of food, shelter and love, the beauty of the framework is that it provides a safe haven. We can rumble on within it, perhaps mildly unfulfilled but not woefully discontent, until one day someone or something flicks a switch. A lightbulb goes on in your mind and lights up a part of yourself you never even knew was there.

Sitting at my desk that day years ago, doing battle with the circles and the grid lines, the lightbulb went on for me. I believed there was something more I could be doing with this precious thing called life. I had no idea what that was, but it was a feeling so overwhelming that it wouldn't leave me alone. It wrapped its fingers around my heart and threatened to stop it from beating unless I listened to it. And I'm very glad I did.

Being on a bicycle, and not just any bicycle – Boudica, to be precise – really allowed me to get under the skin of the USA. I saw and experienced things that no news programme, TV show or tabloid newspaper could have exposed me to. I learned that it is a country so varied and vast that it may as well be 10 countries in one. Within those 50 states, I experienced beauty beyond anything I could ever have imagined. I found solace in the arms of its wilderness, I was in awe of (and often terrified by) the wildlife. I was humbled by its mountains, soothed by the calm of its deserts – my worries washed away by the waters of its great lakes.

I became addicted to getting to know the USA just a little bit better, but I always found myself on the edge of truly understanding it. Because there are layers upon layers, moods and shadows, flashes of bright brilliance and endless cornfield monotonies. Each time I believed that I had got to grips with who or what America really was, I was shown another side. And at the heart of it all are the people.

For a nation that is bold and brash in many ways, the USA is filled with humble, gentle folk. The community-minded strangers who welcomed me into their lives showed that human connection is a force greater than anything nature can conjure up. The South Dakotan blizzard was no match for Dorena Weichmann's home-baked cookies, the thousand-year flood in the Rocky Mountains could do nothing to dislodge memories of Cindy's pancake breakfasts, and even Storm Hercules was forced into submission by a turkey that smelled like farts.

Given that we are all connected in this world, that connection extends to the Dream Dumpers too. I met my fair share of them along the way (Cheveyo-Dave was just one), but I realised that someone likely took a dump on their dream too. Once I understood that, I wasn't so angry any more. You cannot help a Dream Dumper after all, all you can do is help yourself. So my dreams are now officially dump-proof. The dump will forevermore slide off my dream, like water off a duck's back.

Through all the people I met, all the lives I cannonballed into and out of, and all that time spent pedalling into a horizon with nothing but my thoughts for company, I was waiting for the moment I would discover that 'thing' I was supposed to be doing with my life. I was hoping that in someone else's job description I would find that perfect fit for my own. Those I met became my mirror; in their lives I saw the hopes I had for my own future reflected back at me.

Over the course of 11,000 miles, I kept my eyes open. I watched, I listened, I probed, and at the end of it all one thing became abundantly clear: there is no job description for life. It was not going to be something that I would stumble upon one day in the careers section of my local newspaper and cry 'Eureka! There it is!' nor was I going to look at someone else's life and decide that I wanted a carbon copy of it for myself. Instead,

I learned that curiosity can be a great place to start and that perhaps the answer lay in turning my head ever so slightly in the direction of things that intrigued me, pedalling towards ideas that filled me with happiness, and away from those that didn't.

When the 50-state journey was over, I returned to my office job in London. Perhaps unsurprisingly, I lasted a few months before I came to blows with my computer (this time it was an Excel spreadsheet), and I had to accept that nothing would ever be the same again. I had grown so much. Not in the physical sense (although my thighs would beg to differ) but emotionally. My horizons had been stretched so wide that there was no way I could possibly cram all of that experience back into the person I was before I had left the UK. That in itself was frustrating, because there was no way back, only forwards, and forwards felt terrifying. Little did I know that this 50-state cycle would be the start of many adventures to come and that, a year later, I would be heading off to run the length of New Zealand, on my tod and carrying all of my gubbins on my back.

If I could hop in a time machine and go back to getting off the plane in Alaska, I would be less fearful about the things that may or may not come to pass. I would tell myself to take a gigantic chill pill and that it's all going to be alright. And yet, I'm proud that I still went through with something that made me feel so uneasy, so wriggly in my own skin. It's uncomfortable to do things that take us beyond our usual remit because they expose cracks in our character that we try to hide to make us seem like we are functioning members of society. The reality is we are all fumbling around in the darkness, bumping into things and looking for that light switch.

If the 50-state journey taught me one thing, it is that when you put yourself 'out there', way beyond your comfort zone, when you indulge in endeavours that cause your heart to beat fast and your chest to tighten – amazing things happen. Doors open, opportunities arise and, most importantly, the painful chinks in your armour heal. The cracks that threaten to make you fall apart, they seal over. You become far stronger than you'd ever imagined. You stop waiting for permission to start living a life that allows your heart to sing and your mind to soar, and instead you set about building it yourself – shade by shade, piece by piece.

Author Note

Congratulations to you, dear reader, on completing the 50-state journey! I really hope you enjoyed yourself out there. You must be feeling rather tired now, but I would be forever grateful if you could channel the endurance of Betty 'The Hutch' Hutchinson and head over to Amazon right this very moment and leave a review for the book.

Even if it's just a one sentence comment, your words make a massive difference. Amazon reviews are a huge boost to independently published authors like me who don't have big publishing houses to spread the word for us. It's safe to say that the more reviews up there, the more likely it is that this book will land in other people's laps.

If you'd like to be kept up to date with future book releases and adventure shenanigans - then you can join my mailing list here. No Spam, just awesomeness - that's a pinky promise.

www.annamcnuff.com/McNewsletter

And if you'd like to see a picture of me (sometimes posing) with every US state sign – head to:

www.annamcnuff.com/states

If social media is more your kind of fandango, you can say hello here:

On Facebook: **'Anna McNuff'**

On Instagram: **@annamcnuff**

On Twitter: **@annamcnuff**

Or if social media is your idea of hell, I can also be found here:

www.annamcnuff.com

anna@annamcnuff.com

Failing that, send me a pigeon.

Thank You's

This tale of adventure would not have been possible without everyone who supported me along the way or played a part in bringing it to life.

Thank you to my editor Debbie Chapman for being a literary legend (again), to my copy editor Sophie 'Hawk Eyes' Martin, to Jools the proof reader and my great aunt Ann for her extra special read through just ahead of print. Big thanks also go to my fabulous designers Kim and Sally from Off Grid – who worked out how to get my legs on yet another book cover, illustrated all the maps and made the interior of this book look ruddy marvellous.

Thank you from the bottom of my over-laden bike panniers to all of the generous folk across the states who took me in and looked after me or let me come into their school and speak to their kiddywinks – you know who you are, and you will always hold a special place in my heart. Extra special gratitude goes to those hosted me for a long time or really got me out of a logistical fix: Cindy and the Glen family, Jay and Shirley, Larry and Lajunta, Joe and Drea and the Weichmann family.

Thank you to everyone who has followed my journey to Adventuredom from the very beginning; to all of you who 'liked' my vintage 'Big Five-O' page, and also to my lovely colleagues at that office job I left. I hope you see now why I had to spread my wings and head off to sleep in bushes and meet bears.

Lastly, thank you to Lydia for being such a wonderful travel buddy, to my parents for not freaking out (too much) that their daughter wanted go galivanting around the world, and to my partner in crime Jamie, for your unwavering support and love, even (and especially) when I'm a bit mental.

Praise for Anna McNuff: Speaker

Anna has delivered motivational and inspiring keynote talks for schools, corporates, not-for-profits and after dinner events all around the world.

"Absolutely fantastic!"

HRH Prince Edward

"In the same way Jamie Oliver has a kind of innate and interminable positivity that makes cooking and food seem like the best thing ever, adventurer Anna McNuff manages to do that about life."

Stylist Magazine

"You made a huge impact in such a short space of time!"

English Institute of Sport and the GB -Archery Team

"Full of guts, energy, determination, stamina and vision, you placed us right in the heart of the action, and encouraged each and every one of us to try new things and push ourselves more. We can't wait to hear what you get up to next!"

Barclays

"It really felt like we experienced the journey with Anna. Her drive to encourage others to do make the most of life shone through from start to finish."

Cancer Research UK

"Anna is as brave as a wolf and a fire dragon. She is an awesome person because she helps kids around New Zealand. The more money she raises, the more kids get to go OUTSIDE. She is a blue eyed, blonde haired superhero!"

Leonard, aged 7, Deanwell School, New Zealand

"The whole school was buzzing for days after you left!"

The International School, Geneva

"After listening to you speak I just know that I am made for bigger things. I'm now super motivated to work towards doing something really meaningful with my life."

Katie, aged 15, Hamilton, New Zealand

"Great motivational speakers are hard to find. Anna was infectiously positive, and with a real story to tell. Exactly what the kids needed as they head into taking their GCSEs."

Head of Progress -Icknield Community College

Find out more about Anna's speaking at
www.annamcnuff.com/speaking
or email: **hello@annamcnuff.com**

Also by Anna McNuff

"A thrilling, coming-of-age journey that will make you yearn to go on your own adventures."

Runners World

Anna was never anything like those 'real' runners on telly – all spindly limbs, tiny shorts and split times – but when she read about New Zealand's 3,000-kilometre-long Te Araroa Trail, she began to wonder... perhaps being a 'real' runner was overrated. Maybe she could just run it anyway?

The Pants of Perspective is a witty, colourful and at times painfully raw account of a journey to the edge of what a woman believes herself to be capable of. It is a coming-of-age story which will lead you on a roller coaster ride through fear, vulnerability, courage and failure.

For anyone who has ever dreamt of taking on a great challenge, but felt too afraid to begin – this story is for you.

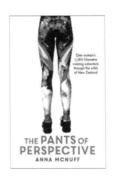

Also by Anna McNuff

**WINNER of the 2020 Amazon Kindle Storyteller
Literary Award**

*"Llama Drama is simply hilarious. If anyone wants something witty
and moving at the same time. Also, something empowering, then this is
the one for them. I literally inhaled it."*
- Claudia Winkleman, TV Presenter and Author

Armed with a limited grasp of Spanish and determined to
meet as many llamas as possible, Anna and her friend Faye
set off on a 6-month journey along the spine of the largest
mountain range in the world – the Andes.

Join the Adventure Queens

Founded by Anna McNuff and her Kiwi best-bud Emma Frampton, Adventure Queens is a not-for-profit women's adventure community – set up with the aim of delicately smashing down the barriers that prevent women from heading off on adventures.

We provide practical information, tips and advice on all things camping, adventure and the great outdoors.

Little by little, bit by bit, Adventure Queens is helping women from the UK and beyond have the confidence to get out there and get WILD.

Website: **www.adventurequeens.co.uk**

Mailing list: **www.adventurequeens.co.uk/joinin**

Email: **hello@adventurequeens.co.uk**

About Anna McNuff

Anna McNuff is an adventurer, endurance athlete and professional speaker. Once upon a time she represented Great Britain at rowing, but after retiring from the sport, she began darting around the world on the hunt for new and exciting endurance challenges.

Named by The Guardian as one of the top female adventurers of our time, Condé Nast Traveller have also included her in a list of the 50 most influential travellers in the world. She is also the UK Ambassador for Girl Guiding.

Aside from cycling the 50 states, she has run the length of New Zealand and spent 6 months cycling up the peaks and passes of South America's Andes Mountains. She has also cycled across Europe directed entirely by social media, run the length of Hadrian's Wall dressed as a Roman Soldier, and the length of the Jurassic Coast, dressed as a dinosaur (as you do).

She is relentless in her search for a decent cup of coffee and will never turn down a good slice of lemon pie.

www.annamcnuff.com

Printed in Great Britain
by Amazon